# THE
# MYSTICAL
# BODY
## *of* CHRIST

FULTON J. SHEEN

# THE MYSTICAL BODY *of* CHRIST

Foreword by Bishop Robert Barron

Introduction by Brandon Vogt

Published by Word on Fire,
Elk Grove Village, IL 60007
© 2023 by Word on Fire Catholic Ministries
Printed in the United States of America
All rights reserved

Cover design by Clare Sheaf, typesetting by Marlene Burrell,
and art direction by Nicolas Fredrickson

Nihil Obstat: Eduardus J. Mahoney, S.Th.D.
Censor Deputatus

Imprimatur: +Joseph Butt
Vic. Gen.
Westmonasterii, Die 30a, Septembris 1935

First published December 1935 by Sheed and Ward, Inc.
Copyright permission was granted by the Estate of Fulton J. Sheen /
The Society for the Propagation of the Faith / www.OneFamilyInMission.org.

---

© 2015 by The Society for the Propagation of the Faith

26 25 24 23    1 2 3 4

ISBN: 978-1-68578-033-3

Library of Congress Control Number: 2022950368

TO MARY
MOTHER IMMACULATE
OF
THE MYSTICAL BODY OF CHRIST

# Contents

# Foreword

*Bishop Robert Barron*

One reason that Fulton J. Sheen was such a successful and persuasive evangelist is that he was exceptionally smart. He was a doctor of theology from the University of Louvain—in fact, one of the rare recipients of Louvain's prestigious *agrégé* degree—an assiduous student of St. Thomas Aquinas, and a professor of philosophy and theology at The Catholic University of America. Sheen had a profound grasp of the Catholic intellectual tradition.

The book you are holding was first published in 1935, when Sheen was ensconced at Catholic University and just beginning his career as a popular evangelist, though long before he would emerge as a television personality. It reflects his thorough immersion in one of the most exciting theological projects of the time—namely, the exploration of the Church under the rubric of the "Mystical Body."

In order to understand the significance of the moves Sheen is making in this book, we have to consider, however briefly, some major themes in the theological thought of the nineteenth century. At the commencement of the 1800s, Catholic theology was in the grip of an arid, tired, and hyper-rationalistic scholasticism that employed the terminology and conceptuality of Aquinas but exhibited little of the vitality and spirit of Thomas' own writings. In regard to the theology of grace, for instance, the standard scholasticism held to an almost physicalistic conception of grace as a created substance infused into the soul. Likewise, the prevalent ecclesiology revealed a highly juridical and hierarchical understanding of Church.

Posing a significant challenge to this regnant scholasticism were two intellectual movements within the German Catholic theology of the nineteenth century. The first of these movements, the so-called "Tübingen school," was associated with two major figures, Johann Sebastian von Drey (1777–1853) and Johann Adam Möhler (1796–1838), both of whom taught on the Catholic faculty of Tübingen at key points in their careers. To some degree under the influence of their Protestant colleague Friedrich Schleiermacher, both Drey and Möhler sought to overcome the cramped rationalism of classical theology and to find a way to reintegrate theology and culture, doctrine and life.

Setting aside Schleiermacher's excessive subjectivism, they attempted to revive two key patristic notions: (1) that the ordinary goal of the Christian life is a real participation in the divine nature, and (2) that the Church is best construed as the prolongation of the Incarnation through space and time. The first point is vital, for it represents an enormous improvement on the extrinsicist and mechanical construal of grace in much of the official theology of the time, and opens the way to understanding salvation as authentic "deification," becoming a sharer in God's own life. And the second point is indispensable in the measure that it permits us to push past an uninspiring ecclesiastical institutionalism and to appreciate the Church as the privileged vehicle by which the divine life is communicated to the people of God.

The second major theological movement I want to highlight is that associated with the patristic theologian Matthias Joseph Scheeben (1835–1888), whom Hans Urs von Balthasar called "the greatest German theologian to date" and to whom Pope Benedict XVI had a special devotion. Like the thinkers of the Tübingen school, Scheeben wanted to instill a greater patristic substance into the scholastic theology of grace. He emphasized, accordingly, that in giving the Holy Spirit, God does not simply convey an isolated gift, but rather "the very Giver of the gifts and the very principle of supernatural power."[1] In a word, the fruit of the sacramental life of the Church is true deification, for in receiving the Holy Spirit, one comes to share in the relationship that obtains between the Father and the Son. Through the Spirit, Scheeben said, we become not merely adopted children of God, but spouses of God.[2]

But then Scheeben went even further, insisting that the supernatural union between the soul and God in deification is like the natural union between the body and the soul. A key Christological implication of this spiritual anthropology is that the purpose of the Incarnation must be re-thought along patristic lines: the raison d'être of Christ's coming into flesh is not merely the reparation of the sinful human condition but also the elevation and transformation of humanity into God: *Deus fit homo ut homo fieret Deus* (God became human that humans might become God).[3]

These two great theological streams flowed into twentieth-century Catholic thought and gave rise to the work of a number of thinkers who profoundly influenced Fulton Sheen. One of these was Karl Adam (1876–1966), a patristic specialist whose greatest work was *The Spirit of Catholicism*. Like his predecessors, Adam argues that the Church is the *locus deificandi* (the place of deifying), which communicates the divine life precisely through the sacraments. His entire approach to liturgy, sacraments, and ecclesiology is predicated on the assumption that the Church is not so much the perfect society as a living organism, the Mystical Body of which Jesus is the Head and the Holy Spirit the Life Force.

Another significant bearer of Mystical Body theology in the twentieth century was Romano Guardini (1885–1968), a theologian who profoundly marked both Karl Rahner and Joseph Ratzinger and who had, consequently, a strong influence at the Second Vatican Council. Guardini's *The Spirit of the Liturgy* is replete with themes from the Tübingen and Scheeben traditions, and his devotional masterpiece *The Lord* is one of the clearest twentieth-century presentations of a Christology correlative to a Mystical Body ecclesiology.

In the United States, a number of pastors, theologians, and churchmen began to take in this theology and apply it in pastoral and liturgical contexts. I have in mind Virgil Michel, a monk of St. John's Abbey in Collegeville, who founded the journal *Orate Fratres*; Godfrey Diekmann, Michel's disciple, who helped to lead the American liturgical movement in the years prior to the council; and Reynold Hillenbrand, my predecessor as rector of Mundelein Seminary. Through teaching, preaching, lecturing, the conducting of workshops, and creative liturgical experimentation, these men brought Tübingen school, Mystical Body theology to a wide audience.

One of their most significant accomplishments—which we see reflected in the last chapter of Sheen's text—is the effecting of a link between the liturgy and the works of social justice, or what was called at the time "Catholic Action." Again and again, Hillenbrand preached that those who have been deified through the Church's sacraments, especially the Eucharist, are now obligated to go forth to effect the deification of the wider society.

It is fascinating to note that Sheen's 1935 text was composed in the midst of this extraordinary theological, liturgical, and pastoral ferment. Adam's *The Spirit of Catholicism* appeared just eleven years before *The Mystical Body of Christ*; Guardini's *The Spirit of the Liturgy* was published just twenty years before Sheen's book; and Hillenbrand became rector of Mundelein precisely one year after Sheen's opus appeared. And just eight years after the publication of *The Mystical Body of Christ*, Pope Pius XII issued his encyclical letter *Mystici Corporis*, which summed up and gave official ecclesiastical sanction to the very themes that Sheen and his colleagues had been exploring.

One would have to be obtuse indeed not to notice that so much of this theology—deification, sharing the divine life, the

Church as Mystical Body and extension of the Incarnation, Catholic Action, etc.—decidedly marked the texts of Vatican II. Even the most cursory glance at *Lumen Gentium*, *Gaudium et Spes*, *Sacrosanctum Concilium*, *Dei Verbum*, and *Presbyterorum Ordinis* reveals the significant influence of the Tübingen school. And to take one more step: these same motifs and themes are on very obvious display in the *Catechism of the Catholic Church* from 1992, a text that would be unthinkable apart from the neo-patristic revival of the last two centuries.

Fulton Sheen's *The Mystical Body of Christ* remains a serious and significant contribution to the Mystical Body theology of the twentieth century. And it provides an intriguing glimpse into the subtle and theologically acute mind of the greatest Catholic evangelist of the twentieth century.

# Introduction

*Brandon Vogt*

In many ways this book finds its roots in 1903, at St. Mary's Cathedral in Peoria, Illinois. There a nervous eight-year-old Fulton Sheen served Mass for the great Bishop John Spalding, co-founder of The Catholic University of America and one of the most impressive churchmen of his day. As the service began, the young Sheen stood, intimidated by the bishop. Yet his anxiety worsened as it was time to carry over a glass cruet to the altar. Along the way, he tripped over his alb and dropped the cruet, which shattered on the cathedral floor.

Remembering this moment of humiliation, Sheen would later write: "There is no atomic explosion that can equal in intensity of decibels the noise and explosive force of a wine cruet falling on the marble floor of a cathedral in the presence of a bishop. I was frightened to death."

After Mass, the boy made his way back to the sacristy, prepared for the worst. Yet when the bishop arrived he knelt down, placed his arms on the nervous boy's shoulders, and said, "Young man, where are you going to school when you get big?"

Those weren't the words Sheen expected. But quick on his feet, the boy answered, "Spalding Institute," referencing the local Catholic high school named after the bishop.

Bishop Spalding clarified, "No, I said 'when you get big.' Did you ever hear of Louvain University?"

The boy answered: "No, Your Grace."

"Very well," the bishop said. "You go home and tell your mother that I said when you get big, you are to go to Louvain, and someday you will be just as I am."[1]

Where that strange prophecy originated, nobody knows. What prompted a bishop in Peoria, Illinois, to predict that a clumsy young altar server would one day attend college in Belgium and someday "be just as I am"? Yet sure enough, the young boy was ordained a priest in 1919, and two years later he set foot in Louvain to attend the university. Then, in 1951, just as Bishop Spalding predicted, he was consecrated Bishop Fulton J. Sheen—"just as I am."

By the time he became a bishop, Sheen was already a well-known preacher and evangelist. He launched his *Catholic Hour* radio program in 1930, which at its peak reached four million listeners. In 1952, decades before "televangelism" became mainstream, Sheen launched his *Life Is Worth Living* television show. Media executives didn't expect much from the program, which they scheduled in the graveyard slot on Tuesday nights at 8:00 p.m. But Sheen's charisma, clarity, and showmanship catapulted the program past ratings giants like Milton Berle, the father of modern television, and Frank Sinatra, the iconic singer. At its peak, the show drew over 30 million people each week and earned Sheen an Emmy award in 1953 for being Television's Most Outstanding Personality. He remains the only religious figure ever to win the award.

In addition to Sheen's radio and television work, the prolific evangelist authored over seventy books. Marked by precision and wit, his writing evokes other twentieth-century apologists like C.S. Lewis, Ronald Knox, Frank Sheed, and G.K. Chesterton (the latter of whom wrote the introduction to Sheen's first book, *God and Intelligence in Modern Philosophy*). Sheen's genius lay in communicating lofty ideas in down-to-earth prose, using an array of humorous anecdotes, clever metaphors, and memorable one-liners. All this made him one of the most-quoted Catholics from the twentieth century.

Among his many books, *The Mystical Body of Christ* shines especially bright. First published in 1935, over twenty-five years before the groundbreaking Second Vatican Council, the book offered a major contribution to ecclesiology—the study of the Church—and preempted many of the council's eventual declarations. For example, Sheen devotes a whole chapter to the Eucharist as the source of unity for the Mystical Body of Christ, a key theme in *Lumen Gentium*, the council's major document on the Church.

Yet what of the book today? It may have foreshadowed Vatican II, but does it still have relevance?

One answer can be found by way of YouTube. Some years back, a young Evangelical Protestant named Jefferson Bethke uploaded a video titled "Why I Hate Religion, But Love Jesus." The four-minute video consists of spoken-word poetry, stirring music, and dramatic cinematography. Bethke professes that "Religion is man-centered, Jesus is God-centered." He suggests that real Christianity focuses solely on Jesus while ignoring unnecessary accretions like doctrines, institutions, and liturgical norms.

While the video doesn't explicitly condemn the Church, its subtle criticisms suggest as much. The video became an immediate hit, garnering over 35 million views and 145,000 comments, making it one of the most-watched religious videos in the history of the world.

The video especially resonated with the rapidly growing "spiritual but not religious" demographic. Although many in this group are still fascinated by Jesus, they want nothing to do with the Church. Cardinal Timothy Dolan described them well: they want to "believe without belonging," and "they don't mind being the sheep, but without a shepherd. They don't mind the family, as long as they're the only child. They don't see the need for a Church."² In other words, they're not keen on the Mystical Body of Christ.

And that's partly why Sheen's *Mystical Body of Christ* remains relevant. Within its pages, Sheen affirms that Jesus can never be separated from his Mystical Body any more than his divinity can be separated from his humanity. For the Mystical Body of Christ is Christ's Incarnation prolonged through space and time. Sheen explains that the Church "continues Christ, expresses Christ, develops all the virtualities, potentialities of Christ, makes it possible for Him to extend Himself beyond the space of Palestine and the space of thirty-three years to prolong his influence unto all times and to all men—in a word, it de-temporalizes and de-localizes Christ so that He belongs to all ages and all souls."³

He puts it even more pithily later in his book: "The Incarnate did not exhaust himself in the Incarnation." This is why the Scriptures describe the Church as the fullness of Christ (Eph. 1:23). The Church is the new Body that Jesus assumed after his Ascension, the instrument he now uses to teach, govern, and sanctify the world.

The Church is not a roadblock to encountering Christ, a barrier to pure Christianity. The Church *is* Christ. As Sheen poetically observes, "[The Church] no more stands between Christ and me, than His feet stood between Magdalene and His forgiveness, or His hand stood between the little children and His blessing, or His Breast stood between John and the secrets of the Sacred Heart."⁴

When we misunderstand the Church and her connection to Christ, we misunderstand Christ himself. That's what has happened today among the "spiritual but not religious" crowd, and that's why it's important that we recommit ourselves to understanding who the Church is and why she matters. It's important we rediscover the Church as the Mystical Body of Christ.

Sheen knew that one of the great difficulties toward that aim is the word "mystical." In our day, just as in his, the word carries a regrettable connotation, suggesting the "genuinely lofty spiritual states of a St. Theresa and St. John of the Cross," but also "the vague, the undefined and the unpractical."[5] However, when the Church uses that term in reference to the Body of Christ, she refers to a hidden yet clear and concrete reality, a Body whose members are united not by external bonds but by an internal, invisible force. Christ's Body is "Mystical" not because it is vague and undefined but because it is invisible and divine.

This confusion is common. As Sheen famously noted elsewhere, "There are not a hundred people in America who hate the Catholic Church. There are millions of people who hate what they wrongly believe to be the Catholic Church."[6] Many people see the Church as an organization rather than an organism—as a "what" rather than a "who." But the Church isn't merely a collection of individuals who decide to form a club, united through common ideals and purposes. Instead, she's a living body of cells, infused by the life of Christ and united by his will and purposes.

Like any living body, the Mystical Body of Christ requires three components to flourish: a head, a soul, and a source of unity. For the Church, her Head is Jesus Christ, who entrusts authority to a visible head on earth: his vicar, the pope. Her Soul is the Holy Spirit, the vivifying, energizing principle of life. And her Source of Unity is the Eucharist. Sheen reveals how each of these pieces fit together, the Head guiding the Body, the Soul enlivening the Body, and the Eucharist uniting the Body, together allowing Christ to move and act in our world.

After explaining how the Mystical Body of Christ operates, Sheen spends many chapters on her implications. For example, he devotes one chapter to scandals within the Body, which seems especially prescient in light of the abuse revelations in recent decades. If the Church is the Mystical Body of Christ, and therefore the prolongation of God's Incarnate Son, why does it seem plagued by sin? Sheen readily admits, along with St. Paul, that members of the Mystical Body are "treasures in clay"—a phrase

Sheen chose for the title of his own autobiography. "The graces of God are communicated through 'frail vessels' (2 Cor. 4:7)," he writes, "where mediocrity is the rule, genius the rarity, and saints the exception."[7]

Therefore, scandals shouldn't surprise us. Members of the Church regularly fall into sin, with few exceptions. But that no more sullies the Church's holiness than dirty hands pollute an entire human body. The Mystical Body may contain sin-stained vessels, but the innate treasure has always remained pure.

Another implication concerns Mary. If Mary is the Mother of Christ's human body, then she must naturally be the Mother of his Mystical Body, the Church. And since all Christians are incorporated into that Mystical Body, then the Mother of the Redeemer is also the Mother of the Redeemed. Her role in the Church today, Sheen writes, is just as active as her role in the Incarnation. Mary continues channeling her Son's grace to us, and for that reason all Christians should draw close to her aid.

The Mystical Body also means that Christians live as the visible, active expression of Christ in the world. Without his Mystical Body he would have no physical presence beyond Jesus' short life in first-century Judea:

> How else could He, as the Incarnate God, console other widows than those of Naim, visit other friends than those of Bethany, attend other nuptials than those of Cana, call other apostles than those of the lake, convert other women than those of Samaria, and other men than the centurions of Calvary? How could He the God-man show meekness to other soldiers' executioners; patience to other timid disciples, love for other publicans, friendliness to other Judases, forgiveness to other malefactors, devotion to other Johns, affection to other Marys, wisdom to other doctors of the Law, except through another Body with whose Feet He could step from Jerusalem

to the world, with whose lips He could speak to us who call ourselves modern?[8]

Christ instituted his Mystical Body to continually serve on this earth and to unite all humanity to himself.

Sheen ends his book by noting, "The dominant religious error from the sixteenth century to the present day has been to believe that religion is a purely personal matter between God and man."[9] Religion has become a private pursuit—think of the "me and Jesus" language among many Protestants—disconnected from corporate expression or ecclesial responsibility.

Many of those drifting away from the Church, who now identify as "spiritual but not religious," still seek an encounter with Christ. However, "they need not go back 1,900 years to meet Christ, for He is already living in His Church."[10] We know Christ best as Peter, Paul, Augustine, Aquinas, Catherine, Newman, Thérèse, and millions of Christians have come to know him throughout history: through his Body. In a world bent on separating Jesus from his Church, Christ from his Body, Sheen's masterful book bridges that divide, affirming that the two are really one.

# Author's Introduction

### I

Of all the tracts of Theology the one which has probably received the least development in modern times is the tract on the Church. A partial and insufficient explanation is that the Church has been subject to but little doctrinal attack in the last 150 years. Just as the spirit of the Church thrives by persecution, so does her mind develop by intellectual opposition. Pelagianism helped the development of the Grace tract; Arianism aided in the deeper study of the Incarnation; the Fideism of Protestantism did much to further a study of Justification; and Modernism, instead of weakening the Church, drew from her greater proof and assurance of the objectivity and historicity of Divine Life. Because the Church has been ignored rather than attacked, during the last century, there has been lacking the stimulus to expand its implications and sound its depths.

This, of course, is only a partial explanation and does not explain why, with a still greater decline of intellectual opposition at the present time, we are about to witness the most intensive study of the Church since the Reformation. The reason is not because logic has been used against us, but rather because it has ceased to be used at all. During the days when Protestantism was strong, it was necessary for apologists to emphasize the external structure of the Church, its hierarchy, its apostolicity and its visible marks. But now Protestantism has reached a stage where its churches no longer claim to be Divine or to be deposits of Divine Revelation. Protestantism has dissolved either into the (*a*) individualistic type of religion in which each man's subjective religious experiences determine the God he will worship and the altar he will serve, or else (*b*) into the purely social form of religion as developed by the International Congresses of Stockholm and Lausanne, and National Federations in which the bond between churches is external and communal, but not internal and spiritual. In other words, Protestantism in great part has ceased to be Christian.

This should give us no great reason for rejoicing. About fifty years ago we could depend on our separated brethren to help us defend the fundamental dogmatic truths of Christianity, such as the Divinity of Christ, but we can depend on them no longer. About twenty-five years ago we could depend on them to help us defend the basic principles of the moral law, such as the evil of sin, eternal sanctions, and the sanctity of the marriage bond; but we can depend on them no longer. To-day we are fighting the battle practically alone. Whether we fully realize it yet or not, on the bloody anvil of the World War we began to beat out a new civilization in which there will be either brotherhood in Christ or comradeship in anti-Christ.

The surrender of Divinity among the prodigal children has left the Church very much to herself. No longer attacked from within the broad body of Christendom with its variety of opposing sects, she is now forced to look at herself, not from the *outside* where she was opposed, but from the *inside* where she lives her most spiritual life. And it is indeed a remarkable thing that every profound treatise on the Church written in the last few years has considered the Church as she is in herself, and not as she is to her opponents. In other words, the *Church is no longer on the defensive; she is no longer on the offensive; she is on the descriptive*—revealing herself to hungry hearts and minds as the Bread of Life. No longer are her theologians, with an eye to Protestantism, presenting a partial aspect of her; rather they are revealing her as an organic whole, or as what she was from the beginning, and what our Lord wished her to be. Already the signs portend such a presentation, and within the next twenty years we will witness a general revision of our *De Ecclesia* manuals, not because they are incorrect, but because they have served their day. The time is ripe for the Church to enter into herself, to understand the spirit which binds her external communicants into a living whole, and to begin once more where she started: as a spiritual leaven in the mass of paganism. The Church will present herself to the world, not under the impersonal "it" as in the days when she struggled against heresy, but as the personal "she" as she was known to Paul, under the title of "The Body of Christ."

## II

One of the great difficulties apologists will meet in presenting the Church as the Body of Christ is the use of the term "Mystical," which, unfortunately, has a bad connotation. It is used to embrace not only the genuinely lofty spiritual states of a St. Theresa and St. John of the Cross, but is identified also with the vague, the undefined and the unpractical. It sometimes is applied in derision to any priest, nun or layman who "prays too much." Despite these associations, the term "mystical" is finding more general acceptance. Those who scruple at its use should remember it is not a substantive, but an adjective modifying "Body," and therefore is not identical with Mysticism. The word is not found in St. Paul. Bishop Myers of London finds that the two words "Mystical Body" are first actually combined by St. John Chrysostom in speaking of the Eucharist. That patristic use of "Mystical Body" for the Eucharist persisted in Rabanus Maurus (856) and in Paschasius Radbertus (860); Alexander of Hales (1245) uses the term of the Church in his *Universae Theologiae Summa*, and it is generally known to be the common teaching in the early part of the thirteenth century.

One reason perhaps why the term "Mystical Body" was not used in the Apostolic Fathers is because they treated the Church with emphasis on the doctrine of ecclesiastical unity, which needed to be stressed in their day. The relatively late association of the word "mystical" with the revealed word "Body" does not, of course, affect the substance of the doctrine. What is more important is to discover why the term "mystical" ever became associated with the word "Body." The word "Body" we know definitely was used by St. Paul, but it is worth remarking that he did not build his theory of the Church on the analogy of a living body, composed of head and members, in order to define the reciprocal rights and duties of the Head and the members. Rather, for him, the Church *existed as a reality anterior to the comparison*. He employed the analogy only to facilitate the understanding of the *reality* which is *one*, *hierarchical* and *possessed of solidarity*, like a living body.

Furthermore, it must not be thought that the doctrine of the Church as the "Body of Christ" differs from the doctrine found in either the Synoptics or St. John. *A priori* such is impossible, for God could not be guilty of contradictory revelations. The different presentation of the Church in the three abovementioned sources is due rather to the audiences they had in mind in preaching the doctrine. In the synoptics, "kingdom" is used; St. Paul uses "mystery" and John uses "life." These three terms at first sight seem quite different, but as Father Emile Mersch has pointed out in his profound historical study of the *Mystical Body of Christ*, these three terms apply to the same reality under different aspects. The first, that of "kingdom," expresses the economy of salvation in function of the prophecies and Messianic expectations of the hearers our Lord met in His customary preachings. The second term, "mystery," is a theology which opposes the immense splendour of Divine decrees to the narrowness and exclusive parochialism of our hearts. It is the word best suited to an apostle whose preoccupation was to vindicate the transcendence and infinite mercy of the Divine gift against the nationalism of the Jews and the short-sighted wisdom of the Greeks. Finally, the third term, "life," shows Christianity in its interior aspects, as closer to us than we are to ourselves. The fundamental reality in all three is the same. The "kingdom" speaks of a membership, a subjection and a consecration; "life" of a rejuvenation; and both imply that we are incorporated into Christ, made children of His kingdom, and the beneficiaries of the "mystery" hidden from the ages.

The doctrine of the "Body" is therefore Pauline only in the etymological sense of the term, but it is equally Synoptic and Johannine as regards its reality. Our unity with Christ and our unity with one another are expressed in the unforgettable words of the Last Supper, even though the word "body" was not explicitly used.

But why add the term "mystical"? Because there are various kinds of bodies, and therefore various kinds of unity. The Church, manifestly, is not the *physical body of Christ*, for that already enjoys its glory at the right hand of the Father. On the other hand, the Church is more than the *moral* body of Christ, e.g., a nation, for in a moral body, unity is achieved through the will of the members alone, that is, through their common service of common ideals and purposes. The Church manifestly has a higher unity than this, for, as our Lord explained, there would be oneness between the Church and Him as there is oneness between the branches and the vine. This oneness between Him and us, based on the unity of Him and His Father, was finally achieved by the Holy Spirit. Just as the Spirit of Love binds Him and the Father in the unity, the Godhead, so the Spirit will bind Him and us in the unity of His Mystical Body. Now, in order to express the higher unity of the members of the Church one with another and with their Head, Christ, and in order to better distinguish the Church as a Body, from a physical or a moral body—because it is infused by a hidden, mysterious, unifying soul which is the Holy Spirit—tradition has coined the term "mystical."

The term, then, is not opposed to the real, for there are realities besides those which we touch and weigh. It implies a sensible sign of a hidden reality, namely, a body whose members

5

are united not by external bonds, but by the Third Person of the Blessed Trinity. Certainly such a unity of members had to be expressed by some specific term, and since none better fitted the transcendent, vivifying power of Christ's Spirit than the term "mystical," it became associated with the Pauline term "Body." The conjunction of the words "Mystical Body" then does not stand for an abstraction; it refers to something visible and invisible, something tangible and intangible, something human and something Divine; it refers to a reality which is the subject of attribution, of properties and rights, to an organism with a supernatural soul, to a prolonged Incarnation, to the extension of Bethlehem and Jerusalem to our own days, to the *contemporary Christ*: the Church.

### III

Occasionally one hears it said that the doctrine of the Mystical Body is "dangerous" and "novel." The work of Father Mersch leaves no doubt that it has always been the traditional doctrine of the Church. The Church of the Orient following Sacred Scripture, this author proves, affirmed that the Church is an organism in which Christ acts, or better still, it is His "mystical prolongation." The Greek Fathers in refuting the Christological heresies say that the Mystical Body is constituted by a union of our nature and eternal life, as Christ is constituted of the union of two natures in the unique Person of the Son. The Latin Fathers and particularly Augustine, and later the Scholastics, spoke of the Church as the expansion of Divine Life in our souls under the Headship of Christ. The Council of Trent stated: "Christus Dominus lavacro baptismi *sui corporis membra* semel effecit" (*Sess.* XIV., cp. 2). Eucharistica est "symbolum unius *illius corporis* cujus *ipse caput* existit, cuique nos tamquam *membra* . . . adstrictos esse voluit" (*Sess.* XIII., cp. 2). This was in keeping with the idea previously defined by the Council of Florence: "Per [baptismum] membra Christi, ac *de corpore* efficimur Ecclesiae." The Council of the

Vatican, at the time of its disruption, had a schema or draft on the dogmatic constitution of the Church awaiting definition which called the Church the "Mystical Body of Christ." Lest anyone should have further scruple, we recommend a diligent reading of the Encyclical of the Holy Father, Pius XI, *Miserentissimus Redemptor.* His Holiness does not give an *ex professo* treatment of the Mystical Body, but rather assumes it, in treating of devotion to the Sacred Heart. Having spoken of the union of the members one with another, and with their Head, Christ, he goes on to say: "The Passion of Christ is renewed, and in a certain manner continued and completed in His Mystical Body which is the Church. Thus Christ who suffers still in His Mystical Body asks us to be His companions of expiation. Our union with Him demands this."

Some excellent treatises are appearing at the present time on this important subject, among which may be noted: Jürgensmeier, *Der Mystische Leib Christi als Grundprinzip der Aszetik*; Anger-Burke, *The Mystical Body of Christ*; Duperray-Burke, *Christ in the Christian Life*; Karl Adam, *The Spirit of Catholicism*; R. Plus, *God in Us*, *In Christ Jesus*, *Christ in His Brethren*; Dom Marmion, *Christ the Life of the Soul*; Emile Mersch, *Le Corps Mystique du Christ* (two vols.); E. Mura, *Le Corps Mystique du Christ* (two vols.).

This modest contribution to the subject was born of a study of St. Thomas' treatise on the Mystical Body of Christ in which the Angelic Doctor emphasizes the triple office of Christ as Teacher, King, and Priest, which offices are prolonged in the Church whose mission it is to teach, to govern, and to sanctify. This idea is fundamental to the whole book. The book is not a rigid theological proof of the Mystical Body, but rather a reasoned exposition. Its purpose is to inspire further study on the subject and also to introduce the subject to those not familiar with it. For this reason matter specially intended for the theologian will be found in notes. The book can be read without them. It seems clear that a thorough knowledge of the Mystical Body is the condition of not only a fruitful apostolate, but also a spiritual priesthood and laity. It will help to make Catholics realize that they need not go back 1,900 years to meet Christ, for He is already living in His Church; it will inspire a love for the Mass or the Sacrifice of the Mystical Body of Christ in which we offer our sacrificial lives to prolong Calvary to the very hour; finally, it will make Catholicism operative in our lives, which is only another name for Catholic Action. If this book, under the protection of Mary, the Mother of the Mystical Body of Christ, brings a single soul to the feet of Christ living in the Church, the author will feel that the book has been a triumphant success. As the book is primarily for Catholics, the relation to the Mystical Body of Christians outside the visible unity of the Church is not made the subject of special treatment.

It is the author's wish to express a debt of thanks to Reverend Walter Farrell, O.P., S.T. Lr., D.D., of the Dominican House of Studies, Washington, D.C., whose help in writing this book has been commensurate not only with the profundity of his theological knowledge, but also with his willingness to share it with those who know much less. Thanks also are due to Mr. E.I. Watkin (author of *A Philosophy of Form*), who has written a beautiful treatise on the Mystical Body and contributed so intelligently to the final editing of this book.

## CHAPTER I

# The Whole Christ

Our Divine Lord and Saviour Jesus Christ is not primarily a moral reformer, but a merciful Redeemer, and not only a good man, but the infinitely good God. We all know that His earthly Life was lived over nineteen hundred years ago, in a small obscure corner of the earth. Simply because it belongs to the past there is grave danger that we may think it has little relation to the present. Many of us, as practical-minded persons, have probably asked ourselves such questions as these: What possible relation can I, in this twentieth century, have to Him, who lived in the first? What influence can His Life of long ago have upon my life at the present? How can any bond of union that I have with Him, differ from my relation to Plato or Buddha or Confucius?

In order to understand the answer, we must remember that there are three ways in which man may influence posterity even long after his death. The first of these is by *teaching*. Anyone who ever wrote or spoke profound truths may yet be heard from the grave. The wisdom of the Greeks, thanks to their teaching, still lives amongst us. Plato and Aristotle are enshrined in our universities, and we talk of them as if we had walked with them through the market places and porches of Athens. Augustine of the fifth century and Aquinas of the thirteenth are made to come from their graves, and by their written word instruct our hearts, minds, and souls in the things of God and men. And who is there to deny that Washington and Lincoln live beyond their

9

day, in their state papers, so full of the finest political traditions of a free people?

Now, our Blessed Lord also can influence us by His teaching. His words of heavenly Wisdom were not allowed to fade away on an evening breeze, but were caught up by His four evangelists— Matthew, Mark, Luke, John—so that all who could read or hear would know the Wisdom of One who spoke, not as the Scribes and Pharisees, but as One having authority, even the authority of God. The Scriptures, then, which contain the teaching of Christ, constitute the first great link between the past and the present, between His earthly Life and our modern existence.

There is a second way in which a character of the past may make himself felt in the present, and that is by *example*. Any man who has ever had a biographer may project the force of his personality into the future, long after his flesh has crumbled into dust. The military example of a Caesar or a Napoleon, the saintly life of a Vincent de Paul or a Don Bosco, the daring exploits of a Columbus or a Magellan, can be told and retold a thousand times, and thus become an inspiration and a challenge to brave and saintly men of other times and different nations.

In like manner, our Lord can influence our day, because He has left us the beautiful example of a holy, moral Life which we should follow. We too can be forgiving, as He forgave those who crucified Him; we can be gentle, as He was gentle to little children; humble, as He was before those who would make Him an earthly king; and prayerful, as He was in the long vigils on the mountain tops. Countless indeed are the heroic, self-sacrificing, and saintly deeds of our own day, which have had as their inspiration the example of Him who came down from the heavens to teach us what manner of men God from all eternity has wished us to be.

Such are the two ways—teaching and example—in which all men, and our Lord in particular, strike root even centuries after their death. But, and this is important, the pity is that there are so many who believe these are the *only* two ways that our Lord could possibly stir the hearts and fire the minds of our day. As a matter of fact, if our Divine Saviour had no other way to project Himself into our day than by the Gospel records of what He said and what He did, how would He differ from Plato or Confucius, Mohammed or Caesar? They too live in the present by their teaching and by their example. I am willing to grant that the teaching and example of our Lord are nobler than those of other men, but if our Lord has no other way to project Himself than that which is common to all men, *then* He is only a *man* and not God. If He has no other way to energize our hearts and minds than by His teaching and His example, then Christianity is only the memory of a man who lived and died; then it can give only human consolation to hearts that cry out for the Divine; then it is just another *sect* and not a religion, only a point of view and not a heavenly gift.

Much modern Christianity is of this very type. It takes a purely emotional and sentimental outlook on Christ, as a humanitarian and nothing more. It bids us look back nineteen hundred years to Galilee; it repeats His words, interprets His actions, as it might those of Caesar or Aurelius—and because it does *only this*, it has lost its hold on the modern man. I think that there is no reason which so explains the decay of Christianity among sects, as this tendency to regard it only as a memory of a man who taught and lived. Indeed, if Christianity is only a memory of the teaching and example of a man, then it *should die*—and the sooner it dies the sooner we can welcome a religion which will put Divine Life into our veins.

Christianity, fortunately, is something more than a memory, because our Lord is something more than a man. He is true God and true man. Being God, He can perpetuate Himself not only by His teaching and His example, but also in a third way, which belongs to Him alone as God, namely by His continuing Life. Others may leave their titles, their wealth, their stocks and their bonds, their doctrines and their biographies, but only our Lord can make a last will and testament bequeathing to posterity that which no one else on dying could ever leave: His Life as the Life of the World. He brought Divine Life to earth at the crib, but He willed not that this Life should be only a temporary visitation of a score and ten years and a localized experience confined to a few hundred square miles. He willed to diffuse it in time until time should be no more, and in space until all the thirsty hearts of earth had drunk of its refreshing draughts.

God is too good to circumscribe the gift of Divine Life to a brief human existence stretching between a crib and a cross. Did He not explicitly state: "Behold I am with you all days even to the consummation of the world"? And Saint John, speaking of the Divine Life prolonged and diffused in all men, says: "Of whose fullness we have all received." It is the fullness of that Christ-Life, beating and throbbing at this very hour in millions of souls, which gives flesh and blood to His teaching and His example. Because He lives to-day, His teaching is *not* a cold record written only on the pages of history, but a teaching bound up with life in a living mind; His example is not something that *has* happened, but something that *is* happening, not an antiquated historical phenomenon, but a living force active before our very eyes.

Naturally, our Lord does not live in the world to-day in exactly the same way as He lived in Galilee; forty days after His Resurrection He ascended into heaven where He sits at the right hand of the Father. He must live on earth to-day in a way different from His Life of nineteen hundred years ago, and in a way other than that in which He inhabits heaven. This new way is called His Mystical Life. There are therefore three phases in the complete Life of Christ or in the Life of the whole-Christ: first, His Earthly Life; second, His Glorified Life; third, His Mystical Life.

## I. THE EARTHLY LIFE

From all eternity the Second Person of the Blessed Trinity is eternally generated by the heavenly Father in the ecstasy of the first and real paternity: "Thou art My Son, this day have I begotten Thee." It was because of this Eternal Life in the Godhead that He could say, "Before Abraham was, I am." The Eternal generation of the Son of God has its temporal counterpart in the earthly generation of the Son of man in the womb of the Blessed Mother, of whom was born Jesus Christ, possessed of a Divine Nature from eternity, a human nature in time, and of both united in the oneness of the Person of the Son of God. This earthly Life began in the manger at Bethlehem, continued through the obedience of thirty years at Nazareth, the three years of teaching, the three hours on the cross, the three days in the grave, and the forty days of Risen Life before ascending into heaven, leaving us an example to walk in His steps. It was not a long Life, as we reckon a life; most of us would consider our work hardly begun at thirty. But it was a Life in which everything was accomplished according to His pre-ordained plan, neither hastened nor retarded by the iniquity of men. He came to give His Life for the Redemption of many, "laid it down" in the "hour of darkness" which He foretold, "took it up again" as He prophesied in the sign of Jonas, and then ascended into heaven, never again to be visible to the fleshly eyes of men. His earthly Life was finished.

## 2. THE GLORIFIED LIFE

The second phase of the complete Life of Christ is pursued in heaven. During the forty days which followed His Resurrection our Lord has completed His instructions concerning His Kingdom on earth, and now can say to His Father: "I have finished the work which Thou gavest Me to do, and now Glorify Thou Me, O Father, with the glory which I had, before the world was, with Thee" (John 17:4–5). The human nature taken from His pure Mother is ready to enjoy the reward of that earthly Life spent in obedience to the Father's Will. On a Thursday, forty days after Easter, He assembles His apostles, leads them to the Mount of Olives, blesses them, and rises by His own Divine Power above the clouds, as He had told them: "Ought not Christ to have suffered these things and so enter into His glory?" (Luke 24:26). Even as the planets sweep round their orbit and return to their starting point as if to salute Him who sent them on their way, so Christ, completing the orbit of an earthly Life, returns to His heavenly Father to enjoy the glory which was His before the foundation of the world.

St. Paul, speaking of this Glorification of Jesus, writes to the Ephesians: "What is the exceeding greatness of [God's] power toward us, who believe, according to the operation of the might of His power, which was wrought in Christ, raising Him up from the dead, and setting Him on the right hand in the heavenly places, above all principality, and power, and virtue, and dominion" (Eph. 1:19-21). The creed of the Church too describes Christ in His glory as "seated at the right hand of God." This is no more than a figurative way of expressing the eternal repose merited by His glorious triumphs and the continued exercise of those Powers, which His Father had given Him, to teach, govern and sanctify man. For we must not picture our Lord in His glorified state as indifferent to the world which He had come to redeem (cf. John 14:2–4, 17:24).

There are two reasons for Christ's Glorification. The first is because He is God's own Son. "I came forth from the Father, and am come into the world. Again I leave the world, and I go to the Father" (John 16:28). The second is because He has humbled Himself and therefore shall be exalted. "Who emptied Himself, taking the form of a servant, being made in the likeness of men, and in habit found as a man. He humbled Himself, becoming obedient to death, even to the death of the cross. For which cause God also hath exalted Him, and hath given Him a name which is above all names: That in the name of Jesus every knee should bow, of those that are in heaven, on earth, and under the earth. And that every tongue should confess that the Son Jesus Christ is in the glory of God the Father" (Phil. 2:7–11).

### 3. THE MYSTICAL LIFE

This text of St. Paul brings us to the third phase of the Life of Christ, in which He begins again to live on earth in a new way, for He had told His apostles on the night of the Last Supper, "I will come again." It was not best (He told them) that He abide with them in His visible earthly form, for He would thus be only something external to them, but if He left them to go to His Father and sent His Spirit, then He would be, not an example to be copied, but a Life to be lived. And so He said to them, while still in the flesh: "It is expedient to you that I go: for if I go not, the Paraclete will not come to you; but if I go, I will send Him to you" (John 16:7). The day of Pentecost, ten days after His Resurrection, was the birth of Christ's new Life on earth, for on that day He sent His Spirit to His apostles, the nucleus of His Church, to make them, in the language of Holy Writ, His New Body, the Church of which He is the invisible Head (Rom. 8:9).

The new presence of Christ on earth in His Church is the third phase of the complete Life of Christ, and in order to demarcate it from His physical Life and from His Glorified Life tradition has called it the Mystical Life. Just as in His earthly Life He took a human body as an instrument for the exercise of His office as Prophet, King, and Priest, so now on Pentecost He assumes a new body, His Church, through the instrumentality of which He still fulfils the same triple role of teaching, governing, and sanctifying. In His earthly Life, He had only one human nature united to Him; in His Mystical Life, He unites to Himself all those human natures throughout the world who receive His Spirit. In His earthly Life, He was redeeming; in His Mystical Life, He is bestowing the fruits of Redemption on the members of His Mystical Body. In His earthly Life, *He* possessed the fullness of the

Godhead; in His Mystical Life, *we* receive of Its fullness. In His earthly Life, He was the Founder of the Kingdom; in His Mystical Life, He incorporates us into that Kingdom. In His earthly Life, He suffered and rejoiced in His physical body; in His Mystical Life, He suffers and rejoices in His Mystical Body. Then He was the Vine, now He is the Vine giving life to the branches; then He was the Leaven, now He is the Leaven in the Mass; then He was the Mustard Seed, now He is the Tree of Life; then He had a body taken from the womb of the Blessed Mother overshadowed by the Holy Ghost, now He has a Mystical Body, the Church, taken from the womb of humanity overshadowed by the same Pentecostal Spirit. Of course, the Mystical union between the Christian and Christ is not the same as the union of His Divine and human natures in His person. The former is by grace and accidental, the latter is personal and substantial. Remember, we always speak with this understanding.

The complete Life of Christ must include these three phases. Those who consider His physical Life alone, either develop a sentimental spirituality or else end by regarding Him merely as a good man and a teacher of humanitarian ethics; those who consider Him only in His heavenly Life of glory, regard Him as an absentee landlord, disregarding both His promise to send His Spirit, and His abiding interest in the souls which He came to save. Just as it would be wrong to limit *The New Testament* to *The Gospels*, so it would be wrong to limit Christ to an earthly career. *The Gospels* are the record of His earthly Life, and the promise of the Glorified and Mystical Lives; *The Acts of the Apostles* and *The Epistles* of Paul, Peter, James, John and Jude are the records of the Mystical Life. Christ is not divided; He is not past; He has not left us orphans; He is with us and more intimately than we are with ourselves. He is still living in the world, moving amongst its poor, instructing the ignorant, comforting the doubtful, and healing the souls of men. Such is His Mystical Life in the Church. As His human and Divine natures are one in the unity of His Person in the Incarnation, so too in His Mystical Life the Church His Body and He the Head are one Person—the Mystical Christ.[1] Christ is our contemporary.

It is within the power of man to prolong himself through space and time by doctrine and example. It is within Christ's power to prolong Himself, not only by doctrine and example, but also by His Life. If you believe that He is God, you must believe this. If you do not believe that He is God, then you cannot believe Him to be a good man, for a good man does not lie, and He *said* that He was God. But if you *do* believe that He is God and consequently that He has projected His Life through all time and throughout the world, then you must seek out that Divine Life. You must discover where It is. And it must be very definitely somewhere, for life is not something vague and undefined like a fog. If that Life is on this earth, it must be found in some organism, since life on earth is never found divorced from a body. Now where is that Body in which Christ is living His Mystical Life? It is for the next chapter to attempt an answer.

## CHAPTER II

# The Mystical Body

In Christ there are two natures: human and divine, and one Person: the Person of the Word, the Second Person of the Blessed Trinity. "And the Word was made flesh and dwelt among us." From all eternity Christ is God; only from the moment of His Incarnation is He God-man. A nature is the principle or source of action. A person, however, is the source of responsibility. For example, the answer to the question: what is crying? gives us the nature; the answer to the question: who is crying? gives us the person. Now in Christ there is the perfect nature of God, and the perfect nature of man. But though there are two natures, there are not two persons in Him, but only One, which is the Person of God, the Eternal Word, the Second Person of the Blessed Trinity. Christ's is a human individual nature without a human personality; in Him the Divine Personality of the Word performs the functions of the human personality, and it does infinitely more, as behoves a Divine Personality. His human nature is as entire and intact as any human nature; He is as perfectly human as any of us, being man in the truest sense of the term. And although the human nature in Christ is something new (for He assumed it in hypostatic union only at the Incarnation), nevertheless the personality of that human nature is not new, but eternal. Such was the meaning of our Lord when answering the Jews concerning the death of Abraham and His comparative age: "Amen, amen, I say to you, before Abraham was made I am."[1]

It follows that the human nature of Christ was a kind of instrument of His Divine Personality. It was not an instrument separate from His Person, as a pencil is separate from my hand, but united as my hand is united to my brain. St. Thomas has found a happy phrase to express this union by calling the human nature the "conjoined instrument of Divinity." The hand of Michaelangelo which painted "The Last Judgment" was the "conjoined instrument" of his brain. To apply this to Christ: because Godhead is united with manhood in one Person, more intimately than brain and hand are united in one organism, manhood is the "hand" of Godhead and does the works of God, just as the human hand does the works of human genius.[2] Thanks to the hypostatic union, a human nature has been raised to such a height as to make it capable of sharing in the whole work of Redemption and Sanctification. Christ's human nature, body and soul, through its union with the Second Person of the Trinity, has acquired unparalleled fitness to be in the hands of God the instrument of every spiritual marvel. Thus His life, death, Resurrection, and Ascension are the instruments of Divinity for our sanctification, our life, our resurrection, our ascension.

But it may be asked: Why should His human nature acquire such power even though it be a perfect human nature? The reason is because of its union with the Person of God. There is an old Latin axiom, which sounds abstract, but which is very easily verifiable in the language of every-day: *Actiones sunt suppositorum. Actions belong to the person*—not to the nature. For example, though it is the nature of my eye to see, the nature of my tongue to taste, the nature of my feet to walk, it is nevertheless true that when it comes to accounting for the source of their responsibility, we attribute these actions not to our nature, but to our person. We do not say, *My eye saw you*, but *I saw you*; we do not say, *My ear heard you*, but *I heard you*. Now, in the incarnate Life of our Saviour, though His human nature is a perfect human nature like unto ours, though it did the perfectly human things such as shedding tears, suffering pain and a bloody sweat, blessing children, and speaking words of comfort, nevertheless each of the actions of His human nature *is to be attributed to His Person*. But His Person is the Person of God—*therefore, each and every action of His human nature had an infinite value because done by the Person of God*. Hence, a sigh, a word, or a tear would have been sufficient to have redeemed the world, because it was the sigh, the word, or the tear of God.

During His earthly Life, extending from the crib to the cross and from the cross to His Resurrection and Ascension, our Blessed Lord did many things. St. John tells us that "if they were written every one, the world itself would not be able to contain the books that should be written" (John 21:25). This beautiful variety of actions, however, can be reduced to three, for our Lord filled a triple role or office. He was Teacher, He was King, and He was Priest.[3] In other words, He taught, He governed and He sanctified. He was Prophet and Teacher, not as the Scribes and Pharisees, but as one having authority, as the Light of the world. Before Him, Plato, Socrates, Buddha, Confucius, and others had said: "I will show you how to discover truth." He alone could say: "*I am the Truth*."[4] He was King, not a king of this world, but King of a spiritual Kingdom whose power extended over heaven and earth, the living and the dead.[5] He was Priest, not merely by holding up His Life as an example for us, but by laying down His Life for the Redemption of the world, in order that we might be regenerated from within as children of God and heirs of the Kingdom of Heaven.[6]

This triple role of Teacher, King, and Priest, our Lord exercised on earth through the instrumentality of His human nature. It was thanks to the body which He assumed from the womb of the Virgin Mary that He was able to make His teaching, His power, and His sanctification visible to men. The plan of the Incarnation was based upon the communication of the Divine through the human, the invisible through the visible, and the eternal through the temporal. It was, in a certain sense, the foundation of a Sacramental universe in which material things would be used as the channels for the spiritual. The footprints of the Eternal Galilean were soon to fade from the sands of the seashore and the dust of Jerusalem's streets; even the beautiful body which He took from His mother would be so tortured by men as to lose all its comeliness before assuming that glorified state in which men could no longer touch it. But though He knew He was soon to leave, He would not be an Architect who lays a foundation and then disappears, nor a Teacher who ceases to teach, nor a King who ceases to govern, nor a Priest who ceases to sanctify. He would be with men even to the consummation of the world.[7] In order that this union might be effective, He said that He would assume a new body which should not indeed be like the physical body which He assumed from the Blessed Virgin, but *another* body, a kingdom, a social unit, a spiritual corporation of regenerate souls,[8] a new humanity,[9] a new race.[10]

This new body which He said He would assume would be bound to Him not by external bonds such as memory, example, documents, but rather by internal bonds. It would be so much a part of Him that His Life would flow through it, just as the same life energizes both branches and vine.[11] This body would possess the characteristic of all living things, namely growth,[12] and although small at first it would develop even as the mustard seed which grows into a mighty tree.[13]

As a growing thing with the power of incorporating all men unto Himself, this body He ofttimes likened to a Kingdom. Not everyone included in it would be perfect: so He compared it to the sowing of a crop, the harvest of which was to come at the end of the world; and to the lowering of a net, the catch of which will be at the end of the world; and to the departure of a king into a far country, whose return would be at the end of the world. There would be tares as well as wheat in the harvest, good as well as bad fish in the catch, foolish virgins as well as wise virgins; there would be scandals, false sheep, jealousy, seeking first places at table, craving to lord it over others—until the final reckoning, when He would come in the clouds of heaven to separate the sheep from the goats, purge the Kingdom of its enemies, and reward every man according to his works.

All worldly standards would be set at naught in selecting the cells of the Body and the citizens of the Kingdom. Gentiles as well as Jews will be members of it; the elder son must not suppose that the sin of the prodigal and his subsequent pardon has excluded him from the patrimony; those who come late into this new spiritual corporation and work as hard will receive just as much as those who bore the heat and burdens of the day; guests who refuse banquets will be replaced by the poor from the highways and byways; and beggars like Lazarus will be preferred to rich men like Dives. But even though there be scandals from within and persecution from without, the members of His Kingdom need never fear that it will perish—for He has founded it upon a Rock against which the gates of hell cannot prevail, and He will be with it all days even to the consummation of the world.

But how would men become incorporated into this new spiritual Kingdom? If it were a mere earthly kingdom they might become citizens of it by some external means, but if the Kingdom be not material but organic and living, then incorporation will have to be effected in some vital way, namely by a birth. Men became members of the body of Adam, or the human race, by being born of the flesh; so Christ declared that they should become members of His body by being born of the Spirit. It was not very clear to Nicodemus how a man could be born again by entering his mother's womb, but our Lord told him that there was another kind of birth than the carnal one of the flesh, the spiritual birth of the waters of the Holy Ghost. Once reborn, membership in His new society was conditioned upon acceptance of every iota of His teachings: "He that believeth not shall be condemned" (Mark 16:16). And the truth which they were to believe would be safeguarded for all times by the Spirit of truth which He would send upon His new body.[14]

Though He more often spoke of this new spiritual organism as a Kingdom, He made clear that it was not of this world; that is why He fled on the day that men tried to make Him king, and that is why He told them that His Kingdom was not of this world. He hinted that this Kingdom, not of this earth, should be joined to Him as a body to a head. When the head suffers the body suffers too, because they constitute one life; when the body is hurt the head feels it, because they are one. Using this analogy, He said that whatever happened to Him as Head would happen to His Body; if He was persecuted His Body would be persecuted; if He was hated His Body would be hated; if the world did not receive Him it would not receive His Body, for the servant is not above the master.[15] In like manner, anyone who heard the members of His new body would hear Him, anyone who despised them would despise Him. The relation would be so close between the members of that Body and Himself, that anyone who gave a drink to the members in His name, or visited them in prison, or received one of their children, or gave bread to satisfy hunger or clothes to cover nakedness, would be doing the service unto Him. It would seem that He had exhausted all analogies to mark the unity between Him and His new body; but the night before He died, He said that He and His flock were not to be one merely as shepherd and sheep, they were to be one as He and the Father were one. The very fact that He spoke these words on the eve of His Crucifixion and but an hour before His Agony in the Garden was a reminder that this new Kingdom or this new Body of His, would not reveal itself in all its glory and beauty until He had purchased that glory and beauty by the sacrifice of His Life. Thus would He prove that He loved His new corporate life, "for greater love than this no man hath, that he lay down his life for his friends." Addressing His heavenly Father in some of the most beautiful words ever heard

THE MYSTICAL BODY OF CHRIST

on this sinful earth of ours, He confirmed this forthcoming union
of His new Body and Himself:

> As Thou hast sent Me into the world, I have also sent them
> into the world. That they may be one, as Thou, Father, in Me,
> and I in Thee; that they may be one in Us: that the world may
> believe that Thou hast sent Me and hast loved them as Thou
> hast loved me.[16]

The new Body was then to be one with Him as He and the
Father were one, but this unity with Christ would not have its
glorious Transfiguration until after the scandal of His Death,
and His Ascension into heaven. Men must first have faith in
Him, as Head, before they can have faith in His Body. And so
He reminded them that He must first be lifted up on the Cross
before He could draw them unto Himself. The Father had sent
Him into the world, and He was prepared now to leave it. Many
times before, His enemies tried to take away His Life, but He said
that He would lay it down of Himself in the hour of darkness and
then go back to the Father.[17] The greater gifts He had for men in
His new Kingdom were conditional on His Death, Resurrection,
and Ascension. His human nature must needs receive the reward
due to it, for obeying the Father's will: "And now glorify thou Me,
O Father, with Thyself, with the glory which I had, before the
world was, with Thee." If He did not leave them after the "folly
of the Cross" and ascend again to the Father, they could never
become a part of Him, like branches of a vine. "A little while, and
now you shall not see Me; and again a little while, and you shall
see Me: because I go to the Father" (John 16:16).

His departure was the very condition of their receiving Him
in a new way. If He left the earth in His human earthly existence
which He had taken from the womb of the Blessed Mother, He
could descend in a new way by overshadowing them with His
Spirit. "But because I have spoken these things to you, sorrow

hath filled your heart. But I tell you the truth; it is expedient to you that I go; for if I go not, the Paraclete will not come to you; but if I go, I will send Him to you" (John 16:6, 7). He had been sanctifying Himself not for Himself, for He was God; rather He was sanctifying Himself in His human nature in order that He might pour forth His Spirit for the sanctification of His Body and for the faith of the world:

> Father, Sanctify them in truth. Thy Word is Truth.
> As Thou hast sent Me into the world,
> I also have sent them into the world.
> And for them do I sanctify Myself,
> That they also may be sanctified in Truth.
> And not for them only do I pray,
> But for them also Who through their word
> Shall believe in me. (John 17:17–20)

But what was to be the nucleus of this new Body which would be one with Him after the scandal of His Crucifixion and the descent of His Spirit? What was to be the embryo of this new living Kingdom which would fill the earth? Its nucleus was to be men, but not men who chose Him, but men whom He chose because the Father had given them to Him.[18] A little band of apostles, who had been witnesses of His Resurrection and who were therefore convinced of His Divinity, were to be the raw material into which He would send His Spirit to quicken them into a living Body. Most of the Gospels are made up not of His teaching to the multitude, but to the chosen little band who were constantly with Him. They are to be the ones who will represent Him when He is gone; they will have to stand before princes and governors and speak the truths which His Spirit will give them to speak; they will be hated as He was hated, and men will think to do a service to God in harming them. The privilege of evangelizing the world is reserved to them. *He* is sent to the lost sheep of Israel, and only with reluctance does He leave His people; but *they* are to go to the Gentiles, to the Samaritans, to the ends of the earth. This "little flock" He called to be His posthumous Self, His prolonged Personality, the scattered reapers of His harvest, the lights kindled at His Light, the syllables of Him who is the Word. They are not to seek to gain the world, but to save souls as fishers of men, to preach, to baptize in the name of the Trinity, to continue the Memorial of His Passion, and to forgive sins. Very simply, they were to do the same three things as He had done in His earthly life: they were to teach, to govern, and to sanctify. Just as He, the Incarnate Word, exercised this triple office through the instrumentality of His physical body, so would He continue to exercise it through the medium of His corporate Body of which they are the elements. He was Teacher because He was Truth itself, and the Light of the world: but they were also to be teachers: "As My Father has sent Me, so also do I send you. . . . Go teach all nations. He that heareth you, heareth Me, and He that despiseth you, despiseth Me." Certainly, if these words mean anything, they mean that just as He taught through His visible form of man, so He would continue to teach through them, the Truth for ever being His and not theirs.

He was also the King whose power extended over the living and the dead, but His apostles too would have His power: All power is given to Me in heaven and on earth. My power I give unto you. Whatsoever thou shall bind on earth shall be bound also in heaven; whatsoever thou shalt loose on earth shall be loosed also in heaven. Once more He reveals that just as He exercised His powers of Kingship in admitting the penitent thief to His Kingdom, so now He would continue to exercise His Kingly power through His new Body—He remaining the King, they being only His ambassadors or the channels by which that power is communicated to men.

He is the Priest who comes to give "His Life for the Redemption of many." They too will be priests: "Baptize in the name of the

Father, the Son and the Holy Ghost." . . . "Do this in commemoration of Me." . . . "Whose sins you shall forgive they are forgiven them; whose sins you shall retain, they are retained." Even the most prejudiced of textual criticism has failed to dislodge the force of these texts; the meaning is clear. Just as through His own Body He sanctified souls, offered His Body and Blood to His heavenly Father, forgave the sins of Magdalene and Peter, so was He now communicating to His new Body the same power of sanctification, He remaining always the High Priest, they the instruments of that Priesthood.

This Apostolic band, however, did not yet fully understand how they were to be so much a part of Him that He would teach through them, govern through them, and sanctify through them. How they were to be His new Body, share His Life, live by His Spirit, be the nucleus of His Kingdom on earth, they never understood until the day on which He had foretold that they would understand—the day of the descent of His Spirit. Before that day, James and John, through their mother, sought places at the right and left of their Master; Philip could not understand His heavenly Father; Thomas did not know where He was going and how He would come back; Peter denied Him to a maid-servant; the chosen three of the Transfiguration slept in the Garden; and when the Shepherd was struck the flock was dispersed. Even after the Resurrection they were tardy to believe, still not understanding the Scriptures. No one needed to be more convinced of its reality than they; one of them even refused to believe until he put a finger into Christ's hands and a hand into His side. Even in the week after the triumph of Easter they were back at their nets and their boats. But all this was foretold: they would not understand how much they were His until He had sent His Spirit. Had He not told them so: "And I will ask the Father, and He shall give you another Paraclete, that He may abide with you for ever. The Spirit of truth, whom the world cannot receive, because it seeth Him not, nor knoweth Him: but you shall know Him; because

THE MYSTICAL BODY OF CHRIST

He shall abide with you, and shall be in you. I will not leave you orphans, I will come to you. Yet a little while: and the world seeth Me no more. But you see Me, because I live, and you shall live. In that day you shall know that I am in My Father, and you shall live" (John 14:16–20).

In order to drive home this lesson that the embryonic Body would not be fully incorporated in Him until the Spirit had made them one, our Blessed Lord on the very day of His Resurrection told Magdalene, who rushed at Him to kiss His sacred feet: "Touch Me not. I am not yet ascended to My Father." In the language of Cardinal Newman:

> *Why* might not our Lord be touched *before* His ascension, and how *could* He be touched *after* it? But Christ speaks, it would seem, thus (if, as before, we might venture to paraphrase His sacred words)—"Hitherto you have only known Me after the flesh. I have lived among you as a man. You have been permitted to approach Me sensibly, to kiss and embrace My feet, to pour ointment upon My head. But all this is at an end, now that I have died and risen again in the power of the Spirit. A glorified state of existence is begun in Me, and will soon be perfected. At present, though I bid you at one moment handle Me as possessed of flesh and bones, I vanish like a spirit at another; though I let one follower embrace My feet, and say, 'Fear not,' I repel another with the words, 'Touch Me not.' Touch Me not, for I am fast passing for your great benefit from earth to heaven, from flesh and blood into glory, from a natural body to a spiritual body. When I am ascended, then the change will be completed. To pass hence to the Father in My bodily presence, is to descend from the Father to you in spirit. When I am thus changed, when I am thus present to you, more really present than now, though invisibly, then you may touch Me,—may touch Me, more really though invisibly, by faith, in reverence, through such outward approaches as I shall assign. Now you

but see me from time to time; when you see most of Me I am at best but 'going in and out among you.' Thou hast seen Me, Mary, but couldst not hold Me; thou hast approached Me, but only to embrace My feet, or to be touched by My hand; and thou sayest, 'O that I knew where I might find Him, that I might come even to His seat! O that I might hold Him and not let Him go!' Henceforth this shall not be; when I am ascended, thou shalt see nothing, thou shalt have everything. Thou shalt sit down under My shadow with great delight, and My fruit shall be sweet to thy taste. Thou shalt have Me whole and entire. I will be near thee, I will be in thee; I will come into thy heart a whole Saviour, a whole Christ,—in all My fulness as God and man,—in the awful virtue of that Body and Blood, which has been taken into the Divine Person of the Word, and is indivisible from it, and has atoned for the sins of the world,—not by external contact, not by partial possession, not by momentary approaches, not by a barren manifestation, but inward in presence, and intimate in fruition, a principle of life and a seed of immortality, that thou mayest 'bring forth fruit unto God.'"[19]

Forty days after the event of this day, during which time He spoke to them of the Kingdom of God (Acts 1:3), He blessed His little flock (Luke 24:51) and ascended into heaven, commanding them not to "depart from Jerusalem," but to "wait for the promise of the Father." "You shall receive the power of the Holy Ghost coming upon you, and you shall be witnesses unto me, in Jerusalem, and in all Judea, and Samaria, and even to the uttermost part of the earth" (Acts 1:4, 8).

Ten days later, as promised, these frail, weak, human creatures, as yet full of their individual doubts and ambitions, were lifted up into a higher unity by the gift of the Holy Ghost, became the earthly branches of Him the Eternal Vine, the living Kingdom of Him the heavenly King, and the new Body of Him the glorified Christ.

What now is this new Body which Christ assumed after He had ascended into His glory, to which He sent His heavenly Spirit, and through which He continues to exercise His office as Teacher, King, and Priest? If I said it was the Church, I would not be believed. I will therefore let St. Paul say it clearly and unmistakably: "Who now rejoice in my sufferings for you, and fill up those things that are wanting of the sufferings of Christ, in my flesh, for His Body, which is the Church" (Col. 1:24).

Here we must pause to ask ourselves why St. Paul uses the term "body" at all, and then press on to inquire further into the nature of this Body.

St. Paul, it must be remembered, did not build a theory of the Church on the analogy of a living body, composed of head and members, in order to define their reciprocal relations. *Rather the Church existed anterior to the comparison.* The term "body" was used, therefore, merely to make it easier for the mind to grasp the unity existing between the head and members. A body is an organic whole, composed of an infinite number of cells and members, all directed by the head and all vivified by the soul and all directed to a common end, which is the conservation of the organism and its ultimate happiness.

Now it happens that all these elements are in the Church in an eminent way.[20] The analogy of the human body is, therefore, employed by St. Paul to aid in understanding the supernatural organism of the Church.[21]

But granted that the Church is a Body, it remains now to inquire: What kind of a Body is it? Is it the *Physical Body* of Christ, or is it a *moral body* of Christ, or is it something yet other?

It is not the *Physical Body* of Christ, for that is now at the right hand of the glory of the Father. Furthermore, since His Ascension into Heaven, our Lord, St. Paul tells us, is the *Head* of the Body which is the Church.

Neither is the Church a *moral body* of Christ, because the union between the Church and Christ is more intimate than the unity of members in a moral body like a club or a nation. The unity of the members of the Church is not maintained solely by the will of the members, for here the will is neither the sole agent nor the principal agent of incorporation as it is in social bodies. There is a hidden, mysterious, non-human, divine unifying power at work which is Charity poured in the souls of the Mystical Body by the Third Person of the Blessed Trinity. A moral body is an organization, but the Church is an *organism* because of its Soul. In no social unity is there such a bond between head and members, and of members with one another as there is in the Church because of the "Spirit of Christ" which makes them one. Hence we must look for another term to qualify "body" than either *physical* or *moral*.

In order to express that transcendent unity of Christ and His Church which is effected not by external bonds, but by an internal bond of charity diffused in our souls by the Third Person of the Blessed Trinity, the theologians have applied the term "Mystical." This word is only an adjective modifying Body and is therefore not to be confused with Mysticism.[22]

Let us now return to the doctrine of Paul, which is the same doctrine as that of the Gospels,[23] and written even before the Gospels. The Church is the Mystical Body of Christ. It is a body because made up of many members who have become incorporated to Christ by being reborn of the Holy Ghost:

> For as in one body we have many members,
> But all the members have not the same office:
> So we being many,
> Are one body in Christ;
> And every one members one of another. (Rom. 12:4–5)

For as the body is one and hath many members;
And all the members of the body,
Whereas they are many.
Yet are One body:
So also is Christ.
For in one Spirit were we all baptized into one body,[24]
Whether Jews or Gentiles, whether bond or free; . . .

Now you are the body of Christ
And members of member. (1 Cor. 12:12, 13, 27)

Just as my body is constituted of millions and millions of tiny
cells, each one living its own individual life and yet living the life
of the whole body, so too the Church is made up of millions and
millions of members incorporated into it by baptism. Just as one
cell is not another, just as the leg is not the arm and the eye not
the ear, so neither is the Christian who teaches the Christian
who labours, nor the missionary who preaches, the mother who
raises her children in the love of God, and yet all are necessary
for the proper functioning of the whole body. There is diversity
of members and yet unity of vital principle. As St. Paul so clearly
puts it:

For the body also is not one member, but many. If the foot
should say, because I am not the hand, I am not of the body; is
it therefore not of the body? And if the ear should say, because
I am not the eye, I am not of the body; is it therefore not of
the body? If the whole body were the eye, where would be
the hearing? If the whole were hearing, where would be the
smelling? But now God hath set the members every one of
them in the body as it hath pleased Him. And if they all were
one member, where would be the body? But now there are
many members indeed, yet one body. And the eye cannot say
to the hand: I need not thy help; nor again the head to the feet:

I have no need of you. Yea, much more those that seem to be the more feeble members of the body, are more necessary. And such as we think to be the less honourable members of the body, about these we put more abundant honour; and those that are our uncomely parts, have more abundant comeliness. But our comely parts have no need: but God hath tempered the body together, giving to that which wanted the more abundant honour, that there might be no schism in the body; but the members might be mutually careful one for another. And if one member suffer anything, all the members suffer with it; or if one member glory, all the members rejoice with it. Now you are the Body of Christ, and members of member, and God indeed hath set some in the Church: first apostles, secondly prophets, thirdly doctors; after that miracles: then the graces of healings, helps, governments, kinds of tongues, interpretations of speeches. (1 Cor. 12:14–28)[25]

St. Paul uses many other examples to show the unity of Christ and His Church; for example, he reminds us that the Church is God's Building, the foundation stone of which is Christ and in which we are a kind of living stones fitted into that temple.[26] On another occasion he used the analogy of marriage, reminding us that the union of the Church and Christ is more intimate than the union of husband and wife, for the latter are only in the flesh, but the Church and Christ are one in the unity of spirit.[27] Hence to St. Paul it is one and the same thing to say that the Church is the Bride of Christ as to say she is His Body; but he prefers the latter phrase, as signifying a closer unity and a common life. Being His Body, she is one with Him, and from Him comes her whole activity, her whole life, her whole growth and development.

The Church is the Body of Christ, but who is its Head? The Head of the Body is Christ—not the visible Christ who was born in Bethlehem, lived at Nazareth, taught in Galilee and Judea, and was crucified in Jerusalem. If we knew Christ according to the flesh, St. Paul tells us, we know Him so no longer. The Christ who is the Head of His Body which is the Church is the Risen, Glorified Christ, seated at the right hand of the Father, the Christ whose redemptive death won for us the outpouring of the Pentecostal Spirit which made us one with Him more truly than John was one with Him, as He leaned on His breast the night of the Last Supper,[28] and brings Him closer to us than we are to ourselves.

The invisible Christ, in glory at the right hand of the Father, is the Head of this Body.[29] From all eternity He was destined to be the Head of a regenerated humanity. In the order of time, He came relatively late into the world, but in the order of existence and Divine intention He was first.

> And He is the Head of the Body, the Church
> Who is the Beginning '. . . *the first-born of every creature*'
> For in Him were all things created
> In heaven and on earth, visible and invisible.
> Whether thrones or dominations, or principalities
> > or powers.
> All things were created by Him and in Him
> And He is before all. And by Him all things consist.
> > (Col. 1:18, 16–17)

The Head of the Church pre-existed it from all eternity, and the present plan of Providence is to make all men conformable to Christ, and to subject all men to Him in love.[30] Christ is the Head of the Church in the eternal decrees as well as in the order of time, for He is the only one in all the world who ever had a pre-history—a pre-history to be studied not in the slime and dust of primeval jungles but in the bosom of an eternal Father.

Since then He is "the beginning, the first-born of every creature" the Church becomes in the order of time His Fullness, "because in Him it hath well pleased the Father that all fullness should dwell" (Col. 1:19). The Church is the plenitude of Christ;

it is the edifice of which He is the foundation (1 Cor. 3:9 ff); the branch of which He is the root; the organism of which He is the vivifying soul. The Church continues Christ, expresses Christ, develops all the virtualities, potentialities of Christ, makes it possible for Him to extend Himself beyond the space of Palestine and the space of thirty-three years to prolong His influence unto all times and to all men—in a word, it de-temporalizes and de-localizes Christ so that He belongs to all ages and all souls. The garments which He wore in His earthly Life He permitted to be stripped from Him, as He began the great work of Redemption, in order to declare to all men that His sacrifice was not peculiar to any race or any hour.

As He existed before His Church as the first-born of creatures, so He co-exists with it in His risen Life as its Glorified Head in heaven. Hence, those who lived during His Galilean existence had no great advantage over us who see His Mystical existence. Faith is required on the part of both. They saw the Head, but they had to have faith in the Body which was to be vivified by His Spirit; we see the Body which is vivified by His Spirit; but we have to have faith in the Head who is one with it in glory.

*Without the Church Christ would be incomplete.* This is a strong statement, and yet it is precisely what the Scriptures mean in saying that the Church is the fullness of Christ, and that Christ must grow to His full stature. *The Incarnate did not exhaust Himself in the Incarnation.* As the earthly Christ grew in age and grace and wisdom, so must the Mystical Christ grow, but neither can grow without a Body. The physical Body reached its perfect stature, humbled itself in death, and was exalted to glory; the Mystical Body must likewise grow, be humbled, and enter into its glory. Through it, Christ re-lives, re-grows, re-dies, and is re-glorified; and without it He would lack His fullness, and would be circumscribed by time and space—His own creation. It certainly is not fitting that the Creator be limited by His creation.

And yet despite the fact that the Church is His fullness it adds nothing to Him, for He is its principle and its origin. Just as after creation there was no more Being than before, but only more things which had being, as there was no more Truth, but only more true things, as there was no more Love, but only more lovely things, so too after the assumption of His Mystical Body, there was no more Divine Life; there were only more human natures possessing it. Every influx of Life and Truth and Love which the Mystical Body receives is the endowment and the gift of the Head. Without Him there would be no Mystical Body. There is no more light in the sun because it happens to shine in one window of a house than because it happens to shine in ten windows. The quantity of light is fixed; those who share it vary. Likewise in the Church, the Life of Christ is Infinite because Divine. It admits of no increase; it remains the inexhaustible Source regardless of how many members of the Mystical Body voluntarily receive it. But without it, the Mystical Body would have no life whatever, for Christ is the universal principle of Life in the Church.[31]

But if Christ is the Head of the Church which is His Body, it remains to inquire if the relation between the two is something like that which existed between the Divine nature of Christ and the human nature in the mystery of the Incarnation. The answer is in the affirmative. In the natural Christ, there was a human nature and a Divine nature in the unity of the Divine Person of the Word; the human nature was visible, the Divine nature was invisible, but their joint action in the unity of the Word constituted what was called a *theandric* action. Now the Church has a human element and also a Divine element, though the union between them is not hypostatic. The human element is we, the regenerated humanity; the Divine element is our Head, the Risen Christ, and the two are one "in Christ Jesus," as St. Paul expresses it. The actions of the Church are therefore *theandric* actions, inasmuch as they involve a human and a divine element, a visible and an invisible factor. When the Church forgives sins through the instrumentality of a priest, the Life of Christ flows into the soul of the penitent, the priest being merely the channel of the grace, but not its creator.

In the administration of the sacraments where the action is *theandric*, something happens similar to that which took place when our Lord cured the blind man by rubbing dust and spittle in his eyes. The mixing of the dust and spittle was the action of human nature, but it was an action inseparable from the action of the Divine Nature in union with the Person where resided the power to give sight to the blind. The Church, then, the *totus Christus* (the whole Christ), as St. Augustine calls it, is continuing the Incarnation by prolonging the theandric actions of the historical Christ.[32]

In a certain sense, therefore, the actions of the Mystical Body are the actions of Christ. *Actiones sunt suppositorum.* Actions are attributed not to a nature, but to a person. In the Incarnation, the actions of the human nature of Christ were attributed to His Divine Person. When His human hand was laid on a child, it was *God* Who blessed the child. Now since the Church and Christ are one, does not the same principle apply with reservations? Is not the action of a Peter who teaches, the action of a Christ? and is not the sanctification of souls through priestly ministrations, sanctification by Christ Himself? Peter, James, and John baptized, but it is Christ who baptizes. The human elements in the Church are merely the instruments with which Christ continues to teach, to govern, and to sanctify, as His human nature was the "conjoined instrument of His Divinity." The actions of the members in this triple work are to be attributed to the Person of Christ.[33] Christ and His Mystical Body make but one Mystical Person. A Mystical Person has a double existence: one in Himself as Head of the Mystical Body, and the other in the Body of the faithful who receive His Life. Inasmuch as He exists in Himself, He is a single Person; but inasmuch as He subsists mystically in His members, He fills the role of Personality. Thus united to us, Christ shares

His Life by a kind of "communication of idioms" somewhat akin to that which is established between His two natures.

Is the theology of the Mystical Body which represents the Glorified Christ as Head of the Church His Mystical Body, a theory based on facts? As to those who might doubt it, let them recall the conversion of St. Paul. This fiery Hebrew of the Hebrews grew up with an unholy hatred of Christ and things Christian. His first appearance was in that role of hatred, when as Saul he watched the garments of those who stoned Stephen, the first Christian martyr. Saul was not just a bigot. He was a learned man, trained under Gamaliel, and so powerful a disputant that the early Christians must often have wondered whom they could find to refute him. In the Providence of God it was reserved that a Paul should refute a Saul. One day he set out on a journey for Damascus, authorized by letters to seize the Christians of that city, bind them, and bring them back to Jerusalem. Breathing out hatred against the Lord, He departed to persecute the infant Church. The time was only a few years after the Resurrection and Ascension of our Divine Saviour. While he was on this journey, suddenly a great light shone about him and he fell to the ground, aroused by a voice like a bursting sea: "Saul, Saul, why persecutest thou Me?" Nothingness dared to ask the name of Omnipotence, "Who art Thou, Lord?" And He answered: "I am Jesus whom thou persecutest" (Acts 9:1 ff).

Saul was about to strike the Church in the city of Damascus, in exactly the same way as the Government of Mexico persecutes the Church in Mexico and the Government of Spain has persecuted the Church in Madrid—and the Voice from heaven says: "Saul, Saul, why persecutest thou Me?" Christ and the Church, are they the same? The risen Christ, only four or five years after He had left this earth, broke open the heavens in order to declare to Saul and the world that the Church is His Body, that in striking that body you strike its Head, that He and the Church are one Person; that, just as the tongue speaks when the foot is trodden upon, so when the Body of the Church is persecuted it is Christ who arises to speak. On Holy Thursday night a soldier in the hall of the high priest struck our Lord with a mailed fist, and Christ said: "If I have spoken evil, give testimony of the evil; if good, then why do you strike Me?" And now that same Christ in His glory, who has incorporated unto Himself His new Body, the Church, still cries out when that Body is struck: "Why persecutest thou Me?" What does all this mean, but that Calvary may be prolonged even beyond Jerusalem's walls; and the Life of Christ in His Church extended beyond the sands of a Galilean seashore and the memorial of an upper-room? No wonder that the transformed Saul, St. Paul, understood so well the nature of the Church! He too knew Christ as well as the other apostles, for he too had touched His Body.

The Church, then, is in the truest sense of the term the prolongation of the Incarnation; it is the new Body which Christ assumes after His Ascension, with which to extend His Kingship throughout the kingdoms of the World; it is the new living instrument through which He teaches, governs, and sanctifies; it is His new corporate human nature under the headship of His Divine Person, of whose plenitude we have all received; it is His fullness, without which His life would be but a memory and His Kingship only a name.

How far removed is this doctrine of the Church from the false conception of those who would accuse the Church of standing between Christ and us? How often we hear it said: "I do not want an organization between Christ and me," or "True religion consists in union with Jesus of Nazareth without priest, or prelate, or sacrament." Anyone who understands the Scriptures will see that the Church does not stand between Christ and me. The Church *is Christ*. It no more stands between Christ and me, than His feet stood between Magdalene and His forgiveness, or His hand stood between the little children and His blessing, or His Breast stood between John and the secrets of the Sacred Heart.

The Church no more stands between the Divine Life of Christ and my soul, than His physical Body stands between me and His Divinity. It was through His human Body that He came to me in His individual Life; it is through His Mystical Body that He comes to me in His corporate Life.[34] Christ *is the Church*: her real, inner self is His Body permeated through and through with His Redemptive Life. We who are members of His Mystical Body are not merely imitators of Christ; we are not merely lovers of His doctrine; we are more! Why, we are the cells in that very Body which is Christ!

All misunderstandings come from regarding the Church as an organization. It is not an organization like a club; it is an organism like a body. It was formed not by men coming together unto Christ, as bricks are piled together to make a building; it was formed by the life of Christ *going out* to men, as the life of a cell diffuses itself from within. The Church was not formed by the faithful; it was the faithful who were formed by the Church. The Church did not spring into being, when the apostles heard the message of Jesus and then agreed on the basis of their common faith to form a society, which is called the Church. No! The Church was in existence before Peter or James or John or the other apostles became believers. It was in actual existence the very moment when the Word was made flesh and dwelt amongst us, for at that moment Christ assumed a human nature, the "pattern-man," like unto which He would mould us by the fingers of His love and the power of His grace.

It should not surprise us to learn that we derive our individual Christian life from the Church. Do we not derive our individual political life from society? How did each of us become an American? Certainly not by reading our history, studying the doctrine of, let us say, George Washington, following his example, and then concluding that we should become members of this nation. No! We were *born* Americans; we belonged to America even before we chose it. So also, we do not become Christians by going back nineteen hundred years and studying the life of Christ and imitating His example, and then concluding that we should like to attach ourselves to that great Personage. No! The Christian is born in the womb of a religious corporate society, just as a citizen is born in the womb of a political society. He lives by it, before he knows it, before he judges it, before he seeks its sources, before he knows its traditions. It creates him spiritually by baptism of the spirit, as his fatherland creates him by the birth of his flesh. Later, he may accept or reject the Body of Christ as a man may expatriate himself from his country, but in the beginning the spiritual society creates him.

The Church begets us; we do not beget the Church. We do not beget the Church because the Church is Christ who first loved us, even before we were made. Any suggestion, therefore, that the Church is an obstacle to our union with Christ, is based upon a misunderstanding of the meaning and beauty of the Incarnation of our Lord. For, just as our Lord lived a physical Life two thousand years ago in a human body taken from Mary, so now He lives a Mystical Life in a body drawn from the womb of humanity. In the eyes of every member of that Church, the Eternal Galilean re-lives the events and crises of His Life in Judea and Galilee. The written Gospel is the record of His historical life. The Church is the living Gospel and record of His present Life. The life of the Church is the Life of the Mystical Christ—a life whose history is already written because it has been lived in pattern by the Christ who is its Head. The Church is the only thing in the world whose history was written before it was lived.

His Eternity cannot be limited by time, nor His Omnipresence by a lake and a mountain country. America, Europe, Asia, the frozen North, the torrid South, the contemplative East, the active West, all parts of the world must show His Presence, feel His Love, and draw healing from His Wings. But how can this be done unless He assume another Body in which He will live and through which He will march throughout the ages as the Eternal

Christ, "the same, yesterday, to-day, and for ever." The Church is
that without which Christ would be limited and imperfect; it is
that in which Bethlehem revives in every baptism and the Cenacle
in every Mass, the instruction of the doctors of the Temple in
every definition, the pardon of Peter in every absolution, and the
Crucifixion in every persecution. Were it not for the new Body,
where would Christ have tongues with which to preach the Word
of Life? Were it not for His Mystical Body, where would Christ
find lips with which to speak forgiveness to penitent thieves? If
it were not for this Body, where would He find hands to lay on
little children, feet to receive the ointment of other Magdalenes,
and a breast to receive the embrace of other Johns? Were it not
for this Body, where would Christ find a visible Head to articu-
late His voice and draw all souls into the unity of one Lord, one
faith, one Baptism? How else could He, as the Incarnate God,
console other widows than those of Naim, visit other friends
than those of Bethany, attend other nuptials than those of Cana,
call other apostles than those of the lake, convert other women
than those of Samaria, and other men than the centurions of
Calvary? How could He the God-man show meekness to other
soldiers' executioners; patience to other timid disciples, love for
other publicans, friendliness to other Judases, forgiveness to other
malefactors, devotion to other Johns, affection to other Marys,
wisdom to other doctors of the Law, except through another
Body with whose Feet He could step from Jerusalem to the world,
with whose lips He could speak to us who call ourselves modern?
The Upper Room is in our cities, as with other hands we lift to
His Father the chalice of His Blood shed for the redemption of
many; Capharnaum is at the border of all our waters, as He calls
to Himself other fishers of men; Nazareth is at Lourdes, as Mary
Immaculate mothers her new children, brothers of Christ and
sons of the heavenly Father! Christ is *at our very door.* If we do not
see Him living to-day in His Mystical Body, then we would not
have seen Him living nineteen hundred years ago in His Physical

Body. If we do not believe the Mystical Body to be Divine, because it is also so human, then we would not have believed the Physical Body to be Divine, because it was crucified. And if we miss the Lord Jesus it is not because He is too far away, but because He is too close. "Behold I stand at the door and knock."

## CHAPTER III

# The Head of the Body

The Church is the Mystical Body of Christ. The Head of that Body is our Divine Lord whom God raised "up from the dead, setting Him on His right hand in the heavenly places, above all principality, and power, and virtue, and dominion, and every name that is named, not only in this world, but also in that which is to come. And He hath subjected all things under His feet and hath made Him Head over all the church, which is His Body, and the fullness of Him who is filled all in all" (Eph. 1:20–23). "For in Him were all things created in heaven and on earth, visible and invisible, whether thrones or dominations or principalities, or powers; all things were created by Him and in Him. And He is before all, and by Him all things consist. And He is the Head of the Body, the Church, who is the beginning, the first born from the dead; that in all things He may hold the primacy."[1]

These texts of St. Paul make it clear that the creation of angels, of men, of all things was ordained to Christ as their Head. Though His human nature is late in the order of time, in pre-eminence He has even been before all. St. Thomas studies in some detail this pre-eminence of Christ. He writes:

> As the whole Church is termed one mystic body from its likeness to the natural body of a man, which in diverse members has diverse acts, as the apostle teaches (Romans 12 and 1 Corinthians 12), so likewise Christ is called the Head of

the Church from a likeness with the human head, in which we may consider three things—viz., order, perfection, and power: *Order*, indeed; for the head is the first part of man, beginning from the higher part; and hence it is that a principle is usually called a head as in Ezekiel 16:25; *At every head of the way*—*Perfection*, inasmuch as in the head dwell all the senses, both interior and exterior, whereas in the other members there is only touch, and hence it is said (Isaiah 9:15): *The aged and honourable, he is the head*—*Power*, because the power and movement of the other members, together with the direction of them in their acts, is from the head, by reason of the sensitive and motive power there ruling; hence the ruler is called the head of a people, according to 1 Samuel 15:17: *When thou wast a little one in thy own eyes, wast thou not made the head of the tribes of Israel?*

Now these three things belong spiritually to Christ. First, on account of His nearness to God His grace is the highest and first, though not in time, since all have received grace on account of His grace, according to Romans 8:29: *For whom He foreknew, He also predestinated to be made conformable to the image of His Son; that He might be the first-born amongst many brethren.* Secondly, He had perfection as regards the fulness of all graces, according to John 1:14, *We saw Him* (Vulg., *His glory*) . . . *full of grace and truth*, as was shown in Q. VII, A. 9. Thirdly, He has the power of bestowing grace on all the members of the Church, according to John 1:16: *Of His fullness we have all received.* And thus it is plain that Christ is fittingly called the Head of the Church.[2]

The Headship of Christ over the Church means not only the Church on earth, but also the Church in its entirety, including angels and men, even those who lived at the beginning of the world.[3] To say that Christ is the Head of *all* men regardless of time and space does not, however, mean they are all related to Him in the same way. St. Thomas explains the matter thus:

> This is the difference between the natural body of man and the Church's mystical body, that the members of the natural body are all together, and the members of the mystical are not all together;—neither as regards their natural being, since the body of the Church is made up of the men who have been from the beginning of the world until its end;—nor as regards their supernatural being, since, of those who are at any one time, some there are who are without grace, yet will afterwards obtain it, and some have it already. We must therefore consider the members of the mystical body not only as they are in act, but as they are in potentiality. Nevertheless, some are in potentiality who will never be reduced to act, and some are reduced at some time to act; and this according to the triple class, of which the first is by faith, the second by the charity of this life, the third by the fruition of the life to come. Hence we must say that if we take the whole time of the world in general, Christ is the Head of all men, but diversely. For, first and principally, He is the Head of such as are united to Him by glory; secondly, of those who are actually united to Him by charity; thirdly, of those who are actually united to Him by faith; fourthly, of those who are united to Him merely in potentiality, which is not yet reduced to act, yet will be reduced to act according to Divine predestination; fifthly, of those who are united to Him in potentiality, which will never be reduced to act; such as those men existing in the world, who are not predestined, who, however, on their departure from this world, wholly cease to be members of Christ, as being no longer in potentiality to be united to Christ.[4]

Christ is the Head of the Church, but He is invisible because He has ascended into heaven. We cannot see the Head of the

Church now any more than those who lived in Galilee could see His Mystical Body. In both cases faith is required. The union between the Head and the Body, or between the Risen Christ and the Church, is vital and intense, for it is modelled upon the union of His Divine and human nature in the unity of His Person. It is only natural therefore to expect that the union between Him and His Church should be in their own order, as intimate as the union between His Divine and human natures. As a matter of historical record, our Lord did assure us that He and His new Body would be one: one, because the life of one is the life of the other as with the branches and the vine; one, because the authority of the one is the authority of the other: "He that heareth you, heareth Me"; one, because he who gives a drink of cold water to a member of that body gives it unto Him; one, because there is one Church, one fold, and one Shepherd (John 10:16); one, because unless a man be baptized and believe, he is for ever outside of Christ and His eternal Life (Matt. 28:19–20); one, because He and His new Body are one as He and the Father are one (John 17:11). If it were otherwise, His Kingdom would fall to pieces, for unity is the condition of life, and a kingdom divided against itself cannot stand (Matt. 12:25). There is no taking back this promise of common life. Heaven and earth will pass away, but His words will not pass away (Matt. 24:35; Mark 13:31; Luke 21:33).

Granted that He and the Church are so much one that when Saul struck at it he struck Christ, this practical question arises: How are men to know where this one body is? Now that our Lord is in heaven, is it not natural for each of the conflicting groups and sects to say that *it* is the one Body of Christ? It was easy enough to know which was His earthly body as He walked among His apostles, for He was manifestly their Head, but after His Ascension how can future generations tell the Body in which His Life is to be found?

Our Blessed Lord did not leave these questions unanswered. He came on earth to leave us Truth and Life, and dying rather than surrender a single iota of it, it seems only natural that He would preserve it, and would leave some definite mark of identification. That sign He gave was the sign of all living things. How does all life manifest itself except by the unity of its organism, and how does the unity of the body manifest itself except by and through a head, which is the source of the movements of the whole body? In the organic order the head is the symbol of the unity of life. Legs and arms, muscles and sinews may be amputated without necessarily destroying the unity of life, but the cutting off of the head, the centre of its unity, spells the end of life. In the social order likewise, we know a club, or a group, or a society, or a nation to be one because of its head—its president, its king or its ruler. So truly is headship the sign of the unity of life that in the psychological order everything tends by its very nature to acknowledge a primacy, aye more, it produces it by the very necessity of law. In an infant, for example, there is a complexity and a criss-crossing of activities and functions, some vegetative, others emotional, others conative, others mechanical, others vital. As the child develops, however, this variety of activities become more and more unified until a time when the child becomes conscious of its personality, and subsumes all these varied manifestations of life under the primacy of the ego with the use of the personal pronoun "I." Life then, by its very nature expresses its unity, in a centre of reference, in a brain, in a head, in a primacy of personality.

Now if the life of Christ and His Church is one, the obvious way in which we might expect Christ to identify His Body after His Ascension would be through a visible head or a primate. He was its Invisible Head,[5] but that would not prevent Him from leaving a visible representative of His headship, any more than His Godhead prevented Him from using men as the preachers of His Word, water as the channel of His regenerative grace, and bread as the means for communicating His Eternal Life. What we would therefore expect Christ to do, in the very nature of things, is what He actually did. He appointed a visible Head for His Body as the symbol of His oneness with both.

Of course, He might have done otherwise, and there may be some of His creatures who imagine they could think of a better plan, but if we are to be Christians we must be guided by what He did, rather than by what we would like to have Him do. The very interesting and amazing thing about our Lord's action in this matter was that He did seem to take into account the opinions of those who differ from Him. It was an evidence of God's patience with His self-willed creatures that He considered their points of view before imposing His own will.

His will was to name a visible Head to whom He would commit His authority and His power, which Head would be the sign of His oneness with His Body. But His creatures could think of two other plans, and they are still thinking of them—the democratic and the aristocratic.

The democratic form of government contends that God should make each individual his own supreme authority, allowing him either to interpret the Scriptures privately or else interpret his own religious experiences without any dictation from without. Religion on this theory is a purely individual affair: each one casts his own vote as to what he will believe, rejects all creeds, beliefs and dogmas which run counter to his moods and prejudices, determines for himself the kind of a God he will adore, the kind of an altar before which he will kneel—in a word, he worships at the shrines his own hands have made.

The second form of Church government which God's creatures think of as something He might have chosen is the aristocratic in which a select group, a council, a federation, a Parliament, or the representatives of different religious bodies themselves determine, in so far as is possible, the beliefs, worship and creeds of those under them.[6] A national church subject to a parliament, as is the Church of England to the English Parliament, is typical of this form of church government. The council or parliament which rules over the Church in this form is very much like a senate which comes to conclusions after a discussion, but which has no executive or judicial power to enforce them and bind them to the hearts of men.

The form our Lord chose was neither of these, but what might be called the monarchical. In this form the Head, who is the sign of the unity of the body, exercises universal and immediate jurisdiction over the whole Church and every member of it. This power of jurisdiction is not conferred upon him by a council, but given immediately by God, a further assurance of the oneness of Christ and His Church. If Christ chose His own Mystical Body, who shares His Life, it is fitting that He chose its Head, who is the visible representative of that unity. Hence, one man, acting in the name of all and with Divine assistance, is the infallible teacher, the supreme judge, the sovereign legislator of all the faithful. His decrees bind the very moment he as Head of the Church promulgates them, and they become binding on the faithful, even without the consent of the Church.

Our Blessed Lord chose the third form, but in order to make a concession to the poorer plans of His poor creatures and show their inadequacy, as well as to drive home the superior wisdom of His own Divine plan, He did not proclaim His choice until He had eliminated the two faulty plans of His creatures.

The important matter was discussed about the middle of His public career, and those who read His Life closely will see that once He revealed the foundation of His Church His whole plan of teaching changed. Up to that time He had spoken in guarded terms of the scandal of His death, but once the foundation of His Church was assured there was no longer reason for secrecy. He could now speak of His passion, His Cross and His Death.

The scene took place in the city of Caesarea-Philippi, a city in which paganism once flourished and even in those very days, it still preserved Pan's grotto, famous in the days of Greek colonists. In that pagan spot, He, the Lord and Master of the world, stopped to ask a question, the true answer to which would put an end to paganism if men would but heed it. The question was the most important one He ever asked in His Life and startled them all into a new birth of faith.

The question He asked was about His inmost nature, for unless men knew that under that human nature was beating the very Life of God, they could never know the secrets the Divine Heart had for men; unless they knew He was God they could never know the Divinity of the Church He came to establish as His Body. And so He asked: "Whom do men say that I am?" (Matt. 16:13 ff.) Note that it was an appeal to the democratic form of Church government. "Whom do *men* say that I am?" i.e., "Whom do men, individually interpreting their own experiences or constituting themselves as individual judges of My revealed Word, or setting themselves up as the last court of appeal, whom do they say that I am?"

The answer was the answer of confusion. Men had arrived at various conclusions; what else could they arrive at? "Some say that you are John the Baptist, others Elias, others, Jeremias, or one of the prophets." All rudimentary guesses of the poor and ignorant! No certainty! No agreement! No unity so dear to the heart of God! Leave the secret of His nature to individuals and the responses are bound to be contradictory, contrary and confusing, one man denying what another has said! If we modernize the language a trifle the answer then is the answer of our day: one religion is just as good as another; the opinion that Christ is God is just as good as that which says that Christ is only a man! But did Jesus, our Lord, in a broadminded way answer: "Yes, one opinion is just as good as another; I am indifferent as to your theological disputes concerning My nature; I am concerned only with how you follow My example; those who say I am Elias are just as pleasing to Me as those who say I am Jeremias"? No, the answer was so stupidly incongruous to His Divine nature, to His mission of truth, that He brought to it the withering scorn of His silence—the democratic principle will not do!

And so He passes on to the aristocratic. He no longer asks the mob. He turns to the aristocrats, the elders, the chosen twelve, to those who represent the people He serves, those who as a group make up His select council, His federation, His parliament, and says to them: "But whom do *you* say that I am?"—*you*, the aristocrats, not *men* now, but "you" . . .

And the twelve do not answer. Why are they silent? Because, perhaps, if they all spoke at once there would only be confusion of tongues; because also, perhaps, if one spoke for the others they would have asked who gave him authority to speak; silence, too, perhaps, because each one was hoping to be supreme, for more than once they had been found disputing which was the greatest amongst them; silence, too, perhaps, because some amongst them had doubts concerning His relation to His heavenly Father, like Philip, or His Divinity, like Thomas, or His economic sagacity, like Judas; silence, perhaps, because they knew down deep in their hearts that if the truth of the Church was to be merely belief of the majority then God's truth would not be absolute, but subject to the play of human passion and the chance grouping of worldly opinions. There was no certitude in the aristocratic body, any more than among the individuals. And why? Because certitude does not necessarily come from a majority vote of a council; the majority as expressed in public opinion may very well be wrong, as it was the day the mob would choose Barabbas in preference to Christ. The aristocratic form was a failure too. Certitude in matters of salvation can come only from above, for faith is not made on earth but given from heaven.

The federation of those who hold conflicting opinions went down to failure that day, and even until now silence reigns amongst them as to what is the nature of Christ, "Who am I?"—for there is no one to speak for them. There is no authority, there is no head; there is therefore no unity.

The democratic and aristocratic forms of Church government which men might have suggested to God as the plan for His Church have been eliminated. There remains now but one other—the monarchical, which focused its expression in Peter.

Peter now steps forward, not because the apostles asked him to do so, nor because he was personally moved to do so as an individual, but because there came to him a great light, a light that was almost too great for him, a light that made him first for eternity, a light not kindled by the sparks of his own reason, but coming from above like the sun that shone upon his head. It formed itself in words which he could not keep back. An interior spirit, an inward light, a heavenly revelation gave him the answer to the question of the master and expressed itself in a testimony which a moment before he would have believed impossible: "Thou art Christ, the Son of the Living God."

Peter knew who He was. He was not John the Baptist! He was not Elias! He was the One to whom the Gentile and Jewish world had been expectantly looking for so many centuries. He was Emmanuel! God with us! The Son of the Living God! Jesus Christ, True God and True Man!

The apostles did not tell Peter who Christ was. He did not even tell himself at that moment. The moment he said it he was certain he had Divine assistance. It was only by some sudden illumination of his mind that he knew, and our Lord assured him it was so: "Blessed art thou, Simon Bar Jona, for flesh and blood hath not revealed this to thee, but My Father who is in heaven."

Here the plan of Christ's visible kingdom on earth becomes complete. One man, Peter, without the consent of the others, without their authority, but with Divine assistance, announces in the name of all, that Christ is God. Our Lord seized upon it immediately to make him the visible sign of the unity of Him and His Church: "Thou art Peter and upon this rock I will build My Church and the gates of hell will not prevail against it. And I will give to thee the keys of the Kingdom of heaven, and whatsoever thou shalt bind on earth, shall be bound also in heaven, and what-soever thou shalt loose on earth shall be loosed also in heaven."[7]

Those words of Christ founded on the rock Peter the mightiest kingdom the world has ever known; words which have emerged through the patient germination of the long centuries, words for which men have suffered and died; words for which nations have fought, swords been unsheathed, societies shaken, families divided; words so solemn, that rather than cancel the least one of them, the Church has stood and stands against the world, until her mystical unity with the Head is revealed as He comes in the clouds of heaven to judge the living and the dead.

The meaning of the words was unmistakable. The Church which was His Body would be one with Him because it would have a visible head—not a head with the primacy of honour, but with the very primacy of jurisdiction. No detail was left undetermined concerning the nature of that jurisdiction. Our Lord spoke of the foundation of His Church, about the outside of His Church, and about the inside of His Church and all three revolved about one man. The foundation is the rock which is Peter; the door to the edifice from the outside is to be opened by keys, and these keys are carried by Peter; and once on the inside, the same rock and key-bearer has the power to bind and loose, to seal and unseal consciences even for registry in the book of life.

Because of that solemn commitment, from that day to this it has never been true to say that the Church would pass away, for it was founded on a rock by the Rock-Maker of the Ages. It has never been true to say that it made little difference which road we took to the Kingdom of God, for our Lord said entrance was to be gained not by roads, but by a key, and only one key fits the lock and that is the key of Peter. And finally from that day on to this, it has never been true to say that religion was purely service to humanity, for Christ made it a matter of conscience—the power of binding and loosing.

The question: How would men know the Body of Christ which is His Church? was now answered. The sign was given; the identification marks were sealed; the brand was stamped. Men would know the Body of Christ and the union of Christ and His Church by the sign of all life, namely, by its Head. They might not accept it; they might disbelieve or reject it. But the sign was there for those who would read it. Mankind would know His Body was one because it had one Head, whose authority came not from below as a gift of men, but from above as a revelation of God. As a nation is one because it has one executive, as a club is one because it has one president, as a body is one because it has one head, so too the Church is one, because its Head is one. That is why there arose from primitive Christians a cry which has been echoed to our own day: "*Ubi Petrus, ibi Ecclesia.*" "Wherever Peter is, there is the Church." Not indeed that Peter is a Head apart from Christ, but only that he is one authority with Him. He is merely the visible representation, the concrete symbol, the vicar of the Sender among the Sent, the foundation-stone conjoined with the Corner Stone which is the Invisible Christ, or as our Lord put it after the Resurrection, Peter was to "Feed His Lambs" and "Feed His Sheep." This meant more clearly than ever that Christ did not lose His Sheep nor His Lambs, nor did He relinquish power over them, but only that He communicated this power to shepherd His flock and shepherd His shepherds to His Visible Shepherd, His Visible Head, the sign of the unity of His Church—Peter the Rock.

Nor was this primacy, the symbol of the unity of Christ and His Body, to cease with the death of Peter, for what Jesus spoke on that day He spoke out of the triumphant Messianic consciousness that He was God, and that His Person and His work, and His Church were indestructible. He told Peter he would die and how he would die, but He the Eternal saw beyond the shadows of a Crucified Fisherman not to a perishable Simon Bar Jona, but to a Peter who would be living as long as His Church would live, to a Peter who would be a foundation of a House until the consummation of the world, to a Peter who would be a Shepherd as long as there were sheep to be shepherded and lambs to be fed, to a Peter who would be an indestructible Rock against the "gates of hell"; to a Peter whose faith would never fail, because He, Christ, prayed for Him when the devil would sift Him as wheat, to a Peter who would live as long as life would live, and as long as thinking men would seek the sign of the oneness of life in a Head appointed by God. He, Christ, would for ever be the Corner Stone of the Kingdom of God in the invisible and mystical order, with Peter as the foundation stone and His Visible Head in the social order, and we the living stones of the living Temple, His Church, which is one day to be presented to the heavenly Father as the unblemished, untarnished Spouse of Christ Jesus our Lord.

This great truth of the natural and supernatural order never dawns on us with such overwhelming force and peaceful consolation as when we enter the great basilica of St. Peter's in the city made eternal not because the Roman eagles carried their might of arms across a world, but because a fisherman went to die there. Under the great dome, the largest thing man ever threw against the vault of heaven, rests the tomb of Christ's first Vicar and Key-bearer, Peter. That humble, ignorant, all-so-human labourer who earned his living beside the waters of the Galilean Lake, and who earned his crown by the waters of Tiber's river, had his abode shifted from a cottage in Capharnaum to the grandest of Rome's temples, to be ever near the Christ on the altar and His successor in the Vatican.

It is impossible for any loyal member of Christ's Mystical Body to describe the emotions that surge through his soul when he passes from that tomb of the dead Simon Bar Jona to the living Peter of the Vatican. He is a man like unto us, subject to all our weakness and frailties, and as likely to err in human things as anyone in the world. His family name we know: it is Ratti, and yet to us who have the faith, it is Peter. The very first moment our

Lord looked upon His first Vicar He said to him: "Thou art called Simon, son of John; henceforth thou shalt be called Peter. Leave off thy name of earth; take on the name of eternity."[8] And that distinction Christ Himself made between the man and his office we make as we kneel before the saintly man in white: "Thou art called Ratti; henceforth thou shalt be called Peter."

To us the Roman Pontiff is Peter appointed by Christ and living in various individuals unto this hour. He is to us also the Rock who built upon the confession of Capharnaum the foundation of the Christian life: "Christ is the Son of the Living God," the Rock without which there is no confession, and the confession without which there is no Rock. He is also the Vicar of Christ, the visible embodiment of the Redeemer of the world, the sign of the unity of Christ and His Body, the Shepherd of Christ's sheep, the Man in whom as an individual virtue might fail and charity grow cold, but in whom as the representative of Christ faith will never fail, for Christ has said: "I have prayed for thee that thy faith fail not," and Christ's prayers are always heard (John 11:42). The Pontiff calls himself the "Servant of the servants of God," but to us he is called by the dearest term of all: "Holy Father." And as we say it, our memories go back to the days of Paradise and the very beginning of the human race, when God created Adam and, in the energetic words of the Scriptures, says: "Adam was made into a living soul" (Gen. 2:7). That is, he was made the source of life, the principle of human existence, the fountain head of mankind in the order of nature. In the hidden Mysteries of the creation of the first Adam we dimly perceive the sacred character of the living Peter, and why we call him so tenderly: "The Holy Father." A father is one who gives life. But he, the Vicar of Christ, gives life, gives life to my mind by keeping the faith of Christ, gives life to my soul by communicating the sacraments of Christ, and gives life to my conscience by guarding the law of Christ.

We kneel for the blessing of that Father of Fathers[9] and have our souls sealed with the triune seal of the Trinity which Christ commanded Peter and His apostles to teach the world, and then make our way back to the tomb of Peter, every step testifying to a chain of two hundred and sixty-three links which holds the Peter of to-day to the Peter of yesterday. And as our eyes glance upwards to that dome above the tomb, even they seem to seal the certainty of our faith in the continuity of Caesarea-Philippi and Rome, as we read in gigantic letters of gold the words Christ spoke to Peter: "Thou art Peter and upon this Rock I will build My Church and the gates of hell will not prevail against it."

Glancing now from that dome above to the tomb below, we seem to catch a new significance in the death of Peter. Our Lord told him he would be crucified (John 21:18–19), and when the moment came for him to surrender his life, on the very spot where his Church now stands, he begged his executioners to crucify him upside down, as if unworthy to die as his Master had died. His Lord was crucified head upwards as if to signify that He, Christ the Invisible Head, was to be in heaven, but Peter asked to be crucified head downwards, for as the visible rock and foundation stone of the Church, he was to be laid like all foundation stones—on the earth, in order that we, the other living stones, might build upon him as the immutable rock, and be compacted together in the bonds of faith, hope and charity for the salvation of souls and the glory of God.[10]

CHAPTER IV

# The Soul of the Church

The Church is the Body of Christ, and Christ the Invisible Head of the Church, with Peter as His Vicar. But there should be some bond of union between the Head and the Body, for what would a Body be without a soul? In like manner, the Church itself must have a vivifying, energizing principle and that soul is the Holy Spirit, the Third Person of the Blessed Trinity.

In the beginning when God formed Adam, the head of the human race, He took dust of the earth, breathed into it the breath of life, and lo and behold! eyes opened, a heart beat and humanity began (Gen. 2:7). This was an imperfect image of what took place at the birth of the Church, the new race of the Redeemed under the headship of the new Adam, Christ. The Church existed in its raw material; its great arteries had been formed; its head had been named; its members were called, but it still lacked a soul. The condition of the Church at this time may be imperfectly compared to America before the Declaration of Independence. The Dutch, the English, the French, the Irish, the Scotch, and the other nationalities were scattered up and down the Atlantic seaboard, but there was no common bond or spirit holding them together. They needed unity—a soul to make them one. And that spark came in the Declaration of Independence which fired them with the spirit of being a free-born American people. The Church was somewhat in this position. The apostles and disciples and the faithful were still separate individuals; they needed a soul to make them one. But here the analogy breaks down. The Spirit which was to make the members of the Church one was different from that which makes any nation. The condition of the early Church can be represented better by the analogy of life. They were like the elements in a chemical laboratory, capable of being part of a body, and yet not a body, because lacking a soul. We know up to one hundred per cent the chemicals which enter into the constitution of a human body, and yet with all our superior knowledge of chemistry, we cannot make a body in our laboratories. Why? Because we lack the power to give a unifying principle or a soul to those chemicals which will make them mutually coalesce into that new emergent which we call life. The apostles were like the chemicals in a laboratory; they were individuals, each with his own outlook on life, each with his doubts, his uncertainties, his points of view. They could not give themselves unity any more than chemicals can make life. The permanent union of their minds was impossible without a certitude from on high, for life is not a push from below, but a gift from above. They needed a soul, a spirit, a vivifying, simplifying, unifying principle which would make the cells of the Mystical Body cohere in unity under the headship of Christ, and this vivifying, unifying spirit did not come until the day of Pentecost. The apostles knew the Spirit would come to them; they never would forget how our Lord promised His Spirit the night before He died: "I have many things to say to you: but you cannot bear to hear them now. But when He, the Spirit of Truth, is come, He will teach you all truth" (John 16:12-13). "... And I will ask the Father and He shall give you another Paraclete, that He may abide with you for ever. The Spirit of Truth, whom the world cannot receive, because it seeth Him not, nor knoweth Him: but you shall know Him; because He shall abide with you, and shall be in you" (John 14:16-17) "... I tell you the truth: it is expedient to you that I go: for if I go not, the Paraclete will not come to you: but if I go I will send Him to you" (John 16:7).

All this was still in the future; it was only a promise. The next day came Calvary, three days later as promised, the Resurrection. Full of majesty as the Conqueror of Death, He said to His apostles, as they crowded about Him: "All power is given to Me in heaven and in earth. As My Father sent Me, so also do I send you" (Matt. 28:18). Then, "He breathed upon them, and said, 'Receive ye the Holy Ghost.'" God had breathed upon Adam and made him a living soul; our Lord breathes on the apostles to make them a living society. But even this was only the preparation for a more solemn investiture of the Holy Spirit. It was fitting that the Spirit came not in secret, but publicly. Accordingly, ten days after the Ascension, the apostles, with Peter as their head, were in the Cenacle where the Saviour had instituted the Eucharist: "And suddenly there came a sound from heaven, as if a mighty wind coming, as it filled the whole house where they were sitting; and there appeared to them parted tongues as it were of fire, and it sat upon every one of them: and they were all filled with the Holy Ghost" (Acts 2:1-4).

In the glow of the Pentecostal gift the individuals, the cells of the Mystical Body, like the bones in the vision of Ezekiel, were drawn together into a living body, animated by the Eternal Spirit—the Third Person of the Blessed Trinity. All they had dimly guessed at and faintly perceived now became absolute certainty in the glow of the Pentecostal fire, all they had hoped for now became a reality. They saw the continuity of Nazareth and the Cenacle: for as Christ, who is the Head of the Church, was conceived by the Holy Ghost in the womb of the Virgin Mary, so now the Church, which is His new Body, is conceived by the same Spirit in the womb of humanity. The Church was now created in the strictest sense of the term: it had its head, Christ; its soul, the Holy Spirit; and its body, which we are.[1]

The Church, then, is not a human society, a mere grouping of men in a collective life; it is the most august of realities. It is a body animated by a living soul—the Spirit of God.[2] To the

Holy Spirit has been committed for all time the sublime office of applying the merits of the Redemption of our Lord. We are members of that body and are, therefore, under the Third Person of the Trinity as truly as the apostles were under our Lord. The presence of the Eternal Son in a visible human nature was the centre of their unity; the presence of the Holy Spirit is the centre of our unity. As the Father manifests His Divinity by sending His Son into this world, so likewise the Son made flesh, in order to render the last proof of His Divinity, asked the Father to send the Spirit, their mutual eternal bond of love. The descent of the Holy Spirit was therefore one of the fruits of the Passion and Resurrection and Ascension of our Lord, the final term of the Mysteries of the earthly life of Jesus, and the beginning of His Mystical Life through the abundant effusion of the Holy Spirit.

In this great drama of Pentecost is revealed the answer to the questions all thinking men must, at one time or another, ask themselves: "How can I know the truths of salvation?" "What is the rule of Faith?" "Where must I go to know Christ and His Mysteries—to a book or to a Church?" Pentecost gives the answer: the Holy Spirit descended upon the apostles not in the form of a book, but in the form of tongues of fire. In other words, the Spirit of Truth, which Christ promised to send and now sends, is to be found primarily, not in a Bible, but in a Voice! Was it not by a living voice that Christ came to us in His physical body? Should it not be by a living voice that He comes to us in His Mystical Body? During His Life, He did not write except once and that was in the sand, when the Pharisees would have stoned the woman taken in sin. There is no record that He ever commissioned His apostles to write. But there is every record to prove that He sent out His apostles *to preach*. He ever reminded them that the Spirit of Truth, which He would send, would recall to their minds the things He had told them (John 14:17).

Fittingly, then, as His teaching in the flesh was not given by the written word, but by the living voice, so His teaching in His

Mystical Body would be not through a book, but through a tongue, and a tongue of fire whose property is to warm, to enlighten, and to purify. The Old Dispensation under Moses was given to Israel in the midst of fire (Deut. 33:2) and the New Dispensation under Peter was also given to the New Israel by fire, but fire without the thunder, as an eternal reminder that the new law is not a law of fear, but a law of love in the Holy Spirit. And since the Holy Spirit came only to the collective whole under Peter, we must always look for its working in and through a corporate community of which that Spirit is the soul.

Where are we to find the truths which we are to believe? If the Church is the Body, and Christ is its Head, then we are to find the truths in a voice, but in the voice of one who was first to speak after the gift of the Holy Spirit and who, ever since, has been first by a Divine commission: the voice of Peter rising in the multitude and saying: "This Jesus hath God raised again, whereof all we are witnesses. Being exalted therefore by the right hand of God and having received of the Father the promise of the Holy Ghost, He hath poured forth this which you see and hear" (Acts 2:32–33).

A Church which is the extension of the Incarnate Life of Christ through space and time can express itself only in a living way, and the living way is by a tongue and not by a printed word. As a matter of fact no living thing can be comprised and expressed in a few sentences, because it is for ever bursting the temporary, throwing off the shackles of the literary, and breaking the bonds of form. A book might reveal a man's greatness up to a certain point, but at any time some heroic act or great deed of charity or pervading reform makes the character break out of the two covers of a book into something as big and large as life. The stream of life cannot be checked and stopped, it flows on despite all our attempts to cast it into a fixed and rigorous form. The moment then, that one starts with the supposition that Christ is Life, that He lives in His Body, which is the Church, and that that Body is growing unto His Mystical fullness and is vivified by

His Eternal Spirit, then one must logically conclude that the rule of Faith of that Christ-Life is to be found in a living voice. It is this fact, and this fact alone, which explains the beautiful submission, the loving obedience and the childlike simplicity which we, the members of the Mystical Body, render to that voice of the successor of Peter, the Vicar of Jesus Christ.

The members of Christ's Mystical Body, therefore, derive their faith *mediately* from the Bible, and *immediately* from the Church. The reason is obvious. The Church was anterior to the Bible. The Church was already waking the souls of men throughout the Roman Empire at least twenty-five years before even the first of the Gospels had been written. Even when oral communications were written down and read in the various churches at Corinth, Galatia, Rome and Ephesus, they were always supplementary to the oral teachings. The Gospels do not answer the question: "What is truth?" but rather: "Upon what authority do you preach Jesus?" Their aim is to convince readers that Jesus is the promised Messias, with authority from on high, which authority is attested by His works. What is more, they are not vindicating the authority of a dead Messias, but of a *living one, who still speaks and acts and teaches* through the apostles whom He called and sent.

The Acts of the Apostles continue the same idea. The truth which they point out is the same as the truth of the Gospels—not the dead letter of the written word, but the voice of the Living Messias. The Epistles introduce a new element, for they give us not the words of our Lord Himself, but the same doctrine. In the Gospels, Christianity is coming; in the Acts, the coming is described. Then there is a gap, and in the Epistles we discover only the after process—the adaptation of Christian principles to the needs and circumstances of the age. In the order of time, the Church actually ante-dates all three written documents by two or three decades. By this time a tradition had begun, the written word confirming that tradition rather than originating it. As Father Leslie Walker has so picturesquely put it: "In the historical books we watch our Lord preparing a banquet to which He invites us; in the Acts He is serving it, but we do not partake; while to the latter books, where we hoped to discover it, is affixed a notice, 'banquet already served,' and inside we discover only menu cards, portions of some of the dishes, and essays on how to digest them."[3]

From another point of view it is impossible for the Bible to be a fundamental rule of faith. The Bible is really not a book, but an anthology embracing seventy-three distinct books. A mind can no more begin with it as fundamental, than it can begin with the *Encyclopaedia Britannica*, for there immediately arise such questions as these: "Who gathered the books together?" "Why do they begin where they do, and why do they end where they do?" "Why were certain books not included, and why were other books, even though not written by the apostles, included?" When one answers these questions, one gets back to something behind the book, namely a board of editors or a Church already in existence. As a matter of fact, it was the Church which gathered the books together, fixed their number, and even this was not done finally until the year 382. The Church preceded the Bible and gave us the Bible; it can, therefore, hardly be alleged that the Bible is opposed to the Church, or the Church is opposed to it. Nor must it be believed that the Bible stands outside the Church as an independent source; rather does it stand within the life of the Church. It is the Church which makes its meaning clear. What understanding could we possibly have of the words: "Do this in memory of Me," were it not for the Mass? Where would be the meaning of the words: "Whose sins you shall forgive," were it not for the Sacrament of Penance? What could St. Paul's stricture of the Corinthians be without a belief in the Real Presence? Within a Spirit-guided Church, whose authority is vested in a Living Voice, a written book may be of inestimable value, for the Church can testify to its inspiration. But without that Spirit-guided Church, a written book is useless, except as a witness to historical fact, or as the expression of human opinion. Once get rid of the Living

THE MYSTICAL BODY OF CHRIST

Voice and the book becomes a dead letter which every individual may twist and turn to his own conceits. As St. Peter himself wrote: "In the Epistles of our most dear brother Paul are certain things hard to be understood, which the unlearned and unstable wrest, as they do also the other Scriptures, to their own destruction" (2 Pet. 3:16–17). Therein lies the reason why the Bible, when once taken out of the body of the Spirit-guided Church became subject to all manner of misguided critics and interpreters, until to-day, they who were once supposed to be its greatest champions now deny its inspiration, and the Church, which was called its greatest enemy, is the only one which believes it to be absolutely the inspired word of God.

Since the Church is a supra-personal unity of mankind reunited to God, a corporate life infused with the Holy Spirit, it has presented to all men from the very beginning the four distinctive marks of any living thing: it is One, Holy, Catholic and Apostolic.[4] The first condition of life is that it be one. The body is made up of countless cells and members, but they constitute a living thing only on condition that they coalesce and cohere into the unity called life. And what is it that makes the variety of cells and members one except a unifying, vivifying soul? Each of us is a person. Each of us is conscious of being the same person now we were twenty-five years ago. But during that time there has been a complete change of the cells of our body. Something has passed away and yet we remain, because the soul, the principle of unity, remains. Were this to depart, a complete disintegration of our bodies would set in; unity would give way to chaos; life to decay. While the soul remains my eyes may act in seeing, my ears in hearing, my feet in walking, and yet all are parts of me because my spirit is one.

In like manner, the Church is one because one Spirit, the Spirit of God, vivifies it.[5] The individual members which make up the Mystical Body perish and die, just like the cells of my body, and yet the Church remains one because that which gives it its abiding personality is the Pentecostal Spirit. When our Lord came to this earth He assumed only one physical body; when He left it He assumed only one Mystical Body, and gave it one soul, one spirit, one principle of unity. The unity is indissoluble, unbreakable, eternal. He willed that His grace should come to men in a compact fellowship, a corporate body made one not by the concessions of the individuals who compose it, but made one by His Spirit. And this method of communicating Himself is in perfect accord with His commandment of fraternal love, for fraternal love implies the union of brethren, and the union of brethren implies a community, and a community implies one head and one soul. Furthermore, it corresponds to the Truth of God. There can be no contradiction, no variety of opinions, no divided loyalties, no half-truths, no schisms, no heresy where God is. His Truth cannot be otherwise than *one* Truth, *one* Life, and *one* Love. If He died for it, it was worth preserving beyond the shadows of the cross. But how could it be preserved unless there was one body and one head, united into the supernatural unity by the Holy Spirit—the Spirit of the Life, the Truth and the Love of God?

The Church was made one on the day of Pentecost; it has been kept one because throughout the nineteen hundred years of its existence it has been animated by the same Spirit. But it has also another characteristic which is the second characteristic of life—it is Catholic. Does not life endure not only because it has one soul, but also because that soul permeates every single part of the body, even to the smallest extremities? Life grows and expands from the inside out. The unity in the course of time becomes enlarged and the organism develops. God not only gave to the first man and woman the command of unity to be two in one flesh (Gen. 2:24) and fulfilled it in the Church through two in one spirit, but He also commanded the communication and diffusion of that life, "Increase and multiply" (Gen. 1:22). Life is too precious to be hidden in a napkin and rendered barren and sterile. Minds write and speak and communicate to society their thoughts and their science; hearts expand and communicate to society their love and their charity; why then should not the Church, which is the corporate Life of Christ amongst us expand by communicating to souls its Spirit which is the Spirit of Christ?

As the unity of the Church is the centripetal force which keeps her one life, catholicity is the centrifugal force which urges her to expand that life by enlarging the Kingdom of God. The tendency to absorb all mankind to herself without distinction of race, colour or nationality is native to her. The redemptive power of mankind is potentially present in her, as mankind was potentially present in the human nature assumed by our Blessed Lord. The same Spirit that led Christ to be catholic in His relations to men, by extending the benefits of His preaching not only to the "lost sheep of the house of Israel" but also to the pagans who came to Him (Mark 7:24; Matt. 8:5 ff., 8:10, 11, 8:28, 15:21), now makes the Church Catholic. On the day of Pentecost men of all languages heard the apostles speak "the wonderful things of God." At Babel the Spirit of God descended to confound the tongues of men and make them separate. On Pentecost the Spirit of God descended to unite tongues which were divided, in praise of a common Father.[6]

That note of Catholicity which is the fruit of the Spirit meant not only that the Church was to be Catholic by embracing all men with a tidal wave of faith and charity, but also in the sense that she was to verify the *whole* content of revelation and not a part of it—not emphasizing one doctrine to the exclusion of all others, not affirming the theology of St. Paul and denying the mysticism of St. John, not teaching only the doctrinal authority of a St. Matthew and rejecting the faith and works of a St. James and a St. Peter, but accepting all the truths that have been revealed by God in all their vitality and fullness, and then developing these truths not erratically and abruptly, but organically from century to century until her accumulated wisdom makes the deepest of scientific discoveries seem like the playthings of a child. Catholic too, not only because her vocation is to all men, or because she embraces the aspects of Truth in an organic whole, but also because she affirms the *whole man* in his completeness, body as well as soul, will as well as intellect, heart as well as senses. When therefore the Spirit of God animates a man with its supernatural life it takes hold of him in his entirety, in his catholicity as it were, elevating his intellect by faith, his will by grace, his heart by devotion, his senses by liturgy, his body by sacramentals, thus taking over the old stones which went into his earthly temple and recasting and remodelling and giving them new meaning and beauty until they become compacted together into a living temple where God Himself dwells. The Church is Catholic because, like life, she tends to diffuse herself through the whole world, through all knowledge and through the whole man. Nationalities are no barrier to her any more than they were to the Church on the day of Pentecost; half-truths are no barrier to her any more than they were the day Peter under the Spirit made his first infallible pronouncement and revealed the truth concerning Christ and Him Crucified; man himself is no barrier any more than man was a barrier the day the same Peter under the influence of the same Spirit declared at the First Council of the Church that "it hath seemed good to the Holy Ghost and to us to lay no further burden upon you." Catholic she is externally and internally, and Catholic she will always be until the consummation of the world, because her Spirit is the Spirit of Life, the Spirit of Growth, the Spirit of Apostleship, the Spirit which embraces everything within her body except one thing—sin.

Life is characterized in other ways than by unity and fecundity. Life, by its very nature, must also be holy, in the sense that it endures only on condition that it keeps healthy and pure. Disease and evil passions are, in the biological order, the forerunners of death. What disease and passion are to physical life, that error and sin are to the spiritual life. Since the Church is the corporate

Life of Christ among men, it too must be holy. But unlike an individual or a purely human society its holiness is not accidental. Holiness comes from the soul which animates the body. Not every soul, however, strives and struggles to be holy and thus to work out its salvation. But the soul of the Church is the Holy Spirit, which is Holiness itself. The Church therefore as regards her Soul is necessarily holy. Sinful members no more affect the intrinsic holiness than a dirty hand means the soul is in the state of mortal sin.

From the moment the Holy Spirit descended on the Mystical Body even unto the end of the age, the Church is committed unreservedly and absolutely to the ideal of holiness—the salvation of souls. She could do nothing else than keep before her mind the words of her Head: "Seek ye first the Kingdom of God and His Justice." This does not mean, of course, that every member of the Mystical Body is holy: "Ye are not all clean." It does not even mean that all her visible heads would be holy, as we shall see, but it does mean that since the Holy Spirit is her soul, the Church must always be holy in her ideal to be "perfect as the heavenly Father is perfect." The spirit incarnated and socialized in the body assures that body that as an instrument for sanctification she is perfect, because holy in her teaching, holy in the means she uses for the attainment of perfection, and holy because she actually produces holiness in her children.

> In the case of the mass of people this ideal must be content with partial realisation. In the organism, the soul which carries the ideal within it does not penetrate all the parts of the body to an equal degree. Such is the activity of our brain, that it has been said, no doubt with some exaggeration, that the cerebral substance of the thinker in the act of creation becomes entirely renewed in less than an hour. But the rest of the body, the muscular tissue, for example, and even the more bony structure, does not share in this vigorous movement. As

THE SOUL OF THE CHURCH

the river flows at the centre and sleeps in shady hollows along its banks, so is the tide of life, the current of holiness in the Church.[7]

But even though not every member attains this ideal, it can never cease to be the ideal of each member and the ideal of the whole body. For the Spirit of God can will nothing else by its nature than the sanctification of souls. The world has yet to point out a single age in which the Church has not produced her heroes whom she calls saints. How could it be otherwise? Did not Her Head "give Himself up . . . that He might sanctify her . . . that He might present her to Himself a glorious Church not having spot or wrinkle or any such thing, but holy and without blemish." He "doth nourish and cherish" her with infinite love (Eph. 5:23, 25–27, 29). Now if the Church, cleansed and sanctified by Christ, is perpetually animated and fructified by His Spirit, she must necessarily bear corresponding fruit at all times and lead at least some of her members to the glorious heritage of the children of God.

Finally, the fourth note of the Church is her Apostolicity. All life must be apostolic in the sense that it must have an origin or a source. The father precedes the son, and because he does precede his son in virtue and knowledge he can guide and direct his son. The Church too must show her parentage and the source of her life. It would be too late for her to begin sixteen hundred years after the life of our Lord; it would be too late for her to begin even twenty years after the life of Christ. She must be in intimate contact with Him from the beginning. In a word, the Church must be apostolic. Its life must come from Christ and His Spirit. The lineage can be traced in every page of the New Testament. Christ was from God;[8] the apostles were from Christ[9] and the Church from the apostles infused with the Spirit of Christ.[10] That is why when the infant Church met to choose a successor to Judas, she insisted that the successor be a witness of the Resurrection, and hence had to be chosen from among those men "who have companied with us all the time that the Lord Jesus came in and went out amongst us, beginning from the Baptism of John until the day wherein He was taken up from us" (Acts 1:21, 22; cf. Luke 1:2). They were made one in the Spirit of Christ, one in faith, one in language. Immediately after they gave testimony to Christ in Jerusalem and Judea and Samaria and even unto the ends of the earth (Acts 1:8). And how did the faith come to these peoples? How was the life of Christ diffused in their souls? Not otherwise than as it came to the apostles: through the living word and the quickening spirit. And how did those who succeeded the apostles give witness that they were spokesmen of the Church? Only by appealing to their apostolic origin, even as Paul. He confessed that after his conversion he went up to Jerusalem to converse with Peter and then later on writing to the Corinthians boasted of his apostolicity and the royal lineage of his Gospel: "For I delivered unto you first of all, what I also received" (1 Cor. 15:1–9, 14–15).

Everywhere in the early Church the test was: "What is the source of your authority and your truth?" If it did not come from Christ and the apostles it was false. Hence the solicitude of the early Church about its catalogue of Bishops. The right of any bishop to rule his Church was attested by his ability to trace his authority back to the apostles.[11] The appeal to authority to teach is the only valid one. God never guaranteed that He would leave historical evidence to keep the Church from error, but He did guarantee to send His Spirit of Truth to preserve it from error "all days, even to the consummation of the world."

In the biological order the maxim is universally true: *omne vivum ex vivo*; it is equally true in the supernatural order. Life must come from life; truth must come from truth; ministry must come from a mission. The Son proceeds from the Father in an eternal generation as God, and in a temporal generation as the God-Man Christ. The apostles proceed from Christ, and as we see them organized by Christ, they are a corporate body with a head appointed by Christ Himself. This apostolic body, with its primate Peter, received on Pentecost the Holy Spirit, thus constituting it the only real link between Christ and us. If we challenge this apostolic body, it can show the origin of its life. And if there is any Church to-day which claims to give Divine Life and certain Divine Truth, it too must show its origin: it must prove its apostolicity by tracing itself back to that apostolic body with Peter as its head, which was the original pattern upon which Christ builded His Church. This is very easy to do. There is only one Church in the world to-day which claims to be apostolic; there is only one Church which reaches back in an unbroken succession to the apostles under the headship of Peter. Pius XI claims to be the Vicar of Christ, the successor of Peter, the head of the Church. Whence his authority? He points to Benedict XV; Benedict XV points to Pius X; and so on over a chain of gold of two hundred and sixty-one links to the first link, Peter, and from Peter we go back to the Divine Life which touched earth at Bethlehem. The Church therefore presents the spectacle of a living organism continuous through time, a conscious unity in a multiplicity of lives. "As My Father has sent Me, so also I send you," said the Saviour. As His own mission prolongs God to us by an Incarnation which makes one unity of God and man, His mission of the apostles to us, vivified by His Spirit, prolongs Him to us, as well as God who is joined to Him, making one unity, in God and in Christ, between all the human beings of all ages.

### INDEFECTIBILITY OF THE CHURCH

Pentecost is also the explanation of the words of our Lord that the Church would exist all days even to the consummation of the world. Organization does not explain its enduring power through the centuries. Nations have had greater organization; they have had armies to insure obedience to commands, and yet these powerful nations have passed away leaving not a trace behind. Where, then, find the source of the unfailing life of the

Church? The answer is: The Church is not an organization; it is an organism, a Divine-human organism modelled upon the Incarnation and infused with the eternal Spirit of God. A human organism remains the same throughout the vicissitudes of life, the changing of bodily cells, the shock of environment, the process of learning, simply because the human organism is informed by an immortal soul. In like manner the Church which is the Body of Christ remains the same throughout the persecutions from the outside, heresies and schisms from the inside, because possessed of the Spirit of God. But even this analogy is imperfect. A human soul may be separated from a human body, but the Holy Spirit can never be separated from the Mystical Body, the Church.

The human soul does not sufficiently dominate its material vehicle to prevent the forces of dissolution. We die because dust calls to the body from which we are made, and to it we must return. But the Mystical Body which the Spirit of God animates, has no other use than that which the Spirit makes of it. She came into being only for the Spirit, and hence once united with It she is an immortal living thing. Her curve is not the parabola of the projectile which loses its force and falls to the earth; rather is it the curve of the hyperbola which flies off unto infinity.

The Church then is necessarily a *living* thing which grows and never dies. She decays in parts here and there, but she never dies; she may be the "ancient of days," but never the antique, because she bears eternity within her.

Three forces have been aligned against her in the course of her earthly life: the force of body, the force of ideas, and the force of passion.

The first, which was the force of body, was the crudest of all and even the weakest of all, and proved the least successful, for "the weak things of the world has God chosen to confound the strong." Force began with Calvary where men, instead of meeting ideas with ideas, met them with crucifixion. Violence is the weakest answer men can give to reasoned appeal. For three centuries the only answer the world had to Christianity was brute strength. Charity they met with the sword; gentleness with the rack; chastity with assault; prayer with curses; and forgiveness with stoning. And when pagan Rome finally sowed enough seeds of Christian blood to reap the harvest of its own salvation, its swords were blunted, its wild beasts were satiated, and the Church was stronger than ever. What had the pagans gained by the use of force? The same thing a man gains when he strikes a woman—dishonour. What had the Church gained? A consciousness of her own immortality. Brute strength had failed to destroy the physical body of Christ, so brute strength had failed to destroy the Mystical Body, vivified by His Holy Spirit. No wonder He said: "Fear not them who kill the body."

Later, when swords were put into their sheaths, a new force arose, this time one which attacked not the visible body of the Church, but its mind, namely, the force of ideas. In the course of time there was not a single article of the creed that was not attacked a thousand times. First the Divinity of Christ was attacked, then His Divine Nature, then His human nature, then His Person, then the Trinity, then His Blessed Mother, then the Primacy, the Eucharist and the Scriptures, and now in modern times even belief in God. And yet not a word of the Creed has been disavowed; not a single idea received from Christ has been scrapped; not a solitary belief has been rejected. Why, the very assault on her beliefs made the Church see more of their depth and their meaning and thus made her love them more than ever. Where now is the memory of those who most strongly attacked these ideas? How many followers have they to-day? Who to-day venerates Eutyches? Where are his disciples? Who to-day knows of Novatian? Where is his army of devotees? The Church that saw them arise lives to chant a requiem over their graves and a Te Deum for the preservation of her own intellectual life. With her dogmatic integrity preserved, whenever someone to-day renews the attack she merely goes back to the storehouse of her memory and recalls that the new attack which boasts of its modernity, is really something very old, and is called modern only because those who enunciate it do not know what is ancient. In face of the revival of old errors with new labels, the Church is like a schoolmaster who merely recalls at each new intellectual offensive that pupils of former generations who passed through her hands made the same old mistakes, cultivated the same outworn poses and suffered from the same conviction of their originality. Does a father who has the mathematical certitude that two and two make four, overthrow the certitude of this arithmetic because his child says two and two make five? How then could the Church, whose certitude is not mathematical, but divine, because possessed of the spirit of eternal Truth, ever be inclined to doubt, much less ever to overthrow, the deposit of faith confided to her by our Lord and Saviour Jesus Christ? That is why the Apostles' Creed was recited this morning by every loyal member of the Mystical Body.

The Christian world is now over nineteen hundred years old, and therefore old enough to have seen spent two of the forces against the Mystical Christ. Violence has ceased on a great scale; intellectual opposition has even ceased as the world settles down to a brain fatigue. Hence the time is ripe for the birth of the third force—the force of passion. To-day the Church is assaulted not in the field of thought, but in the field of action. The spirit of the world opposes her not because of the way the world thinks, but because of the way the world lives; not because the world cannot accept the Creed, but because the world cannot accept the Commandments. In other words, the force of passion so characteristic of our era of carnality, manifested in a general softening of lives, weakening of wills and the glorification of sex, is the new power which would kill the indefectible spirit of the Body of Christ. But this force will have a shorter life than violence, or ideas, because it will tell first against those who use it. Even now those who speak of the force of passion realize it also as a weakness, and many who were not driven to God by the appeal of the baptismal font are pulled to Him by the trial of the world. The very emptiness the satisfaction of their passions created has made them cry out more than ever for the refreshing waters of everlasting life. The Church, in her turn, has met this new force by drawing from her bosom and emphasizing with greater zeal than ever before, the Divine Remedy for passion, namely, the Body and Blood of Christ. If the world's love is misdirected to the senses, the Church instead of killing it purifies it by the thrill of an intimacy which surpasses that of flesh with flesh—union with the "Passionless Passion and Wild Tranquillity" of "Jesu voluptas cordium" in the Eucharist of His altars. The force of passion cannot stand the counter-attack of Divine love, any more than Magdalene could resist it in the house of Simon. Men will discover that they are really seeking Love whose Spirit is the soul of the Church, which conquers the force of passion by satisfying it with the irresistible force of the love of God.

Organization has nothing to do with this marvellous vitality of the Church, nor has any other human explanation. If the Church were left to her human elements she would have perished long ago before this triple assault. The secret of her immortal life is her eternal spirit which cannot be touched by the world, or destroyed by the world any more than the soul of an infant can be destroyed. Hence in face of the force of violence the spirit manifests the immortality of her being; against the force of ideas the spirit shows the immortality of her ideas; and against the force of passion the spirit shows the immortality of her love.

If there is any picture which adequately describes the Church in time, it is that of a person living through the changes of 1900 years. A man who is fifty to-day is the same identical person as fifty years before, despite the changes in his bodily life and the historic upheavals of our times. He can say: "I saw mankind exalt itself to a god in the pre-war period; I saw that same humanity prove it was not a god, but only weak humanity in the battlefields of the World War; I saw it settle down to a false peace without ever learning the lesson that man cannot survive without God." In like manner, the Church is an abiding person through nineteen centuries. The only difference between her now and then is the difference between the acorn and the oak, the mustard seed and the great tree. Her members have come and gone, like the cells in a human body, but her Spirit has remained one and the same. And since it is the Spirit which makes the Body, the Church which is the Mystical Body of Christ has been contemporaneous with the centuries. When therefore we in this twentieth century wish to know about Christ, about His early Church, about history, we go not only to the written records, but to the living Church which began with Christ. That Church, or that Mystical Person who has been living all these centuries and is the basis of our faith, says to us: *"I live with Christ. I saw His Mother and I know her to be a Virgin and the loveliest and purest of all women in heaven or on earth; I saw Christ at Cæsarea-Philippi, when after changing Simon's name to Rock He told him he was the rock upon which the Church would be built and that it would endure unto the consummation of the world. I saw Christ hanging on a cross and I saw Him rise from His tomb; I saw Magdalene rush to His feet; I saw the angels clad in white beside the great stone; I was in the Cenacle room when doubting Thomas put fingers into His hands; I was on Olivet when He ascended into heaven and promised to send His Spirit to the apostles to make them the foundation of His new Mystical Body on earth. I was at the stoning of Stephen, saw Saul hold the garments of those who slew him, and later I heard Saul, as Paul, preach Christ and Him crucified; I witnessed the beheading of Peter and Paul in Rome, and with my very eyes saw tens of thousands of martyrs crimson the sands with their blood, rather than deny the faith Peter and Paul had preached unto them; I was living when Boniface was sent to Germany, when Augustine went to England, Cyril and Methodius to the Poles, and Patrick to Ireland; at the beginning of the ninth century I recall seeing Charlemagne crowned as king in matters temporal as Peter's vicar was recognized as supreme in matters spiritual; in the thirteenth century*

*I saw the great stones cry out in tribute to me, and burst into Gothic Cathedrals; in the shadows of those same walls I saw great Cathedrals of thought arise in the prose of Aquinas and Bonaventure, and in the poetry of Dante; in the sixteenth century I saw my children softened by the spirit of the world leave the Father's house and reform the faith instead of reforming discipline which would have brought them back again into my embrace; in the last century and at the beginning of this I heard the world say it could not accept me because I was behind the times. I am not behind the times, I am only behind the scenes. I have adapted myself to every form of government the world has ever known; I have lived with Caesars and kings, tyrants and dictators, parliaments and presidents, monarchies and republics. I have welcomed every advance of science, and were it not for me the great records of the pagan world would not have been preserved. It is true I have not changed my doctrine, but that is because the 'doctrine is not mine but His who sent Me.' I change my garments which belong to time; but not my Spirit which belongs to eternity. In the course of my long life I have seen so many modern ideas become unmodern, that I know I shall live to chant a requiem over the modern ideas of this day, as I chanted it over the modern ideas of the last century. I celebrated the nineteen-hundredth anniversary of the death of my Redeemer and yet I am no older now than then, for my Spirit is Eternal, and the Eternal never ages. I am the abiding Personage of the centuries. I am the contemporary of all civilizations. I am never out of date because the dateless, because the timeless. I have four great marks: I am one, because I have the same Soul I had in the beginning; I am holy, because that Soul is the Spirit of Holiness; I am catholic, because that Spirit pervades every living cell of my Body; I am apostolic, because my origin is identical with Nazareth, Galilee, and Jerusalem. I shall grow weak when my members become rich and cease to pray, but I shall never die. I shall be persecuted as I am persecuted now in Mexico and Russia; I shall be crucified as I was on Calvary, but I shall rise again, and finally when time shall be no more, and I shall have grown to my full stature, then shall I be taken into heaven as the bride of my Head,*

79

*Christ, where the celestial nuptials shall be celebrated and God shall be all in all because His Spirit is Love and Love is Heaven."*

Such is the Church to every Catholic—the abiding personality of Christ living now in His Mystical Body overshadowed by the Holy Ghost, as He once lived in His physical Body overshadowed by the same Spirit.

Since then the soul of the Church is the Eternal Spirit of God; how foolish and vain it is for anyone to try to kill it. You can kill individual members of the Church, but you cannot kill the Church, for her Body is vivified by the Eternal Spirit of God. Violence has been tried a thousand times before, as it is being tried now in Mexico, but it is to no avail. Attack her with force, and you will discover the immortality of her being; attack her with lies, and you will discover the immortality of her truth; attack her with the force of passion, and you will learn the immortality of her love. Violence cannot kill her, because violence cannot kill the Spirit of God; that is why it has endured 1900 years; that is why it will endure until the end of time.

But even though violence will not harm the Church, violence will do harm to the world which uses that violence, for it will turn the earth into a Good Friday Jerusalem, where men, like frightened birds, will fly from the wrath they have called down upon themselves. Violence against the Church will only make it more difficult for men to be honest, for children to be loving, for the aged to be hopeful, for the suffering to be resigned. Persecution will not destroy the Divinity of the Church simply because she is Divine; it will not kill the Mystical Christ for He has the power to lay down His Life and take it up again; it will not slay the soul of the Church for that cannot be touched; it will not weaken her whose love increases with each new vision of the cross. Persecution will not drain the sacraments of their Divine Love; it will not empty heaven of angels and saints; it will not scale the parapets of eternity; it will not dethrone God. It will only lay waste the earth.

CHAPTER V

# Scandals

Thus far we have spoken of the Church as an *ideal*: The Risen Christ at the Right Hand of the Father is its Head; we the baptized members are the body, and the Holy Spirit of Truth, the Third Person of the Blessed Trinity, is the soul.

But in *fact* does the Church always realize that ideal? Historically has she always been the "immaculate spouse" of Christ? Has her visible head always been a saint? Has her body always been virginal and saintly? The Church herself need not answer these questions, for the world has already answered them for her at least ten thousand times. Let the world reveal the worst, for it will only help to make clear her true nature. These are the questions by which the world attacks her visible head, Peter, and then the body, which we are: "How dare you say that the successor of Peter is the vicar of Christ? Do not the sinful lives of men who have sat in the chair of Peter prove that they are not infallible? How can anyone be infallible who is a sinner? Could a wicked man like Alexander VI, who was a sinner, be the infallible vicar of Jesus Christ?"

"Furthermore, is it not always blasphemy to say that Catholics, many of whom have been guilty of grave scandals, murders, political intrigues, dishonesty and shameful sin, constitute the Body of Christ? Is not the Church full of bad Catholics? Would you dare assert that they were part of the body of the All-Holy Christ? How could He who is pure have a body which is soiled?"

Despite these seemingly strong objections we still believe that the Holy Father is the vicar of Christ, and the Church is the Body of Christ. Consider first the objections against the successors of Peter.

The root of error on this subject is that the enemies of the Papacy fail to make a distinction between *infallibility* and *impeccability*. Infallibility means inability to teach what is wrong; impeccability means freedom from sin. Hence this question arises: When our Lord conferred primacy on Peter and his successors did He make them infallible or impeccable? The Gospels themselves clearly reveal that our Lord, while making Peter infallible, did not promise immunity from sin. Peter made the confession of our Lord's Divinity, whereupon our Lord made him the Rock of His Church with the guarantee that the gates of error would never prevail against it; later on our Lord told Peter that his faith would fail not, because He had prayed for him when the devil would try to sift him as wheat.

Immediately after this promise of freedom from error and guarantee of faith, our Blessed Lord tells His apostles that He must "go to Jerusalem, and suffer many things from the ancients and the scribes, and the chief priests, and be put to death" (Matt. 16:21).

Poor, weak, human Peter, who was evidently puffed up with pride because he had been made the Rock of the Church, was yet to learn the limitations of his gift. Like a boy given authority and anxious to exercise it, Peter now "takes our Lord aside," and in the language of the Gospel "rebukes Him." He goes on to say: "Lord, be it far from Thee, this thing shall not be unto Thee" (Matt. 16:22).

Whereupon our Lord, whose back was to Peter, turned around and said to Peter: "Go behind Me, Satan, thou art a scandal unto Me: because thou savourest not of the things of God, but the things that are of men."

A moment before Peter was called the Rock; now he is called Satan! Think not that the Divine Mind had so quickly changed! Our Lord did not take back the gift of Primacy, for He re-emphasized it again after His Resurrection. He was just driving home to Peter the distinction between the office and its man, between infallibility and impeccability, between freedom from error and freedom from sin. In so many words our Lord was telling him: "As Peter, the Rock upon which I build My Church, wherever you speak with the assistance of heaven, you shall be preserved from error; but as Simon, son of John, as a *man*, you are so weak, so human, so apt to be sinful, that you may become even like unto Satan. In your office you are infallible; as a man, you are peccable." That, too, is why, when our Lord confirmed the Primacy shortly after the triple denial of Peter on Holy Thursday night, He addressed him as "Simon, son of John"—as the man who had fallen, and only after the triple confession of love was he given the full power to feed the lambs and sheep of the Divine Shepherd. Every priest who has ever sat in a confessional box and heard the confessions of saintly souls and has given absolution to those who he knew were more holy in the eyes of God than he, knows this distinction between the man and his office. Most of us, too, who examine our relations with our fellow-men are conscious of the distinction our Lord made at Caesarea-Philippi. If an officer of the law holds up his hand and orders us to stop in traffic, we do so; and why? Because he is the representative of law and order. And we would do so even though we knew that as a private citizen he was known to beat his wife. It is very likely, too, that in the providential ordering of His universe, God permitted the fall of Peter immediately after the gift of primacy to remind him and all his successors that what he received as Peter was not his as Simon; that infallibility would belong necessarily to his office, but virtue would have to be acquired by his own merit; that God would keep His own doctrine safe for the Church, which is what infallibility means; but for saintliness every man, the Pope included, must co-operate freely with God's grace.

Why then should one object to the infallibility of the successors of Peter on the ground that some of them were wicked men? Did not our Lord Himself imply that an immutable rock might sometimes as a man be as Satan? Why then, if Peter is described as Satan, should not Alexander VI be described as vicar? Does not the distinction between the office and the man apply to him as well as Peter?

Our Lord gave no guarantees that all His vicars would be saints. There would always be Peters who would fail (Matt. 14:30), but there would always be Christ to "stretch forth His hand" and take hold of them and remind them their faith would not fail: "Why didst thou doubt?" There would always be Peters who would have recourse to earthly arms as the first Peter who, in excessive zeal, cut off the ear of Malchus, but there would always be Christ to tell him: "Put . . . thy sword into its place" (Matt. 26:52). There would always be Peters who would warm themselves by a fire in a moment when Christ needed them most, but there would always be the Peters whose very speech would betray they had been with Christ and whose very tears would testify their sorrow and their love (Mark 14:66–72). There would always be Peters who would be weak; there is yet to be a Peter who denied his faith to save his life.

Admitting then the weakness of the man, because he is himself, and the power of the office, because that is Christ's, does history justify the emphasis the enemies of the Church have placed upon her failing Peters? To read some histories one would think the Papacy was nothing but a scarlet river of blood. Scandals have the unfortunate quality of attracting attention. A murderer receives more space in our newspapers than a sacrificing mother. Saints never make the headlines. It is generally safe to say that those who know everything about the few bad successors of Peter, know nothing at all about the very many good ones. A partial truth about scandal can often result in total error about the Papacy, simply because the evil receives the attention and the good is ignored. How true it is "the evil that men do lives after them; the good is oft interred with their bones." The wickedness of one man in authority is allowed to obscure a million saints. But why not get things into proportion? How many who dwell on the Papacy for thirty years during the Renaissance ever dwell on the history of the Papacy for the other hundreds and hundreds of years? How many of those who exploit the bad few ever admit that of the first thirty-three successors of Peter, thirty were martyrs for their faith and the other three exiled for it? How many of those who dwell on the bad example of a few will know or ever admit that of the two hundred and sixty-three successors of St. Peter eighty-three have been canonized for their heroic virtue, and that over fifty were chosen over the protest of their own unworthiness for such a high office? How many who know of the few stains ever mention the courage of a Gregory VII or the great line of saintly and learned men since the Council of Trent, or the saintliness of a Pius IX, the learning of a Leo XIII, the faith of a Pius X, the peace efforts of a Benedict XV, or the saintly wisdom and prudence of a gloriously reigning Pius XI? Anyone who attacks such a long line of martyrs, saints and scholars must be certain of his own sinlessness to lay his hand on the few who revealed the human side of their office. If they are holy, pure and undefiled, let them pick up their stones. For it is the privilege only of those without sin to cast the first stone. But if they are not above reproach then let them leave the judgment to God.[1] But if they are without sin, then they belong to a different race from you and me, for from down deep in our hearts a cry comes to our lips: "Be merciful unto me a sinner."

Unto the Primacy of Peter, then, the visible Head of the Church, the honour which is due. Saintly men and indifferent men will sit in the Chair of Peter but the office itself will never die! If it were mortal it would have long since been killed; if it were only earthly it would have long since died; if it were only human it would have been long since corrupted. Great nations, powerful institutions, and strong states are founded by great men. Our Blessed Lord came to establish the greatest kingdom on the face of the earth; but He did not found it on a great man; He did not build it upon a saintly John; He did not raise up a superman. He founded it on a weak man, a *human* man, to whom He gave His Divine assistance to be the first link in the long chain of Pontiffs until the end of time. That is why the Church will never die. No chain is stronger than its weakest link, and the weakest link is first and is held in the hands of the Eternal Lord and Master of the world, our Saviour Jesus Christ.

As Christ never promised that His Visible Head would always be a saint, neither did He promise that the members of His Mystical Body would all be saints. Sacred Scripture nowhere guarantees that those called to intimate union with God would be without sin. There were eight in the ark and one was a reprobate; there were twelve tribes and one was rejected for the final sealing; there were twelve apostles and one of them was a devil; there were seventy-two disciples and some walked no more with Christ. The kingdom of God on earth, our Blessed Lord assured us, would be made up of foolish virgins as well as wise virgins, of cockle as well as wheat, and of bad fish as well as good, and the final rejection of the bad would not take place until the end of time. Assuming the very imperfection of the members of His Body, He said He came not to heal the just but the wicked, for those who are well have no need of a physician, but those who are ill.

In ideal then the Church would always be the "immaculate spouse" of Christ, but that ideal will never be fully realized here below. The world is full of half-completed Gothic cathedrals, of half-written epics, and of unfinished symphonies, and in the Church our Lord Himself told us: "Scandals must come." And this is natural when one remembers that the graces of God are communicated through "frail vessels" (2 Cor. 4:7), where mediocrity is the rule, genius the rarity and saints the exception.

Quite apart from the Divine warrant that such failings are to be expected, does it not seem to be implied in the very nature of the Mystical Body? In the Incarnation our Lord assumed a physical body, a human nature, like unto ours in all things save sin. The remarkable thing about the assumption of that physical body from the womb of the Blessed Mother was that He, though God, did not dispense that body from the physical imperfections of all human bodies. He was subject to fatigue and thirst, when He rested at Jacob's well; He was subject to grief, when He wept at the grave of Lazarus; He was subject to a bloody sweat, when He bowed down to the Father's will in Gethsemane's garden; and He was subject to pain, anguish, pierced hands and feet, torn body and bruised brow in what He called the "scandal" of His life—the Crucifixion.

Is it not natural then to expect that in assuming a Mystical Body, which we are, He would permit this Body to be subject to mystical and moral weakness; such as loss of faith, sin, scandals, heresies, schisms and sacrileges? And why, when these things do happen, should we deny that the Mystical Body is Divine in its inmost nature, any more than we should deny that our Lord was Divine because of the weakness of His own physical body? The Crucifixion did but appear to obscure His Divinity; and so it is with scandals when we find them, as He foretold, in His Mystical Body. The scandals or sins of its members do not affect the intrinsic sanctity of the Church. Because our hands are dirty, the whole body is not polluted. The scandals, sins and imperfections of the members of the Church no more destroy its substantial holiness than the Crucifixion destroyed the substantial wholeness of Christ's physical body. The evangelist, in recording those terrible scenes on Golgotha, recalls the fulfilment of a prophecy that not a bone of His Body would be broken (John 19:36). His flesh would hang like purple rags about Him, wounds like poor dumb mouths would speak their pain with blood, pierced hands and feet would open up torrents of redemptive life, but His *substance*—His bones—they would not be broken. So with His Mystical Body. Not a bone of it shall ever be broken; the substance of her doctrine will always be pure, though the flesh of some of her doctors fail; the substance of her discipline will always be sound though the flesh of some of her disciples disobey; the substance of her faith will always be Divine though the flesh of some of her faithful will always be so human. Her wounds shall never be mortal, for her soul is holy and immortal, with the sanctity of the Third Person of God.

Hence it is no great objection against the Mystical Body to urge that some Catholics are bad. The Church no more expected to have perfect Catholics than our Lord expected to have perfect apostles. Catholics may be bad, but that does not prove Catholicism is wicked, any more than a few bigots prove America is bigoted. If the Catholics are bad it is not because they are Catholics; it is because they are not. Faith increases their responsibility, but it does not force obedience; it increases blame, but it does not prevent sin.

Why is it that the world is always so scandalized at a scandal in the Church? Why does it always blame a bad Catholic more than it blames a bad Mohammedan, if it is not because it expects so much more of the Catholic? Any fallen-away Catholic whose name is quoted as a by-word of sin, and who is supposed to be an argument against the Church, is really a strong Catholic credential. The seriousness of any fall depends on the height from which one has fallen, and since one can fall from no greater height than union with Christ in His Mystical Body, the fall is accordingly greater. Nowhere does evil become so visible as when contrasted with the ideal. The very horror the world expresses at the fall of a Catholic is the measure of the high virtue it expected of him.

That too is why the greatest enemies of the Church are not the persecutors who bear the rack and the sword, nor the pamphleteering bigot with his lies and half-truths, but rather her own children, who have been cradled in her sacred association, who have been thrilled at her peace-giving pardons, and who have sat at her Eucharistic Banquet. Only those entrusted with sacred secrets can betray effectively. It was only Judas who knew where Jesus could be found after dark: in the olive trees of the garden; only he and his posterity who have been with the Master can lead soldiers and brigands to the vulnerable parts where Christian faith can be most deeply pained; only they can go straight to the very object of their hate without error or hesitation and utter the "Hail, Master" amidst the clinking of thirty pieces of silver which testify that Divine Truth is always sold for something wholly out of relation to its real worth. And the betrayal itself always takes place by a sign of affection, like the kiss of Judas. It would seem that Christ and His Church are so sublime that public opinion requires nothing less than a kiss to disguise the betrayal. So true is this that the littlest and greatest of her fallen-away children find it necessary to preface an assault on her truth by the expression of some concern for it. However they betray, the extent of their bad influence is beyond reckoning here below. There is many a prospective convert who has reached a stage where the lies of the blackest of bigots could no longer keep him from the Church; only the word of a bad Catholic could keep him from Catholicism. To justify his break with the Mystical Body of Christ a man may give many reasons, but the world has yet to hear of anyone who ever left the Church because he wanted to live a more saintly life. They abandon it not for a more beautiful Christ; they abandon it for *things*.

Because such scandals must be because of the imperfections of mankind, the Church must always be reforming herself. There are moments when she is triumphant with palms beneath her feet; but there are moments when palms are turned into spears as her own children shout "Crucify!" Shadows will follow lights, and sinners will follow saints. There will even come times when our Lord will seem asleep in the bark and when the whole Church will appear to be submerged with want of faith, but not even her greatest enemies, her own children, can cause her ruin. Infused with the Spirit of God, she has the power to repair her own organism, to grow new members and to surmount herself by a reform. The very fact she can do this despite the weakness of her own members is in itself a proof of her Divinity. Her system of reformation is always the same in the sense that she reforms only one thing. There are two things that might be reformed: faith and discipline. Others may "reform" faith and ruin it, but she refuses to touch it. The faith is sound because it is the faith of Christ. The faith is not hers but God's and hence she dare not touch it. But discipline affects not Divine truths but human beings; it is on these she lays her rod, drawing from out her own bosom the penances which make for a holier life. That is why the tenth-century humanity and the fifteenth-century humanity, which offered such poor material for Christ's Mystical Body, was immediately followed by the great disciplinary reforms of Gregory VII and the Council of Trent. She still bears the traces of those evil days as Christ still bears in His Body the scars of Calvary. As her Divine Head she can show these scars and say: "With these was I wounded in the house of those that loved Me," but they are now her greatest glory—the pledge to the world that when scandals come it is not the faith of Christ, but the hearts of men that need to be cleansed and purged.

The Mystical Body then is no less under the headship of Christ because some of His vicars are not saints, nor because some of her members are not holy. The Mystic Christ will not have grown unto His full stature until the advent of the heavenly Kingdom, when the earth shall pass away and there shall be only love.

Looking at the Church now from another point of view, would not those who object to her because her members are not all holy be just as scandalized if she were all they wanted her to be?

Suppose every vicar of Christ were a saint; suppose every member of His Mystical Body were another St. John the Baptist or another St. Theresa. Would not her very perfection accuse and condemn us who are not saintly? Too high an ideal often repels rather than attracts. She would be so saintly that she would no longer allure ordinary mortals. She might even appear to the struggling souls as a terrible Puritan, easily scandalized at our failings, and might even shrink from having her garments touched by sinners like ourselves. Where then would faith be for those who doubted? Where would hope be for those who were unholy? Where would charity be for those who were in sin? No, a perfect Church would be a stumbling block. Then, instead of us being scandalized at her, she would be scandalized at us, which would be far worse.

Our Lord did not make His earthly Life one prolonged transfiguration. In those few, brief moments He did reveal the glory which was really His, but at all other times He appealed through the humanity which was like unto ours. His fatigue at Jacob's well, His tears over Jerusalem, His agony in the garden, His sufferings on the Cross—all the "weakness" of His human nature have won more souls to Him than the blazing garments and the heavenly Voice of Thabor.

In like manner, if the life of the Church had been one triumphant, blazing transfiguration on a mountain top, apart from the woes and ills of man, she would never have been the comforter of the afflicted and the refuge of sinners. She has been called, like her Divine Head, to be a redemptress, lifting men from the shadows of sin to the tabernacles of grace where saints are made. She is not a far-off, abstract idea, but a mother, and though she has been stained with dust in her long journey through the centuries, though some of her children have left her and saddened her soul, yet there is joy in her heart because of the children she has nourished; there is gladness in her eyes because of the faith she has preserved; there is understanding in her soul for she has known the frailty of our flesh, and how to nourish us back to life.

And in these qualities one divines the reason why our Blessed Lord chose, not a sinless man like John, but a weak, frail, fallen man like Peter as His first vicar, in order that through his weakness he, and the Church of which He is the head, might sympathize with the weakness of his brethren, be their apostle of mercy and, in the truest sense of the term, the vicar of the Saviour and Redeemer of the world, who came not to save the just but the sinner.

## CHAPTER VI

# Infallibility

The Eternal Word in becoming Incarnate assumed a human nature like unto ours. With this human nature as an instrument He fulfilled the triple role of Prophet, King and Priest. On Pentecost He assumed a new Body, the Church, through the instrumentality of which He continues as its Head to teach as Prophet, to govern as King and to sanctify as Priest. Each of these three functions we now propose to study in detail, beginning with Christ the Teacher or the Infallibility of the Church.

To understand just how the infallible Church prolongs the teaching office of Christ it must be borne in mind that Christ is God. Being God as well as man, He has the Wisdom of God. From all eternity as the Divine Word, He is the Thought of the Godhead, the abyss of knowledge which includes all that is known or can be known. The world itself was created by the power of that Word; human intelligence is a feeble reflection of that Word; the sciences and arts, inventions and discoveries are echoes of the Eternal Word who is the Wisdom of God. Then, at a time pre-ordained by God, the Word became flesh, appearing in the form of a Babe and growing to His full stature as man. His coming into the world was not like that of a sightseer to a strange city, but rather like that of an artist visiting his own studio, or an author paging the books he himself has written, for in becoming incarnate the Divine Word was tabernacling Himself in His own creation. His human nature in no way limited His Divine Wisdom, but it did give Him a new way of communicating it to men, and one quite conformable to the nature of man. Through a human tongue like their own and one speaking their own dialect men heard Him say, "I am the Light of the World"; they saw His lips move; they saw His fingers point to a harvest field to remind them of the harvest awaiting them as He bade them: "Go and teach all nations." Under the appearance of a torn body, after a night spent at the mercy of rough hands, Pilate saw Kingliness, and heard One apparently defeated utter words of victory: "I am come to give testimony of the Truth." St. John, at the end of his life, recalling the deeds of his Master, declared they were so rich and multiplied that if they were written down the world would not be large enough to contain the books thereof.

The truth and wisdom of God, our Lord communicated through the medium of His human nature. There were no infusions of wisdom in the minds of His hearers; there was no sudden lightning flash penetrating their brains. It was all the very simple process of teaching; He taught and He commanded others to teach in His name.

Now it is quite unthinkable that all this Wisdom should be lost, for it is the Wisdom of God Himself. It is even unthinkable that He who was so emphatic about every "iota" of His Truth being accepted, and who condemned those who would not believe (Mark 16:16), and who remained three years on earth to teach its details to the tardy intellects of His time, and who died rather than surrender the Truth of what He taught, should allow this same Divine Truth to be forgotten, to be twisted, turned, misinterpreted, interpolated and explained away as if it were worth no more than the babble of a child. One need only recall how the earthly wisdom of an Aristotle was altered by his disciples, to realize the need of an agency to preserve truth. It hardly seems consonant with the nature of God to allow the branches of His Vine to be poisoned, or to go back on His Promise that He would send the Spirit of Truth which would preserve His followers from the gates of hell.

If God in His Providential ordering of the universe bestows on vegetables and plants and flowers the power of drawing up from the soil and out of the atmosphere what is good for them and rejecting what is evil; if He has implanted in the birds and beasts an unerring instinct which enables them to ward off the forces of decay and preserve the original endowment of life; if He gives to man the light of reason to enable him to choose what is good for his human perfection, and to reject that which cannot be healthily incorporated into his moral fibre; if God has answered the hunger of an infant with the breasts of a mother; if He has met the cry of man for light with the sun to guide his steps and illumine his way, then why should not He meet the instinctive cry of our hearts that the beautiful Truths of His earthly life be preserved by something higher than the erring reason of man? Should not He who is Truth Itself find a way to preserve that Truth as He has found a way to preserve the earth He has made and mankind created to rule it? I could never doubt the Divinity of Christ after hearing His prophecies and learning of His miracles; there is only one thing that could make me doubt it, and that is that He should leave this earth without leaving the salt to preserve His Truth. If His own Life could not be taken away from Him by a crucifixion, how could we believe that His Truth which is identical to that Life could ever perish through the fickleness of men?

He should have left a means to preserve His Truth, a channel to prolong His teaching, or an instrument to communicate His voice. The way He chose is so very natural both to *His* way of dealing with men and to *our* way of learning truth, that it often escapes us because of its simplicity. *The way He chose to prolong His teaching is the same as that which He chose to communicate it originally, namely, through human nature.*

It was through a physical body assumed from the womb of the Virgin Mary, overshadowed by the Holy Ghost, that He communicated to us His eternal Truths; it is through the Mystical Body assumed from the womb of humanity, and overshadowed by the Pentecostal spirit, that He prolongs and preserves and teaches those same eternal Truths. He promised to send to that corporate apostolic body under the headship of Peter, the Spirit of Truth, the Spirit that would recall all things He had taught to their minds, the Spirit that would preserve them from error even unto the consummation of the world. When, therefore, He did send that Divine Spirit on the day of Pentecost to His New Body the Church, we have no more reason for disbelieving the teachings of that Body under the visible Head, than we had for disbelieving His teachings because He spoke them through a physical body. When, therefore, the Mystical Body the Church teaches, we know Christ is teaching through it. Hence to that Church we give the same obedience as if we had heard Christ Himself speak in His human body. In other words, the Infallibility of the Church is nothing more than the Infallibility of Christ. If Christ is God, and therefore infallible, then the Church which He founded under a visible Head and infused with His Spirit, must necessarily be infallible.[1] Infallibility is nothing more nor less than the gift of Christ's Spirit to His Mystical Body which enables it to speak the mind of Christ. The infallibility of the Vicar of Christ, the Head of that Body, is merely the visible expression of the invisible Head who is Christ. "He that heareth you heareth Me" (Luke 10:16). There is, for example, in my mind a truth: two and two are four. That truth has no weight, no colour, no latitude, no longitude; it is real, but invisible. Now suppose I write it out in symbols on a piece of paper, or speak it so that others may hear it. In that case it becomes visible or objective or concrete, but it does not become a *new truth*. The truth in my mind and the truth on the paper or repeated aloud are one and the same. The only difference is that in the latter case I articulated what was previously invisible and spiritual. This rather imperfect analogy does afford some hint of the relation of Christ the Invisible Head of the Mystical Body, to Peter the visible head. When the Vicar of Christ, the successor of Peter, proclaims an infallible truth he does not make an absolutely new and personal pronouncement; he merely articulates the Mind of Christ. He enunciates no new truth apart from Christ; he does not speak in his own right but only as the visible pledge of the unity of the Body of Christ in space and time. Infallibility is thus a prolongation of the Incarnation of our Lord in which the Wisdom of God speaks eternal Truths through human nature that would have spoken error, had it not been one with the Word and overshadowed by His Holy Spirit. Just as the human nature of Christ would have spoken error had it not been one with His Divine Person, so the Body of the Church and its visible Head would also speak error, had she not been one with her Divine Founder and infused with His Spirit. Once given the fact of Pentecost and the fulfilment of the promises of Christ, then the teaching of error becomes impossible. I know men are liable to error; I know the Church is composed of men; I know the conclusion follows that therefore the Church is liable to error. But the premises are false. Suppose the men who make up the Church transcend themselves, suppose they are lifted up into a higher unity with higher powers, like twelve men in a jury, who individually have no power over life, and yet who in virtue of their new unity are given the power of life and death; better still, suppose, as is really the case, that individuals like Peter, James, John and the other apostles are lifted into an organic unity governed by a higher personality, as food is incorporated into my body and subsumed under the primacy of my ego; suppose, further, that this Personality under whom the members of the Church and its visible Head are subsumed, is Divine; and suppose He lets flow His Divine Spirit of Truth back into that body, then that body must necessarily be infallible. The Church is infallible because Christ is infallible. There is no escape except to say that Christ is not Truth, that He did not prolong His Truth, that He did not guarantee its preservation, and that He did not mean what He said when He promised to keep the Church from error until the end of days. But to say that is to surrender even the hope of living.

The notion of the infallibility of the Church derives from the teaching office of Christ, and from the fact that He uses the Church as the *social instrument* of His teaching now, as He used His human nature as the individual instrument of His teaching while on earth. The Mystical Body is not united with Him, as it has already been pointed out, hypostatically, but there is nevertheless a unity of Life as there is in the vine and the branches. This reservation made, it is true to say that as the Spirit makes Him and the Father one, so too the Spirit makes Him and the Church one. There is only one Teacher: Christ. Only the *method* or the *instrument* of His teaching has been changed since Pentecost. Since Christ is infallible because God, and therefore possessed of the Spirit of Truth, it follows that when He sent that Spirit of Truth into His new Body, the Church, it too became necessarily infallible. The details of the Life of Christ the Teacher and the delegation of His teaching office to the Church are familiar to all readers of the Gospel. First of all our Lord commissioned His apostles to teach: "Going therefore, teach ye all nations, baptizing them in the name of the Father, and of the Son, and of the Holy Ghost. Teaching them to observe all things whatsoever I have commanded you" (Matt. 28:19, 20; Mark 6:7–13; Matt. 10:5–15). Now the peculiar characteristic of the Divine commission was that the apostles and others were bound to believe the truth which Christ taught them under pain of damnation. "Go ye into the whole world, and preach the Gospel to every creature. He that believeth and is baptized shall be saved; but he that believeth not shall be condemned" (Mark 16:15, 16). But why should there be a severe penalty for not believing His doctrine? The answer is because He is God, and therefore infallible. "I am the Truth" (John 14:6). "For this was I born and for this came I into the world; that I should give testimony to the truth. Everyone that is of the truth heareth My voice" (John 18:37). These words imply that as

He came from the Father with Divine Truth, so too the apostles who were sent by Him bore that same Truth: "He that believeth in Me, doth not believe in Me, but in Him that sent Me. . . . The thing therefore that I speak, even as the Father said unto Me, so do I speak" (John 12:44, 50, 8:26, 29, 5:36–38). "As the Father hath sent Me, so also do I send you" (John 20:21). "As Thou (Father) hast sent Me into the world, I also have sent them into the world" (John 17:18). "Amen, Amen, I say to you, he that receiveth whomsoever I send, receiveth Me, and he that receiveth Me, receiveth Him that sent Me" (John 13:20; Matt. 10:40). "He that heareth you heareth Me; and he that despiseth you despiseth Me; and he that despiseth Me despiseth Him that sent Me" (Luke 10:16; John 12:44–48). These texts reveal that there was to be an active co-operation of Christ in their teaching, for they were His Mystical Body, through whom He would continue to teach.[2] This Truth which the Church received of Him, and He of the Father, was not given to them *externally* as a diploma or a book, but *internally* as a *Spirit*. On three successive occasions Christ promised to send His Spirit, the Spirit of Truth.[3] This Spirit would not be temporary, i.e., for this lifetime, but would be the permanent possession of His Mystical Body for ever.[4] Furthermore, the Spirit would be a living Teacher, i.e., the Truth which the Church would communicate would not be a *dead truth* like the fact of the battle of Waterloo, but a *living truth* invested in a person.[5] This Spirit of Truth would not only bear witness to Christ, i.e., it would not only be a proof that He was God because He sent the Spirit, but it would also bear witness to them, that they were one with Him.[6] It is therefore not surprising, that when the glorified Christ kept His promise on the day of Pentecost, the Apostles were filled with the Holy Ghost and began to speak.[7]

It is noteworthy that they did not begin to *read*—and why? Because the Spirit of Truth is a living Spirit, and therefore descended not in the form of a book, but in the form of tongues of fire. Hence the absurdity of claiming that the Rule of Faith is

THE MYSTICAL BODY OF CHRIST

either a book, or the first five or seven councils of the Church. Did the Spirit of Christ *die* after the first few councils of the Church? If the Spirit of Christ is Eternal, why then did it not speak at the Council of the Vatican as well as at the Council of Chalcedon?

The Church has always been conscious of possessing the Spirit of Truth. Hence it is not surprising to find that the apostles were just as much convinced of their corporate infallibility under their Head as the Church to-day is convinced of it under its head, the successor of Peter.[8]

The Spirit of Truth was communicated not to the apostles individually and separately, but to them as a corporate body which our Lord Himself called under the primacy of their Head, Peter—the visible mark of their unity. Neither Peter nor the apostolic group were ends in themselves, in the sense that one was endowed with that gift apart from the others. In like manner neither the Vicar of Christ nor the Church are ends in themselves, they are relative entities: "They look towards the Church." As the Virgin Mother of God had nothing for herself (except habitual grace), but all for her Son; and as the Son of Man graciously condescended to be what He was for our sakes, so are popes and general councils provided with certain charisms, not for themselves, but for the Church of God.

So, too, may it be said in a very true sense that the gift of Infallibility resides primarily in the Church rather than in the popes or general councils. We may make this clearer by a comparison. A human being is composed of body and soul, or of matter and life (i.e., living force). By itself matter is distinct from force. The law of inertia comes to mean that matter can receive force, but cannot change it. That highly organized form of force which is called life comes from the soul. Yet, strictly speaking, we do not say, "The soul lives." On the contrary, we say "Caius lives—he lives—the man lives—the person lives." The soul is therefore the principle whereby the being or person is said to live. Indeed, it is a most profound remark of St. Thomas that it is not this or that fragment of a composite being or person, it is the whole being or person that acts through the parts,[9] as a king is said to rule through his officers and ministers. In the same way, though popes and general councils may be looked upon as the proximate principles or organs of the Church's Infallibility, yet it is true to say that in a certain sense Infallibility resides primarily not so much in popes or general councils as in the Church. When, then, it is recognized that Faith demands objective Infallibility though not insubordinate to the Infallibility of the Church, matters are seen in their true light.[10]

This statement makes clear the meaning of the words of the Vatican Council when it declares that the Roman Pontiff when he speaks *ex cathedra* is, by the *Divine Assistance*, "possessed of the Infallibility with which the Divine Redeemer willed that His Church should be endowed in defining doctrine regarding faith and morals; and that therefore such definitions of the Roman Pontiff are of themselves and not from the consent of the Church irreformable."[11]

Peter, in answer to the question of our Lord, spoke in the name of all, but without their consent. On that Rock Peter Christ built His Church. In like manner the successor of Peter is infallible when he speaks as head of the Church, even though he speaks without the consent of the Church: *etiam sine consensu Apostolorum* becomes *etiam sine consensu Ecclesiae.*

The Gospel of St. John tells us how our Lord after His Resurrection confirmed and fulfilled the promise made to Peter that he would be the Rock upon which His Church would be built, and that the gates of hell would not prevail against it. "When therefore they had dined, Jesus saith to Simon Peter: Simon, son of John, lovest thou Me more than these? He saith to Him: Yea, Lord, Thou knowest that I love Thee. He saith to him: Feed My lambs. He saith to him again: Simon, son of John, lovest thou Me? He saith to Him: Yea, Lord, Thou knowest that I love Thee. He said to him: Feed My lambs. He said to him the third time: Simon, son of John, lovest thou Me? Peter was grieved, because He had said to him the third time: Lovest thou Me? And he said to Him: Lord, Thou knowest all things: Thou knowest that I love Thee. He said to him: Feed My sheep. Amen, amen, I say to thee, when thou wast younger, thou didst gird thyself, and didst walk where thou wouldst. But when thou shalt be old, thou shalt stretch forth thy hands, and another shall gird thee, and lead thee whither thou wouldst not. And this He said, signifying by what death he should glorify God. And when He had said this, He saith to him: Follow Me" (John 21:15–19). This text is not to be understood apart from the text "And other sheep I have that are not of this Fold. Them also must I bring. And they shall hear My Voice, and there shall be one flock and one Shepherd" (John 10:16).

The unity of a Church is therefore the unity of a flock and a shepherd. Now our Lord after His Resurrection commissioned Peter to "Feed My lambs." Evidently, the flock commissioned to Peter's shepherding is not his but our Lord's, who remains the Chief Invisible Shepherd.[12] Our Lord, in giving Peter headship over His Church, under the symbolising of shepherding, as He had promised under the symbolism of keys, used one word, which means *to give food*, to feed with food; and another, which means to shepherd, to lead, to rule, to direct as a ruler. It follows then that towards the lambs (laity) St. Peter has the duty of feeding, but towards the sheep (clergy, bishops), who can feed and lead the lambs, St. Peter has the duty of feeding and leading. It was evident that our Lord, the Chief Shepherd, before quitting His little flock, was commissioning another shepherd whose power of order and jurisdiction would endure as long as there was error (gates of hell), i.e., until the consummation of the world. As Father McNabb has so well expressed it: "In failing to see to-day in the world the authority of Peter, the failure cannot be caused by lack of a claimant to that authority. The claim to succeed Peter in his apostolic power is made, as it always has been made, by the apostolic see of Rome. But this claim is not effective with men who think that the undoubted primacy of power granted by Jesus to Peter was granted for a time only and not for ever. They are persuaded, on what sufficient grounds we do not know, that Peter's prerogative ended with Peter; and ended not when he was put to death, but when he had fully organised and brought the Church to life. In other words, Peter's power, far from outlasting his death, did not last out his life; so that, in consequence, he could not transfer to a successor powers which were no longer his to transfer. . . . Whoever seeks to reach the heart of St. John's teaching must gradually realise what was meant by the weighed, deliberate words of the last of the apostles. . . . His message is no clearer, even though more fundamental, on the Divine Nature and authority of Jesus Christ than on the divinely-given power and authority of Simon Peter. Moreover, this divinely-given power, if we may believe the Son of Thunder, was not put finally to death on the cross of Peter. It rose again in Linus, Cletus, Clement of Rome. It is still extant, not in the one living apostle, John, but in the undying successors of Peter. In that See which had been set up by Peter, the Rock chosen by Jesus was still upholding the House—the Key-bearer was still opening and shutting the Door—the Greater and Leader was still strengthening his brethren—the Shepherd was still feeding, leading and 'dying for' his lambs and sheep."[13]

A word now concerning the nature of Infallibility. Infallibility, as the word itself signifies [in (not) fallor (am deceived)], means I am not deceived, or the power of not being misled into error. It is thus a negative rather than a positive gift. Furthermore, infallibility is not *revelation* or the manifestation of a supernatural truth or mystery, or the impression of Divine ideas on a human mind. Neither is infallibility the same as *inspiration* or the infusion of light to judge ideas. Infallibility means Divine assistance for the prevention of error. It is a supernatural gift conferred upon the Church by her Divine Founder in virtue of which she is free from error in safeguarding, proclaiming and explaining the deposit of

Divine Truth confided to her care. As the Council of the Vatican stated it: "For the Holy Spirit was not promised to the successors of Peter, that by *His Revelation* they might make known new doctrine, but that by *His Assistance* they might inviolably keep and faithfully expound the Revelation or the Deposit of Faith delivered through the apostles."[14] Infallibility, then, lays down nothing new; it only safeguards and explains what is old. The content of revelation closed with the Apocalypse. As our Blessed Lord told His apostles: "The Holy Ghost, whom the Father will send in My name, He will teach you all things, and bring all things to your mind, *whatsoever I shall have said to you*" (John 14:26).

There are some who think that the Vicar of Christ should be making infallible pronouncements about all the trivial details of life. The fact is that "infallibility is not on tap." As Arnold Lunn puts it, "Infallibility is more like a dam than a tap. It is something which dams back heresy rather than something which releases orthodoxy."[15]

It is not to be imagined that the Holy Father is possessed of this gift of infallibility at all times and on all subjects. In order that his decision be infallible certain conditions must be fulfilled.

(1) He must speak *ex cathedra*, that is, as Doctor and chief shepherd. The gift does not belong to the first vicar as Simon, but as Peter, and so it belongs to his successors not as private persons but as visible heads of the Mystical Body and successors of Peter. As a private person the Roman Pontiff has the Divine assistance no more than any member of the Church, and is just as liable to error as anyone. Neither as man, nor as a savant, nor as a priest is he infallible any more than he is impeccable. John XXII's successor condemned what John XXII had written concerning the beatific vision.

Infallibility belongs not to a person as an individual but to a function. Divine assistance is accorded the Roman Pontiff only when he speaks from the chair of Peter (*ex cathedra*), i.e., with the authority promised to Peter and his successors as Vicar of Christ and visible head of the Mystical Body.

(2) A second condition required for an infallible decree is that the Roman Pontiff "define a doctrine of faith or morals." On questions of history, literature, art, science, the Vicar of Christ has only the certainty of his own human knowledge. Hence, if tomorrow the Holy Father made an *ex cathedra* pronouncement concerning the nature of the atom, it would be no more infallible than if Millikan or Jeans made it. It would even have less certainty, for these men are specialists on the atom and the Holy Father is not. Peter was made the Rock of the Church to teach us the truths necessary for salvation, and his successor enjoys the privilege of his office only when defining those same eternal verities.

(3) and (4) The third and fourth conditions are that he define the truth explicitly so as to render all discussion and all hesitation in matters of faith or morals impossible—*pro suprema sua apostolica auctoritate . . . definit.* It would not suffice for an infallible declaration for the Holy Father to give his personal opinion on a question of faith, or to give directions for a solution. The *ex cathedra* power is exercised only when the unity of faith is made obligatory, by affirming a truth with infallible certitude. The fourth condition is that the decision be imposed on the entire Church, and not on a part of it—*ab universa ecclesia tenendam.* The reason for this is obvious. The Roman Pontiff does not act as chief shepherd of his flock unless he obliges the whole Church to accept the truth which he has defined.

It is worth observing, in conclusion, that just as Peter made his confession concerning the Divinity of Christ without the assent of the other apostles, so likewise when the successor of Peter speaks he does so even without the consent of the Church—*ex sese, non autem ex consensu ecclesiae.* The Church can never say no to his infallible decision but only *Credo.* This does not mean that the Roman Pontiff is independent of the Church when he defines. The head is never independent of the body. *Ubi Petrus ibi*

*Ecclesia.* The head speaks with the body and never apart from it. The decisions of councils are not infallible by themselves without the approval of the Holy Roman Pontiff.

The dominant note of the modern world is confusion. It has not only lost its way; it has even thrown away the map. It stands bewildered, lost, stunned, afraid to enthuse or even trust lest its new love prove as unfaithful and as fickle as the others. Some solace for its bewilderment it finds by repeating: "We must just go on experimenting, for we know not where we are going, or why we are here." But it is only for a moment. Each con has its pro; each pro its con. Every lunatic has his "case"; every fool admits "another side," and every sphinx a thousand answers to every ten questions. When brought face to face with the certitude a Catholic has in his faith, or the peace of soul and security and the feeling of "being at home" a convert has in coming into the Church, the confused modern attributes it to excessive credulity, to the surrender of reason, to priestcraft, in a word, to anything and everything except the real reason, namely, the discovery of Truth.

What are we asking for in the world to-day? The bankers' money? The power of kings? The plaudits of the mob? None of these things do we seek. What we are asking for, if we are honest with ourselves, is certainty—a tiny atom of unquestionable Divine Truth. We cannot live without it; we scan every eye, knock at every door, watch every lip and fathom a thousand hearts to catch but a ray of certainty and truth. Who among us who has listened to the babel of confusing voices, who has read the oldest and latest wranglings of prophets, who has turned an ear to inner voices, has found that truth that strikes us prostrate on the earth like a flash of Divine lightning? Truth is what we seek—a belief that cannot be shaken; a knowledge that cannot be debated; a truth that lays hold so firmly on the mind that to conceive its opposite is impossible; a truth that is the last and most solid prop of reality—a truth even that is worth dying for!

And where is that Truth? That Truth came to this earth nineteen hundred years ago and spoke through a physical body like unto our own. That Truth is now living on earth to-day and speaking in a new body, the Church. Whenever then the head of the Mystical Body, the Holy Father, teaches, I believe that Christ teaches; when the Holy Father canonizes, I believe Christ canonizes; when the Holy Father condemns an error, I believe Christ condemns an error; when the Holy Father says this is true, I believe that Christ says this is true. "He that heareth you heareth Me," said our Lord. Hence the obedience to the commands of the Holy Father because Christ is speaking through Him. That is why there is on the part of the Holy Father no complacent re-echoing of the inanities of the hour, no revision of eternal truths to suit the new astro-physics, no compromising with morals to suit immoral ways of living; no attempt to please the world to win its favour; but there is an unmistakable effort to salt the earth, to save men's souls, and to lead them to God.

Some there are who hate Truth and nail Him to a cross; some there are who half believe in Truth like Pilate, who turned his back upon Him; some there are who love Truth like Peter, and die like the Master died. And from that day to this—it is Divine Truth that makes the difference. It is Divine Truth that makes the Church the stumbling-block of the sceptics, the scandal of the half-hearted, the reproach of the ignorant. But no one escapes her, for they realize she stands in a drab civilization as the only rock of security and Truth.

## CHAPTER VII

# The Authority of the Church

Christ is God and God is Truth. Therefore, His teaching, whether communicated through His physical body or through His Mystical Body, must be necessarily true, or infallible. It remains now to show that what is true of Christ as Teacher is true also of Christ as King.

When He came to earth in the form and likeness of man, He exercised the power and authority of God as King not only of men, but of all created things. He showed His power over nature, as He stilled the seas and the wind, and made the dead walk in the newness of life; He showed His power over men, as He read the secrets of their hearts in anticipation of a judgment which was yet to come; He showed His power over angels, as He told timid apostles that He could summon legions of them to His assistance. He promised to exercise this power later on through another body, the nucleus of which would be the apostles under the headship of Peter, who were to be made one with one another and one with Him by the descent of His Holy Spirit. As unto that body and His Vicar, Peter, He communicated His Truth, so unto it He communicated also His power and His authority.[1] "All power is given to Me in heaven and in earth. . . . Going therefore teach ye all nations . . . to observe all things whatsoever I have commanded you; and behold I am with you all days even to the consummation of the world" (Matt. 28:18–20). "As the Father hath given Me commandment, so do I" (John 14:31). "As the Father hath sent Me, I also send you" (John 20:21). "He that believeth and is baptized shall be saved; but he that believeth not shall be condemned" (Mark 16:16). "He that heareth you, heareth Me; and he that despiseth you, despiseth Me; and he that despiseth Me, despiseth Him that sent Me" (Luke 10:16).

When this apostolic body under the headship of Peter on the day of Pentecost exercised authority, they did so in the name of Christ.[2] The ascension and glorification of Christ at the right hand of the Father did not mean that He relinquished His power and authority any more than He relinquished His truth. It only meant that instead of governing through an individual human nature, He began to govern through co-operative human natures: His Mystical Body, the Church. While living in His physical body He exercised His power through the touch of a finger, the motion of His hand, the sound of His voice, all of which were acts of God.

Now that He lives in His Mystical Body, His power and authority remain the same; the only difference is that now He manifests it through human natures such as the apostles and those who have succeeded them even to our day, namely, the Bishops of the Church. They are to Christ in His glory much like His physical body was to Him during His earthly pilgrimage. In those days the power of God rang out in a voice to the storming sea: "Be calm"; in our day that same power rings out in the voice of a successor of the apostles—the power behind the voice remaining always the same. If the Kingship of Christ could be hidden in the form of a helpless babe, why can it not be equally hidden in the form of a Peter, a James, or a John? If God can communicate His power to a human nature made one with His Divine Person in the Incarnation, why can He not continue to communicate it through other human natures made one with Him by the unifying Spirit of Pentecost? Is God so limited by His creation that He cannot act through a corporate body as well as through a physical body? If men were pure spirits without bodies, then the Divine Son would never have taken on a human nature to have revealed His power; but since we can know the invisible only through the visible, the spiritual only through the material, God revealed His invisible power through a visible human nature. But are we who live posterior to the Incarnation in any less need of a continued visible revelation of that power than were those who saw Him in the flesh? If God has chosen to reveal His invisible Divinity through a visible body, why should He suddenly stop that condescension? Once that human nature was glorified in heaven, why should He not continue to manifest Himself through other human natures made one by His Spirit of Truth? His Mystical Body, the Church, is therefore the very thing we should expect of the goodness of God, for it is modelled upon the plan of the Incarnation. It, too, is a union of the Divine and the human, the visible and the invisible, the spiritual and the material, in which Christ is the Eternal King and the Power of God.

If I am scandalized at the thought that Christ gives His power to the apostles and their successors, why should I not be more scandalized that the power of God once manifested itself in a human nature that could be nailed to a cross? If I am scandalized that the bishops of the Mystical Body exercise power in His name, then why should I not be scandalized that the power of God should teach the doctors of the law in the form of a child only twelve years of age? How else could this power and authority be preserved except by communicating it to a new body which would preserve it because it was filled with His Holy Spirit? A book could not preserve His authority, for the book needs interpretation, and who would interpret it? There has never been a society without a government, a family without a head, a nation without a ruler, or a body without a brain; and in each instance the authority is vested not in a code or a constitution, but in a person who safeguards, applies and judges it. Only a living body united with Christ as branches and vine can meet the demands of living men and women. And there is no more reason for doubting the authority of the bishops of that body, to whom the fullness of His power was communicated, than there is for doubting that the voice of Christ, who once spoke a crude Galilean dialect to His fishermen, was in very truth the Voice of God.

The Church is not a vague brotherhood or a vacuous "good fellowship" without external ties; it is a Divine-human society, a hierarchy, a spiritual organism with a subordination of part to part under the headship of Christ. The authority of this body is not from below, but from above. The apostles did not choose Christ, but Christ chose the apostles. The bishops who are their successors are not chosen by the people, it is the Mystical Body under Christ's Vicar that chooses them. Their authority therefore is not in a horizontal line with authority of priests and people; it is in a vertical line extending downwards from God to Christ and from Christ to the apostles and from the apostles to them. The bishops throughout the world therefore are not to be regarded as the police of a central government and therefore mere accidents in a plan, who might be displaced at the will of the Head. Rather they enter into the very substance of the Mystical Body as the nerves of the body enter into the very substance of the brain, or as children enter into the very notion of a family, as citizens into the notion of a state. Christ is in the bishops somewhat as the Father who sent Him is in Christ. The penetrating type–union (*circumincession*, in the language of theology) by which the Father is in the Son and the Son is in the Father (John 14:10) is the exemplar of the union between Christ and His apostle-bishops. "I am in My Father and you in Me, and I in you."[3]

The authority of the bishops is not theirs; it is His who chose them and sent them. The power they exercise over their priests and people is not personal to them; they are merely the ambassadors of Christ. When the vicar teaches, Christ teaches; when the bishops govern, it is Christ the King who rules. To every Catholic the command of the bishops within his own sphere is in this sense the command of our Lord Himself. When bishops speak as shepherds of their flocks we do not see them; we see

Christ who gave them power; they are not opaque, like curtains; they are transparent, like window-panes; we see the Divine Christ through them as the women of Jerusalem saw Divinity through the bleeding face and cross-torn body of a Man on the road to Calvary. When then the bishops of the Church in union with Peter give commands to the universal Church, their authority is for us in the truest sense of the word the very authority of Christ. The lifting of my hand in obedience to an act of the will is only the visible expression of the invisible resolution; so too the commands of the Church are the visible expressions of the invisible Christ. We would think it just as serious to disobey their legitimate authority in the Mystical Body as it would be for us to disobey Christ if we saw Him in His physical body along the shores of Galilee. They are the very voice of Christ ringing through His Mystical Body, the kingly branches of Him, the King Vine, the apostles of Him who is Apostolicity, the shepherds of Him who is the Shepherd of all—and whatsoever they bind on earth shall be bound also in heaven, and whatsoever they loose on earth shall be loosed also in heaven. If we deny this then we shall have to deny Christ, who certainly meant what He said in saying: "My power I give unto you. . . . He that heareth you, heareth Me. . . . And behold I am with you all days even to the consummation of the world." Take away the apostles and the first words are meaningless; take away the bishops who are their successors and the second words are vain. Accept both apostles and bishops and the words are meaningful. And so it happens once more that without the Church the Gospels would be an enigma. It is the Church which makes the Gospels clear.

There are three characteristics of the Church's authority: It is *impersonal* in its visible expression; it is *divine* in its essence; and it is *free* in its effect. The authority of the Church is impersonal. That is, the lawfully constituted apostolic body does not possess authority in its own name, but only because it is representative of Christ Himself. The executive, judicial, and legislative functions of the episcopacy do not belong to any bishop as an individual person, however great the profundity of his learning or the sanctity of his life. The human natures in the Church are impersonal in their office as governors; they are merely the instruments of the Mystical Personality of Christ. Our Blessed Lord in the Incarnation assumed a human nature but not a human personality. There was only one Person in Christ—the Person of God. Hence every action of His human nature, every command, every law, every precept, belonged to His Divine Person as the Word of God. Now this impersonal character of His human nature He has communicated to His corporate nature, the Church—His Mystical Body. Just as the action of the pencil in writing is not to be attributed to the nature of the pencil but to the person writing, so is the action of the episcopacy in the Mystical Body of Christ not to be attributed to the human natures who govern, but to the Person whose instruments they are, Christ, the Eternal King. The apostles and their successors are merely the voice of Christ, the spokesmen of the Invisible Head, and the mouthpieces of the Word Incarnate. It is therefore a great error to say: "I do not want a Church, or a Pontiff, or a bishop to stand between Christ and me." The Supreme Court, the Congress, and the President do not stand between the authority of the United States and me. These three bodies are the Government of the United States and they derive their powers from the consent of the governed. The Church is even less of an intermediary because her authority comes not from below as in human governments, but from God. The Church does not come between Christ and me. The Church is Christ—*the total, permanent Christ of the centuries.* The human instruments of Christ the King are therefore to be judged not by themselves, but by Him who sent them in His name, just as the general is to be judged not by the tone of his voice but by his right to command. "He that heareth you, heareth Me," said our Lord. These words imply that He, Christ the King, would govern through others, and that those who accepted the commands of those whom He sent

THE MYSTICAL BODY OF CHRIST

would be obeying Him. The commands are the words of human natures, but the authority is the authority of God.

When, therefore, the episcopacy under the headship of Peter binds and looses, rules and governs, we always look to the Person of Christ behind it, just as when we hear a voice on the radio we always look for its source, not in the machine which communicated it, but in the living person who sent it forth. It may happen that the human failings of one exercising authority may make it difficult to envisage Christ speaking through him, but that should not make us doubt that Christ speaks any more than static on our own radio makes us doubt that the tones of the one who speaks from the studio are clear and distinct.

Simon was a weak man, but Peter was the rock. The man is not the office, the person is not the message. Why have the later successors of Peter, after the manner of our Lord who changed Simon's name to Peter, dropped their family names to receive a Christian name like Leo, Pius, or Gregory; and why do the successors of the apostles, the bishops throughout the Church, under the same inspiration drop their family names whenever they are prayed for in the Memorial of Christ's Passion and Death, if it were not to remind themselves and us, that their authority is impersonal; that they are only the instruments and representatives, and that even in the strongest of their commands the words of our Lord ring for ever: "One is your master—Christ" (Matt. 23:10)?

The second characteristic note of the authority of the Church is that it is *Divine*. This follows from the fact that those who exercise authority are merely the representatives of Christ; they have no rights over the Kingship of Christ and cannot alter either His laws or the end and purpose of their existence, namely, the salvation of souls. In other words, the Church, because her authority is Divine, must be intolerant: the two ideas are inseparable. If we are shocked at hearing that the Church must be intolerant about the truths committed to her it is because we have lost all respect for the uniqueness of truth. It is too often generally assumed that tolerance is always right and intolerance always wrong. This is not really so. Tolerance and intolerance apply to two totally different things. Tolerance applies only to persons, but never to principles; intolerance applies only to principles but never to persons. We must be absolutely intolerant about the truths of mathematics, but we must be tolerant to the mathematician. We must not be broadminded when we receive our bills and say that twenty and twenty *may* make sixty, but we must be tolerant to the grocer who makes the error. Nothing is so fearfully exclusive as truth. We must be intolerant about truth, for that is God's making and not ours. We must be tolerant to persons, for they are human and liable to error—perhaps their education, their training, their want of opportunity for learning, or their inherited prejudices and bigotries, received in good faith, keep them from knowing the truth. Most bigots are not to blame; they hate only because they have never been given an opportunity to know, and therefore never an opportunity to love. I dare say that most of us Catholics, if we were trained on as much false history as many of them, and if we had heard only lies about the Church since childhood, and had never been given an occasion to know the Church at first hand, would probably hate her as much as they do. They do not really hate the Church; they hate only that which they mistakenly believe to be the Church. To them, therefore, we must be tolerant, kind, and sympathetic. We must even pray for them as Christ prayed for those who nailed Him to the cross. But about the truths of the Church we must be intolerant, for they are divine.

Intolerance is essential when truths are at stake, otherwise we would degenerate into the spineless inconsistency of jelly. The stronger the life, the stronger the skeleton; the more divine the truth, the more intolerant we must be about error. The truths of the Church are the truths of Christ, and are therefore divine. The Church consequently has no power to change them. Human institutions may change their creeds and beliefs because they

THE MYSTICAL BODY OF CHRIST

are man-made. But the truths of the Church are God-made, and hence man may not unmake them. The Church is merely the trustee of the talents, and when the Bridegroom cometh she must not only return to Him the original deposit of truth, but she must also show an interest on them in the increased harvest of those who have faith in His Word. Her jealousy of truth is merely the love of the Master who died rather than compromise the Truth received from His heavenly Father. Heaven and earth might pass away, but His Word would not pass away. Those who would not believe it would be condemned. This did not mean contempt for persons, for He loved all men. When He spoke this and when He called Herod a "fox" and the Pharisees a "brood of vipers" and "whitened sepulchres," He was not showing His hatred of these persons, but only showing His tremendous love for the truth which they so wilfully rejected.[4] Neither in His historical existence nor in His Mystical existence in His Church does He force belief, for belief must be free; but once incorporated into His body no one may accept some of the truths and reject others. They are an organic whole and to deny one is to deny all, just as to cut an electric cable at any one point is to break the communication of its energy.[5] It may seem harsh to the outside world that the Church should be so intolerant of error, but that is not because the Church is narrow; it is only because she is a lover of truth. A heresy is like a poison in an organ of the human body, endangering the life of the organism. Just as the human body must sometimes submit to the amputation of a diseased member in order to preserve the life of the body, so, too, the Church must occasionally amputate some of the erroneous members of the Mystical Body who refuse to accept Divine truth—because they endanger the health of the Body of Christ, and that amputation is called an excommunication. If we thought just as much of eternal truth as we do of human life we would think heresy just as serious as disease; and if we loved eternal truth—as we ought—more than human life, then we would think excommunication more necessary than amputation. The body is worth more than the raiment, the soul is worth more than the body. But though the heresy is condemned it does not follow that the heretic is lost. Due reparation made, the Church will always accept a heretic back into the treasury of her souls, but never the heresy into the treasury of her wisdom.

The third characteristic of the authority of the Church is its freedom. This statement may seem strange not only to those who believe that the authority of the Church is enslaving, but also to those who think liberty means freedom from all law and restraint. Liberty, it must be clearly understood, does not mean freedom from law; rather, obedience to law is the condition of all freedom. Aviators are free to fly only on condition that in the construction of their machine they respect the law of gravity; we are free to use words only on condition that we accept the standard meaning of those words and the authority of the dictionary; we are free to drive automobiles on the street only on condition that we obey the traffic laws; an artist is free to draw a triangle only on condition that he respects its intrinsic nature and draw it with three sides—if in a sweep of broadmindedness he drew a triangle with four sides he would very soon discover he was not free to draw a triangle at all. Every traveller who follows a road submits to a restriction of his freedom. The road limits his freedom, for if it were not for it, the whole forest primeval would be his road; but in submitting to the limitation of a road he finds he is more free to travel.

So it is with the laws of the Church. They are limitations imposed on us by Christ, it is true, but obedience to them is the gateway to freedom. The Church does not dam up the river of thought; she builds dams to prevent it from overflowing and ruining the countryside of sanity. She does not build great walls around rocky islands in the sea in order to prevent her children from playing; she builds them to prevent her children from falling into the sea and thus making all play impossible.

THE MYSTICAL BODY OF CHRIST

If obedience to law is the condition of freedom, it follows that the more we obey the laws which make for our perfection, the more free we become; and the more we disobey those immanent laws which make for our development the more enslaved we become. In the physical order, for example, if I judge freedom to be exemption from the laws of health, the more I enslave and weaken myself. If in a stroke of false liberty I eat as much as and whatever I please, drink as much as and whatever I please, my health is destroyed and I thus become less free to enjoy my life. I become a slave to my ailments. Self-determination of this sort means self-termination. What the laws of health are to the physical order, truth is to the intellectual order. The more I submit myself to the truths of geography, the more free I am to travel; the more I bow down to the necessities of mathematics, the more free I am to know the stars and the secrets of the universe; and, on the contrary, the more I reject the truths of history, the more I become enslaved to ignorance. This is precisely what our Lord meant when He said: "The truth will make you free."

Now we are not only physical beings like animals; we are not only rational beings limited to the knowledge of our weak reason, we have been called to be the children of God, partakers of His Divine knowledge. It follows then that the more I submit myself to the laws of Christ and His Church, which is the Kingdom of God on earth, the more my perfection grows and the more my freedom increases. By submitting my reason to the higher light of faith I do not enslave my reason any more than a telescope enslaves my eye; when I bow down my will to the law of Calvary, I do not surrender my liberty any more than an acorn loses its nature when it dies to itself to be reborn in the oak; when I obey the truths of the teaching authority of the Church I no more relinquish my freedom than I relinquish my freedom of writing when I submit to the laws of grammar. When I obey the commands of the Mystical Body of Christ, I am obeying that which makes me perfect not only in my body, because it subjects it to reason, not only in my mind, because it subjects it to the higher knowledge of faith, but perfect in my being, body and soul, because it leads me to perfect union with Him who is God. If liberty means freedom from that which restrains the joy of life, freedom from that which darkens the mind from discovering truth and binds the will to the sweetness of love, then how could I be more free than by submitting myself to the commands of Him who is Perfect Life, Perfect Truth, and Perfect Love? I become free only when I begin to possess myself, I become free only when I abdicate the slavery of death, of error, of hate—and I abdicate these only when I become a sharer in the Life of Him who has conquered them all.

Such is the liberty of the children of God; such is the freedom we, the cells of the Mystical Body, enjoy. We obey only what Christ wills through the representatives of His Body, we think only what He thinks in the ambassadors of His Body, and we love only what He loves through the shepherds of His Body. We are enslaved, if you will, but only at one point: we are slaves to the Kingship of Christ; but that one point is like the fixed point of a pendulum and from it we swing in beautiful rhythm with the freedom of Him who can do all things, and therefore can make us free from everything except the joy of having eternal bliss. Consciousness that He, the Truth, speaks through His Body alone accounts for that beautiful childlike spirit and simple obedience which we render as sheep to the shepherds of His flock. That is why there wells up from our hearts at all their commands and bursts on our lips the cry of joyful acceptance. "Speak, Lord, for Thy servant heareth." Speak, Lord, for Thy servant heard Thee in a physical body at Galilee; speak, Lord, for Thy servant hears Thee now in the Mystical Body which fills the world. Speak, Lord, for Thy truth makes us free from error; speak, Lord, for now we see that the root of all the liberties of the Church is the most glorious liberty of all—*the freedom to become a saint.*

CHAPTER VIII

# The Priesthood of the Church

Thus far we have considered how the Truth of Christ lives in His infallible Mystical Body and how His Power lives in the Episcopacy of that Body. By the first the human intellect was perfected with Divine Truth; and by the second the human will was perfected with Divine Authority. There yet remains to consider one other office of Christ more intimate than either of these, namely, His Priesthood, by which His Divine Life is poured into the Mystical Body to sanctify it with the holiness of God.

In the natural order there is no such thing as spontaneous generation: the mere juxtaposition of physical and chemical elements does not produce life. Life can come only from life. What is true in the natural order is true also in the supernatural order: Divine Life does not come from human life, any more than a child comes from a chemical. "He that is born of the flesh is flesh; and he that is born of the Spirit is Spirit." There is no such thing as a man being kind, philanthropic, and generous in the human order, and then by increase of those purely natural deeds becoming a child of God in the supernatural order. Divine life is not an urge from the dust; it is a gift from heaven.

God alone is Divine Life. Earth never saw Divine Life and Holiness until God walked the earth in the form of man. Until that time men knew life only in its broken fragments; now they saw Him in whom it pleased the Father that all fullness should dwell. Until then men saw sanctity mingled with the dust of weakness and sin; now they saw the Holy One of God, who was God's response to the world's desire for higher life in Him. Thanks to His human nature assumed from the Virginal Flower of the human race, He became possessed of an instrument for sanctification.[1] Through its instrumentality, He, the Person of the Word, forgave sins, He blessed, He commanded apostles to baptize, He saved that which was lost (Luke 19:10; John 3:15–17), and above all He gave His Life for the Redemption of many. This supreme act of love, by which He atoned for the sin of man, restored man once more to union with God. Having sacrificed Himself for His "purchased people" (1 Pet. 2:9), He seeks to apply His Divine Life and the merits of His Passion and Death to us,[2] for as St. John tells us, "of his plentitude we have all received." How will that Fountain Head of Divine Life communicate that Life to man after His Ascension into Heaven? He will communicate it in the same way He communicated His Truth and His Power, namely, through His Mystical Body, the Church. Since He had chosen a human nature as the instrument for the sanctification of men during His historical Life, so would He use a corporation of human natures as the instrument for the sanctification of men until the end of time. He the Head is one with that Body. From that invisible Head who sits on the Throne of God there issues forth as from an inexhaustible source to His Mystical Body in earth, that fountain of living waters which elevate men unto life everlasting. Just as the invisible energy of my brain descends into all parts of my body, giving movement to arms and legs, muscles and sinews, so there descend beams of glory from the glorified Christ to the members of His Mystical Body which we are because one in His Spirit.

But the Mystical Body is made up of many members, not all enjoying the same function or the same authority. It remains to inquire which particular members Christ has chosen to be the living instruments for sanctifying souls with the merits of the Cross. He prolonged His Truth by appointing a visible Head. He prolonged His Power by appointing an Apostolic Body of Bishops in union with that Head. But how has He prolonged His Divine Life?

He used persons as the channels for His Truth and His Power; He uses persons and *things* as the channels for the giving of His Life. The things would be the matter of His sacraments, and persons the ministers of those sacraments. In the whole of religious history there is nothing so full of wonder and wisdom as the sacraments of Christ—the ordinary means by which the Invisible Head sanctifies the individual members of His Mystical Body.

What is a Sacrament? In the broad sense, a sacrament is a material thing used as a channel for the spiritual; it is a visible sign of an invisible grace or favour.[3] The world is made up of sacraments of the natural order. A handshake is a sacrament, in the sense that through the visible clasping of hands something invisible is communicated, namely welcome and friendship. The eye, the tongue, the hand, are sacraments in the broad sense, because they are the material signs of what is going on invisibly within us. It is the character, the personality, the soul that speaks, and yet who has ever seen the soul? We know it only through its visible signs by which it manifests itself by the look of an eye, the sound of a voice, the gesture of a hand. The universe of science is a sacrament too, for the order of the heavens reveals the God who made them, and the beauty of the sunset tells the Beauty of the Artist who painted it on the canvas of the West.

> To him, who in the love of nature, holds Communion with her visible forms, she speaks a various language.

When our Lord came into the world He took a sacramental outlook on the work of His hands. The lilies of the field were material signs of an invisible Providence; sheep and goats were symbols of the good and bad; the coin of Caesar was the tell-tale of Caesar's power. His countless parables were so many instances that He was always seeing the eternal through the temporal, the Divine through the human, the Invisible through the visible and God through things.

But why look to nature and to His teachings as examples of sacraments? Was not He Himself a living "sacrament"? What else is the meaning of "the Word became flesh and dwelt amongst us"? The Word is God and God is Invisible. But when the Word became flesh and dwelt amongst us, then men for the first time came, touched, heard and saw Him who is in Truth the Eternal God.[4] God is in Christ. The flesh was the visible sign and the invisible thing signified, namely the Divine nature, united to the human nature in the Person of the Son of God—the *sacramentum* and the *res*. Virtue was going out of Him as it did when the blind saw at His touch, when the woman with the issue of blood touched the hem of His garments.

If then the universe is a sacrament because through its matter spiritual things are signified, as a flag is a symbol of a country; and if man himself is a sacrament because made up of body through which the soul reveals itself, and if Christ Himself is a "Sacrament," then why should not our Lord after His Ascension make the sacramental principle universal and use material things as the channels for the communication of His Divine Life? If we were just spirits like angels, then it would not be necessary for Him to use a visible sign for His Divine Life, but as we are a compound of both matter and spirit then sacraments are necessary, otherwise how would we know when we received Divine Life? Furthermore, why should not our Lord extend His redemption to material things as well as to man? Man had sinned in Adam, but since all created things were subject to man, these too in some way rebelled against God. The sin of Adam had a repercussion upon all creation. One even wonders if the exceptions to nature's laws are not a dim reflection of the revolt of man against the Law of God. Just as when the Head of a nation betrays his trust, the

servants under him revolt against his authority, so too when the
Head of the human race fell, the material things subjected to him
by the Creator rebelled against him. If he would not serve God
his Master, then they would not serve their master: man. This
seems to be the thought behind St. Paul's profound reflection that
"Creation was groaning for redemption." Was it not fitting then
that our Lord not only chose men out of His Mystical Body to be
the ministers giving His Life to men, but also that He chose bread,
wine, oil, water from the material universe and lifted them back
into union with Him by making them the signs of His Invisible
Grace? Why should not Christ the King be the King not only of
hearts, but also of the material things which once pulled hearts
away from Him; why should not His Dominion extend to men
through things, since through things men broke away from Him?
Why should not Calvary have its repercussion on the material
universe as well as Eden, and the second Adam as well as the first?
And so in order that all things might be restored in Christ, He,
the Head of the Mystical Body, lifted up the crude matter of the
visible world to be the exalted signs of His Invisible Life poured
into the hearts of men. Why should not He, the Divine Pharmacist
who made minerals, roots, and vegetables as medicine for the
natural life of man, also make use of the corn and the grape and
the oil as the medicine for His supernatural Life? Thus would all
things once more serve God through man, and sing with the three
youths in the fiery furnace a living *Benedicite* to God the Creator.
Such is the wisdom of God in instituting Sacraments, the visible
signs of the Invisible Grace by which our Lord and Saviour Jesus
Christ vivifies the members of His Mystical Body.[5]

How many Sacraments has Christ chosen to vivify His Mystical Body? Since the supernatural Life is modelled upon natural
life, we would expect that there be seven, and such the number
actually is. But why seven? Because there are seven conditions
upon which we live; five that condition our individual life, and
two that condition our social life. In the individual order the

first condition of all life is birth, for obviously unless I am born, I cannot live. In the supernatural order too unless I am born to Christ, I cannot live His Life, and this is the Sacrament of Baptism.[6] "Unless a man be born of water and of the Spirit he cannot enter the kingdom of heaven." The material sign of the Invisible Birth to Divine Life is water, because in the natural order water is the ordinary means of purifying, and baptism purifies us from the stain of original sin.

Secondly, in the natural order in order to continue living, once born, a man must grow from infancy to maturity. In the supernatural order a soul must grow to a perfect cell in the Mystical Body unto the spiritual maturity which enables it to overcome obstacles against that Divine Life, and this is the Sacrament of Confirmation. The visible sign of this sacrament is oil, for in the natural order oil is used for strengthening the muscles, and Confirmation is the sacrament of the strengthening of faith in the Spirit of Christ who animates the Mystical Body.

Thirdly, in order to live naturally a life must nourish itself; in the supernatural order a soul must nourish the Divine Life already within it, and that is the Eucharist. The material sign of the invisible Divine Life communicated is Bread, for in the natural order bread is the ordinary means of nourishing physical life, and the Eucharist is the Food *par excellence* because the very Life of Christ Himself.

These three Sacraments represent in both the order of nature and grace the three vital functions of birth, growth and nutrition. The fourth Sacrament is necessary after the manner of a medicine which comes to the aid of a sick organism. In the natural order it sometimes happens that a part of the body may become injured, in which case the wound must be bound and healed. In the supernatural order, it may sometimes happen that a soul may sin, in which instance a member of the Mystical Body becomes wounded, or even dies. The spiritual wound must be healed, and the inanimate member revivified and the Sacrament which restores it to the Life of Christ after sin is the Sacrament of Penance. The visible sign of the Sacrament is the confession of the sin of the penitent and the resolution to amend, just as in the natural order the body is not healed of its diseases except by a diagnosis of the disease and by a co-operation of the organism with the medicine of the physician.

The last condition of life in the individual order is the driving out of the effects of disease, for a body may not only be wounded; it may suffer from physical weakness which follows a disease. In the supernatural order the soul must be freed from the remains of sin, or the moral weakness which comes in the wake of sin. The visible sign of this Sacrament is oil, for in the natural order oil is used as the athletic refreshment for the final contest, and Extreme Unction is the Sacrament which heals the last moral weakness and prepares us to receive the everlasting crown at the throne of God.

We are not only individuals, but also members of society. In the natural order social life is conditioned upon the procreation of species; in the supernatural order the growth of the Mystical Body is conditioned upon the raising up of children of God, and this is the Sacrament of Matrimony. The visible sign of the invisible grace is the man giving himself to woman and woman to man, for the Sacrament of Matrimony is the unity of two in one flesh as a symbol of the union of Christ and His Church as two in one spirit.

Finally; as a social being man must also be governed. This necessitates officials whose business it is to apply the fruits of law and order to him and his neighbours; in the supernatural order too, the members of the Mystical Body must be governed, and this means ministers in order that the effects of the Redemption may be applied to their souls. Such is the Sacrament of Holy Orders. In the natural order the visible sign of power and authority is the conferring of the symbol of the office; and in the Sacrament of Holy Orders the imposition of hands signifies the conferring of the Holy Spirit and the delivery of the chalice and paten signify the power over the Body of Christ.[7]

The seven Sacraments are thus the channels by which Christ in heaven builds up His Mystical Body on earth by the infusion of His Divine Life. They are the bridges between Christians and Christ in His Glory; the veins of the Mystical Body carrying the Blood of Redemption from the Sacred Heart to the members of that Body; the channels through which the waters of everlasting life pour forth into the garden of the soul. The Sacraments are the kiss of God under the visible sign of which He floods the soul with the riches of His Love.

One day, as our Lord was seated at the side of a well in Samaria, a woman came to draw water, and He said to her: "Woman, give Me to drink." The Samaritan answered, "How dost Thou, being a Jew, ask of me to drink, who am a Samaritan woman? For the Jews do not communicate with the Samaritans." And Jesus answered, "If thou didst know the gift of God, and who He is that saith to thee, Give Me to drink; thou perhaps wouldst have asked of Him, and He would have given thee living water." The woman, full of the obscurities of one without the fullness of faith, was so limited in her outlook that she could understand nothing more than the well before her. But our Lord would not leave her in darkness, and He continued, "Whosoever drinketh of this water, shall thirst again; but he that shall drink of the water that I will give him, shall not thirst for ever. But the water that I will give him shall become in him a fountain of water, springing up into life everlasting" (John 4:7–14). Jacob's well and the water thereof were only a sign and symbol of the sacramental waters which would nourish the soul with God.

"Nourish the soul with God." Dwell on that expression. Think out its tremendous implications and you have some idea of what goes on in a soul as the Charity of God is diffused in our souls (Rom. 5:5) by the Sacraments of the Mystical Body. Real love comes not from flesh and blood, but from the beauty of God present to the soul by faith. A heart that has loved and found joy in the love of another is but a spark of the great flame of love which burns in the soul ravished with the love of God in the Sacraments. Judge not the existence of those Divine outpourings by the matter you see in the Sacraments which are but the sign of the life within; judge not baptism by the water, or the Eucharist by its bread any more than you judge the joy of friendship by a handshake or an embrace. What is the spoken word but the air put in movement? But when the soul is in it it becomes eloquence, justice, truth, courage to do and die. Think of what a word is when God puts His soul into it! What is water but a union of hydrogen and oxygen? Put the genius of man into it and it becomes vapour, commerce, power, civilization. Think of what water is when God puts Himself into it. What is bread but the mere chemical combinations of wheat, water and yeast? Unite it with the soul of man and it becomes strength, life, food, joy. Think of what bread is when God unites His Life with it. And so on for the other Sacraments: that which strikes the eye in them is weak and poor, but that which strikes the soul in them is Divine. They, too, like the men who receive them, are made up of body and soul, and, like the Christ who instituted them, made up of the visible and the Divine which the visible reveals. Thanks to them the words of our Lord are fulfilled: "I am come that they may have life, and may have it more abundantly" (John 10:10). In all the shocks of life He meets us with His Life and the Redemption of His Cross—at the cradle when we are born, at the moment of our death; when we are at peace, and when we are in sin, when we share our life socially, and when we share it religiously, and in each and every instance He has used visible signs that we may know when we receive an inrush of the Life of God.

In no instance does that Divine Life depend on the minister who administers the Sacrament. Like the authority of the Church, the Sacraments are impersonal, neither the sin nor the sanctity of the minister in any way alters the grace which we receive. The human intermediaries play a secondary role and no more affect the Divine Life than a messenger boy affects the message which he brings. The Sacraments sanctify through themselves and not through men; for all grace and pardon within the Mystical Body come from the Head of that Body. The bishop and the priest are merely the human instruments of Christ in the administration of Sacraments; as members of His Mystical Body they supply the voice, the gesture, and the visibility to Christ, but the Life which is given is not theirs but His. Hence when the priest says, "I baptize," it is Christ who baptizes; when he says, "This is My Body," it is Christ who consecrates; when he says, "I anoint," it is Christ who anoints; when the priest says, "I absolve you from your sins," the world may ask, "How can man forgive sins?" Man cannot forgive sins; only God can forgive sins. The priest is merely the visible minister of Christ who forgives, for He that leaveth him leaveth Christ, and whose sins he looses Christ has promised to loose also in heaven. The priest at the baptismal fount, in the Confessional box, at the altar, at the sick bed, the bishop at the Communion rail and laying his hands over his priests are the human natures in which Christ walks the earth to-day. Their actions are not their own; like the action of the human nature of Christ, they belong to the Person whom they represent—the Son of the Living God.[8]

The Sacraments therefore really bring the Life of God to our souls independently of the merits of the minister; they really convey Divine Life independently of our subjective attitude toward them. Just as it is not our mental attitude toward a pipe that makes it contain water, so neither is it our subjective outlook on the Sacraments which make them contain Divine Life. We may or may not turn on the faucet; we may or may not receive the sacraments, but the Reservoir of Calvary is full to overflowing if we would allow it to flood our souls. As our minds cry out for Truth, and our wills cry out for Power, so our whole being, like the hart, panteth after the fountains of Divine Life.

No vague theories about life, no humanitarian service, no natural fellowship, no aphorism, no preachment can really fill the emptiness of a soul made for the very life of God. Only the sun and rain can slake the thirst of the flower, only food and drink can please the body of man, only the soul can give life to the body, and only God can give life to the soul. When therefore Christ communicates His Divine Life to the members of His Mystical Body in the Sacraments He is like a mother drawing her babe to her breast to give unto us the very substance of His Life. Unless He gives it how shall we possess it? Unless He bestows it how shall we thrill with it? The life of the plant must come down to the lifeless sunshine and rain if they are ever to live in its palpitating roots and stem and flower; the life of man must come down to the birds and beasts and take them into his organism if they are ever to live the higher life of a thinking living being; and in like manner, the Divine Life of God must come down to the physical life of man if man is ever to share Divine Life as the branches share the life of a vine. The Sacraments are the ordinary channels God has chosen to let loose upon our souls the torrents of His Divine Life.

The procession of life is not upwards from the beast to man, but downwards from God to man. The source of Divine Life whence the great procession starts is in God: Father, Son and Holy Ghost. From out of that Immensity the Procession of Life moved as the Father sent His Divine Son into the world of broken hearts. Assuming a human nature from the Blessed Mother the Procession of Divine Life moved on the earth in the Person of Jesus Christ, and finally wound its way up the hill of Calvary, and on Good Friday a soldier struck a lance into the side of that Sacred Humanity—blood and water poured forth: blood the price of our Redemption, water the symbol of our regeneration. The Son sent by His Father now returns to the Father, and from the Eternal Godhead the Procession of Life moves on as the Father and the Son send their Holy Spirit full of Truth and Love to the Mystical

Body on the day of Pentecost. Striking that Mystical Body as the brightness of the sun striking a prism splits up into the seven rays of the spectrum, the Procession of Divine Life broke up into the Seven Sacraments to flood the members of that Body with Divine Life for the seven states from the cradle to the grave. For 1,900 years Life has flowed from the Head in heaven to the Body on earth, without increase or decrease, for as Creation added nothing to the Being of God, so the Church added nothing to the Life of God.[9] And the Procession of Life moves on as Christ once more walks the earth in His Mystical Body. The River Jordan flows into every baptismal font as Christ baptizes a soul into that Body of which He is the Head; the Pentecost fires blaze again at every Confirmation as Christ sends His Spirit to make us valiant soldiers of His Body on earth. The Cenacle table is moved to our Communion rails as Christ once more gives the Bread of Life that the members of His Body may be one as He and the Father are one. Simon's House is become a Confessional box as Christ once more raises His Hands to penitent sinners bidding them go in peace and sin no more. The cross at the right of Calvary's central cross becomes the symbol of a million deathbeds as Christ once more purifies the soul for its last journey into Paradise even on the very day of death. Cana's nuptials are repeated at the foot of every altar as Christ once more blesses the love which unites man and wife in an unbreakable bond, as the Holy Spirit has united Him and His Spouse the Church in a union of bliss through the endless eternity. The Last Supper is revivified at every ordination ceremony as Christ once more says to those whom He has chosen out of the world, "Do this in commemoration of Me."

And, finally, when the great Procession of Life has wound its way through all nations and all peoples, infusing them with the Divine Life unto the fullness and perfection of His Mystical Body; when Christ shall have grown to His full stature, then will the Procession turn back once more to its Source in heaven, where all nature will be subject to man as in the sacramental principle, where man will be subject to Christ as in the Incarnation, where Christ in His human nature will be subject to the Father, and where God shall be all in all.

## CHAPTER IX

# The Individual and the Mystical Body

What does it really mean to be a Christian? The general answer to this question to-day is that any man is religious who is devoted to moral beauty and humanitarian ideals, and that those fair-minded, tolerant, public-spirited citizens who contribute to the social good, practise fair play in their dealings with others, possess a natural beauty of character and crystallize within themselves the finest of human traits, are in the real sense of the term, Christians.

This definition of a Christian in no way coincides with that which was given by Christ Himself. If there is any one thing ringing clear in the Scriptures it is the important distinction our Lord made between two classes of men; the *once-born* and the *twice-born*. The once-born are those who are born of the flesh; the twice-born are those who are also born of the Holy Spirit. Nicodemus heard this from the lips of the Master Himself. One night when he came to visit our Blessed Lord to inquire into salvation the Saviour said: "Amen, Amen I say to thee, unless a man be born again, he cannot see the kingdom of God." He did not say "he *will* not," but "he *cannot*." Nicodemus, being a public-spirited man, a member of the Sanhedrin, and therefore a symbol of the naturally good, could not understand the meaning of a twice-born man, and so he asked: "How can a man be born when he is old? Can he enter a second time into his mother's womb, and be born again?" Our Lord's answer was a reminder that there are other realities than those of the flesh: "Amen, Amen I say to thee, unless a man be born again of water and the Holy Ghost, he cannot enter into the kingdom of God. That which is born of the flesh is flesh; and that which is born of the Spirit, is spirit. Wonder not that I say to thee, you must be born again. The Spirit breatheth where He will; and thou hearest His voice, but thou knowest not whence He cometh, and whither He goeth; so is everyone that is born of the Spirit" (John 3:5 ff).

In making this distinction between the flesh and the spirit, our Lord was re-emphasizing the preaching of the Baptist, the forerunner of the kingdom: "He that believeth in the Son hath life everlasting; but he that believeth not the Son shall not see life; but the wrath of God abideth on him" (John 3:36). In both these texts the assumption is made that men already possess physical life, but as long as they are not born of the Spirit and believe in the Son, they do not possess that other life which alone can enter the kingdom of God. A man therefore may be physically alive and spiritually dead; that is, his body may live because his soul is in it, but his soul may be dead because the spirit of Christ is not in it. Our Lord often taught in paradoxes to bring out in clearer relief this double life. "For whosoever shall save his life shall lose it and he that shall lose his life for My sake shall find it" (Luke 9:24). "He that loveth his life shall lose it; and he that hateth his life in this world keepeth it unto life eternal" (John 12:25). This double meaning of the term "life" is certainly behind the words of St. John in the Apocalypse: "Thou hast the name of being alive: and thou art dead" (Rev. 3:1). A good man in the natural order is not, therefore, the same thing as a good man in the supernatural order. The humanitarian spirit which stops with the love of the brotherhood is not the ideal of the kingdom of heaven; if it were, our Lord would never have said: "And if you salute your brethren only, what do you more? Do not also the heathens this? Be you therefore perfect, as also your heavenly Father is perfect" (Matt. 5:47–48). Neither is a man whom the whole world acclaims as its own, necessarily a member of the race of the twice-born. Why, it may even be that those who were born of His Spirit will be hated by the world: "If you had been of the world, the world would love its own: but because you are not of the world, but I have chosen you out of the world, therefore the world hateth you" (John 15:19). The world judges things only by their outward appearances: and therefore it misses their high reality which alone matters in the eyes of God: "The spirit of truth the world cannot receive, because it seeth Him not, nor knoweth Him: but you shall know Him; because He shall abide in you, and shall be in you" (John 14:17).

There are in the sight of God only two classes of people; the once-born and the twice-born; those who are born of woman, and those who are born of the spirit of God. The first are just men; the second are children of God; the first are humanists, the second are Christians; the first are of the world, the second are of the kingdom of God. The womb of a mother is the birthplace of the man; and the womb of the waters of the Holy Ghost is the birthplace of the Christian. The Christian life therefore consists in the introduction of an entirely new principle into man which lifts him out of the natural order; the infusion of a new vital force which does not belong to man as man. That new force, or energy, or life, no more belongs to man than the gift of poetry belongs to a dog, or blossoming belongs to a stone; it is something even more above the nature of man. By nature man is a child of his parents, and a product of the Creative Power of God, but by grace man is a child of God and member of the family of the Holy Trinity. It is a tremendous and overwhelming thought when we dwell on it, that we should be "children of God," and yet such is the energetic language of the opening of the Gospel of St. John: "He came into His own and His own received Him not. But as many as received Him He gave them power to be made the *sons of God*, to them that believe in His name, who are *born, not of blood*, nor of the will of the flesh, nor of the will of man, *but of God*" (John 1:11–13). "Born of God"—that means to have God as a Father, to be an adopted son of God, to be a brother of Christ the Natural Son of God, to be "joint-heirs with Christ" of the kingdom of heaven (Rom. 8:14–17; Gal. 4:1–7); it means also to be a "partaker of the Divine Nature" and to have the very Life of God flow through our soul as the life of our parents flows through the veins of our body. It means to be suffused through and through with the Divine Life as the cathedral windows are suffused with the light of the sun; to possess God in my soul as my intellect possesses a truth and my will possesses a love, to be one with Him as the branches are one with the Vine; to be re-born in Christ, to re-live His Life; to re-die His death; to re-enact His Resurrection and His Ascension, to re-glorify His Glory—that is what it means to be a Christian.

The human eye sees no difference between the once-born of the flesh and the twice-born of the Spirit; for there is no sensible difference in a child before his baptism and after. But that is because the new life of the soul is so profound. The really profound things of life always escape the eye. There is very little difference in the human embryo and the embryo of a rabbit, but later on the difference becomes manifest. And so the Divine command has gone out, "Let both grow unto the harvest." Let the once-born and the twice-born live together in the world until God comes to judge motives and the inner realities of the soul, and then shall those who possess the nature of God hear the Son say: "Come, ye blessed of My Father: I am the Natural Son; you are the adopted children; come to the kingdom prepared for you from all eternity."[1]

Man's true end lies not in mere humanity, but in a kind of super-humanity where he is governed by new laws, vivified by a new soul, and thrilled with new joys. His nature after the manner of the Incarnation has been "assumed" by a higher nature and elevated unto a higher life. As the air and sunshine live in a new way when they are absorbed into the life of the flower; as the plants begin to live a higher life when taken up into sentient life of an animal, and as chemicals, plants, and animals begin to live the life of a thinking, loving man when taken up into his body as food, so, too, man begins to live a Divine Life without ever losing his identity once he is re-born to the higher life of God. He lives his human life because he has a soul; and so he can say: "I live"; yet he lives a Divine Life because his soul is possessed of the Spirit of God, and so he can add: "Now, not I, but Christ liveth in me." Once that assumption into the Life of God takes place man ceases to call the Power that made him, God. He begins to call Him "Father," as he prays "Our Father, who art in heaven." The more conscious he becomes of his filiation, the less he considers the world and all that is in it; the more he realizes the love of God who died to redeem him, the less he is afraid of becoming a "fool for Christ." The salvation of his soul purchased by love of God and love of neighbour becomes his all-absorbing occupation, like that typical Christian, Sir Thomas More, who died rather than deny his faith.

A second important characteristic of the spiritual life is that it is not a purely individual relation of the soul and God or a personal affair between man and God. Man is not only an individual; he is also a social being. His relations to God are in some way relations to his neighbours. The Divine law of love embraces both: "Love God and love your neighbour." The spiritual life therefore, in addition to the enrichment of our personal life, also commits us to the social life of the kingdom of God. Hence in the greatest of all Christian prayers taught by our Lord Himself we do not say: "My Father, who art in heaven," nor do we say: "Give me this day my daily bread"—which we would say if religion were a private relation between God and the soul. Rather were we told to say: "*Our* Father who art in heaven" . . . "Give *us* this day *our* daily bread." These very words, "Thy kingdom come," imply that we as individuals are incorporated into a supernatural society, the Mystical Body of Christ.

It may strike us as strange that God should make the normal growth of our spiritual self depend upon our membership with his Mystical Body or His kingdom on earth; but once we look over the natural order we see that such is the law of all life. Is not every living thing in the universe in some way conditioned by its environment? Does not each individual life live in a kingdom? The fish, for example, can live only in the environment of water; the plants live by communion with the sunlight and moisture; the cells live through their membership with other cells in the kingdom of the body; the bee lives in the hive, the child in the family, and the citizen in the nation.

Now the supernatural order is built upon the order of nature. Hence the Christian is a part of a whole, a citizen of the kingdom of God, a child in the family of the Trinity, a cell in the organism of the Whole Christ and a member of the Mystical Body. As St. Paul tells us: "You are the body of Christ and members of member," for "it is the one and the same Spirit working and dividing to everyone according to His Will for the edifying [building up] of the body of Christ . . . unto the perfect man, unto the measure of the age of the fullness of Christ" (1 Cor. 12:27, 11 Eph. 4:12–13).

The Church does not stand between Christ and me any more than the nation stands between me and patriotism. It is just as natural for my soul to live in it as it is for my eye to live in the environment of beauty, my lungs to live in the environment of air. The great broad world of Nature does not cramp my intellect, but enlarges it by giving it an opportunity to study the secrets of Nature, to tame its forces, and to harness its energies; and the great broad world of supernature, the Church, does not cabin, crib and confine my spiritual life; it gives it an opportunity to expand its faith by belief in a larger whole, and to enlarge its charity by kindness to the other cells of that body. The Church is the native air of the soul in the state of grace; the blood of the heart in love with God, the common ground where Christians meet in Christ;

the altar where individuals forming part of the world-life of Christ kneel to say in common "Our Father."

When therefore I ask what the Church means to me, I answer that it is the Temple of Life in which I am a living stone; it is the Tree of Eternal Fruit of which I am a Branch; it is the Mystical Body of Christ on earth of which I am a member. The Church is therefore more to me than I am to myself; her life is more abundant than mine, for I live by union with her. She could live without me, for I am only a cell in her body; but I could not normally live without her. I live only as a part of her as my arm lives only as part of my body. So absorbing does she become that her thoughts are my thoughts; her loves are my loves; her ideals are my ideals. I consider sharing her life the greatest gift God has ever given to me, as I should consider losing her life the greatest evil that could befall me. Dependence is the very essence of my creaturely existence, for no man is sufficient unto himself. I am not a speck in a moral void, nor a wanderer without a home nor an isolated unit in creation; rather am I dependent on the God-appointed destiny whereby I *share* my love of God with others who love God in the unity of the Mystical Body of Christ. In that Body which is the fullness of Christ I find the spiritual environment for my spiritual life. In her I live and move and have my being; from her seven fountains I draw the waters of everlasting life; from her Book of Seven Seals I learn the secrets of the lamb; from her tabernacles I receive the Bread of Life. My life is her life, my being is her being, she has my love, my service, as I myself have the entire devotion and service of my hand. She is the living organism, I am but an organ; she is the body, I am but a member; she is Life, I am a living thing; she the Vine, and I the branch. "Abide in Me; and I in you. As the branch cannot bear fruit of itself, unless it abide in the vine, so neither can you unless you abide in Me— I am the Vine and you the branches. He that abideth in Me and I in him, the same beareth much fruit: for without Me you can do nothing" (John 15:4–5).

We must not think that because the fullness of our spiritual life is in the Church she absorbs us and leaves no room for our individual development. Just as in the natural order the individual cell has its own growth even though it dwells in the body, so in like manner the individual Christian has his own personal development even though a member of the Mystical Body. There is only one sun to shine upon all the flowers of the world, but their mutual dependence on the sun does not prevent the sun from drawing out of each flower its own particular beauty, and its own special perfume. So does Christ in His indwelling in the Church give life and beauty to all who receive Him, yet to each individual soul the Mystical Body gives its special life and beauty, so that there is consummated in the Church the union of the soul and its Divine Beloved, which death does not part but seals in everlasting bliss. The body is made up of many members and countless cells, each with its own personality, though all draw upon a common life and are animated by a common soul. The eye does not lose its power of vision, nor does the ear lose its sense of hearing, because they are part of the body. Neither does the soul who has a natural bent for an active life, nor the soul who has a natural bent for contemplation lose their personalities when united to the Body of Christ, for the Church still has her Marthas and Marys. As a matter of fact, there is no legitimate natural bent or leaning of any personality in the world that cannot find its development in the organism of the Church. The vast multitude of religious communities in the Church give free expression to the most varied personal inclinations; a Francis who loves the poor may become a Franciscan; a Teresa who loves penance may become a Carmelite; a Dominic who loves study and preaching may become a Dominican; an Ignatius who loves spiritual action may become a Jesuit; a Paul who loves the Passion of Christ may become a Passionist; a Paul who loves preaching the Gospel may become a Paulist; a Vincent who loves the orphans may become a Vincentian, and so on for the hundreds of communities within the Church. Moreover, in each of these communities each individual still has his special personal devotions to his Lord and Master. While living His historical Life our Blessed Lord did not destroy the personalities of His twelve apostles because they were one with Him, nor did He destroy the passions of a Magdalene after her conversion. He merely changed the direction of their inclinations, making them flow upwards instead of downwards, transforming an impetuous Simon to a daring Peter; a hating Saul into a loving Paul; a flesh-loving Magdalene into a spirit-loving Mary. Now that He has ascended into Heaven and sent His Spirit into His Mystical Body the Church, He continues to draw all souls into the common life of that body without destroying their individuality as a member or a cell of that body. The simple little girl of Lisieux did not cease to be a Little Flower because she became a Carmelite in the Mystical Body of Christ. Ignatius was a soldier both before and after he became the founder of the Jesuits; Louis IX was a king even though he was a subject of the King of kings; and, in like manner, each of us may continue to live our distinctly different lives in the office, in the field, at the machine, and at the university, in the humble duties of a routine world and in the lofty position as leaders of men. There is no destruction of nature by grace, but only its elevation to another order. Tears are a common fountain for joy and sorrow. Passions too are common outlets for virtue and vice. It is not a different passion that makes a man into a saint or devil; it is the same passion going in a different direction. The Church then in embracing our lives within Her common life does not destroy our personalities—she does not even destroy our most wicked passions. She transmutes them by the magic of her Sacraments, provides new outlets, fixes new goals, and digs new channels, for she knows that only a soul that hates like a Saul can ever love like a Paul, and only a soul that can be wicked as Magdalene can ever be as virtuous as Mary. The heroes of the world are not so different from martyrs; the same natural courage which would make a man die for Caesar on a battlefield, the Church would transmute into a supernatural courage which would make him die for Christ. Bigots are potential missionaries, for the same zeal that makes them unwittingly serve falsehood can be elevated by the Church to make them serve Divine Truth. Great scientists are incipient theologians, for that same curiosity which drives them to a knowledge of secondary causes the Church transmutes by leading them to a knowledge of the First Cause, which is God. We would not say that the hero who became a saint, or the bigot who became a missionary, or the scientist who became a theologian lost their personalities once incorporated into Christ's body, any more than we lose our personalities when we become citizens of a nation. But we would say, and they would be forced to confess, that in their union with that common life of grace they had found the sublimation of their distinct personalities, and the crown of their individual selves. They would see, as we see, that Christ's Mystical Body is like a beautiful garden, formed by the blossoming of individual flowers in their varied beauty blending into one harmonious delight. Each flower of that garden has its own beauty revealed as in no other flower, yet each flower grows in beauty by contrast and by blending with the other flowers all rooted in a common soil and lighted by a common sun. So is it in the mystical life in which Christ dwells in His Church, revealing Himself anew in each individual soul, and never in two wholly alike, here manifesting Himself as Peter, there as Paul, here in Martha, there in Mary, in a lover of His infancy, or a lover of His cross, in a rose with thorns, or a thornless flower, each more beautiful by fellowship with other flowers, all rooted in the same Christ-Life and all lighted by the same Christ-truth. In the Church's garden is fulfilled the prayer of our Lord as He went into the Garden of Gethsemane: "That they may be one, as Thou, Father, in Me and I in Thee; that they also may be one in Us" (John 17:21).

## CHAPTER X

# The Prolongation of the Christ-Life

As society stands in the background of individual life, a nation in the background of the citizen, a family of the child, and an organism behind the life of the cells, so is the Mystical Body the environment in which a Christian lives his normal personal spiritual life. But it must not be thought that because the individual lives in a society, his individuality is crushed by it, any more than a cell loses its identity because it is part of an organism. It is therefore important to dwell at some length on the relation of the individual soul who is a member of the Mystical Body to his Lord and Saviour Jesus Christ.

How often we hear people lament that they are so distant from Galilee, so removed from Jesus. We hear them say that they long to have lived when He walked the earth, to have heard Him speak the Beatitudes with sweetness and authority, to have watched Him dignify common labour at the carpenter's bench, to have stood beneath the Cross with Mary, and on Easter, like Thomas, to have put their fingers into the wounds and their hands into the side of their Lord and God.

Others wish not so much that they lived in His day, but rather that He lived in our own. What a joy if He walked our earth today, if we could go to Him in moments of doubt and be consoled by His Divine Peace, or kneel at His feet and have Him wash away our sin. Would He but lay His hands upon our children, enter the cathedrals that bear His name, above all, preach the doctrines of economic and social justice and heal the lame and halt, walking the streets of our city as He once walked through Jerusalem.

The world is full of men and women who think of our Lord solely in terms of what their eyes can see, their ears can hear, and their hands can touch. Many start with the truth that He was a great Teacher of commanding influence who walked the earth 1,900 years ago, gather up the details of the scenery of lake and hill country of Galilee, and use their imagination to portray the exact circumstances of His earthly Life; but there they end. They have learned to think of Him as someone who belongs to human history, like Cæsar, Washington or Mohammed; they think of Him as One who lived on earth and passed away. But where He is, what His nature is, whether He can act upon us now, whether He can hear us, be approached by us, are thoughts contemptuously dismissed as belonging to the category of theological abstractions and foolish dogmas. These very souls may follow His example in such and such an instance, apply His Beatitudes to this or that circumstance of their life, look upon His Life as a great Sacrifice and an inspiration to their own lives, but to them Christ is no more than that! He is the greatest Man who ever lived; but He is nothing more. They indeed are among those of whom St. Paul has said, that they know Christ only according to the flesh.

It must be admitted that the continued sensible and visible presence of our Saviour would have been an inspiration to our lives, but we must not forget that He Himself said the night before He died: "It is expedient for you that I go" (John 16:7). Strange words these! Why should they be spoken at a moment when He had weaned the hearts of His apostles from their nets, boats and custom tables, and had drawn them so closely to His own Sacred Heart? How could it be expedient for them that He go? How could it be expedient for travellers on the sea of life, that their Captain should be taken from them? How could it be expedient for them to be left alone when He was sending them out as sheep among wolves? How could it be expedient for men who live so close to the material and the sensible, to lose their Lord from sight and touch? And yet it was expedient for us that He go, otherwise He would not have told us so. Perhaps we can see reasons why it was expedient for Him to go.

First, if He had continued His earthly life to our own day, then the most important questions of life would have been left unanswered. What is the reward for virtue? What lies beyond the tomb? Does a saintly life purchase anything better in the next world? Has heaven any crown for those who, like good shepherds, lay down their lives for their sheep? Certainly, if Jesus has not merited eternal glory because of His earthly Life, then wherein lies the value and the worth of a good earthly life? Did not our Lord Himself tell us that "it was fitting that the Son of man should suffer in order that He might enter into His glory," and did not Paul, repeating that lesson in other words, say that "if Christ is not risen again, then is our preaching vain, and your faith is also vain" (I Cor. 15:14)? Hence one of the reasons why it was expedient for our Lord to go was to show that the reward of an earthly life is not an earthly reward; that each of us has an appointed task to do in this world; that we were sent into it to work out our salvation, and that, like Him, we must press onward to our "supernal vocation," which is everlasting glory with Him in heaven.

But it was expedient for Him to go for still another reason.

If in our prayers and meditations we lived only in the memory of Jesus of Nazareth we would never know Him as He really is. We would know Him in His outward appearance; we would know Him "in the form of a servant," subject to all the limitations of His human nature: a lowly birth, a homeless apostolate and ignoble cross; we would know Him as a figure who passes before our carnal eyes and judge Him as we judge anyone whose hands we can clasp and whose garment we can touch. But knowing Him this way we might be too inclined to love Him only as man, however good, and forget that He is God, whose pre-history is hidden in the bosom of an Eternal Father. Our exclusive attention to His physical movements might make us forget that in becoming man He thrust His Divine Glory into the background, that His humanity was but the humble instrument of Divinity, for in it God "emptied Himself"; and that the Cross represented only the last act in time of the "Lamb slain from the beginning of the world." The exclusive emphasis on the earthly Life would becloud His inner knowledge; leave unexplained the new Organic Kingdom He came to found and, above all else, the astounding fact that He never spoke so intensely about living and dwelling within our souls, as the night before He went to His Redeeming Death.

Finally, it was expedient for us that He go in order that He might be nearer to us. This is the very reason He gave for His going: "for if I go not, the Paraclete will not come to you; but if I go, I will send Him to you. . . . I have yet many things to say to you, but you cannot bear them now. But when He, the Spirit of Truth, is come, He will teach you all truth. He shall glorify Me: because He shall receive of Mine, and shall show it to you. . . . A little while, and now you shall not see Me: and again, a little while, and you shall see Me: because I go to the Father. . . . I will see you again and your heart shall rejoice; and your joy no man shall take from you" (John 16:7, 12, 14–16, 22).

In these solemn words, spoken on the eve of His Crucifixion, He explicitly stated that He was going back to the boundless depths of His Father's Life whence He came, but His going would not leave them orphans, for He would come again in a new way, namely, by His Spirit. Our Lord was here equivalently saying that if He remained on earth in His Physical Life, He would have been only an *example to be copied*; but if He went to His Father and sent His Spirit, then He would be a *Life to be lived*. If He remained on earth He would have been merely the subject of prolonged observation, of scientific study and imitation; but however noble

His example, however inspiring His words, He would always have been *outside us, external* to us—an *external* Voice, an *external* Life, an *external* Example. He could never be possessed other than by an embrace. The very physical body which housed that Divine Life would have been an obstacle to our loving Him by a unity of mind and heart and soul whence all true love must end. If He had tarried on earth all would have stood still. It would have been the perpetual promise of a day, a lingering blossom, a retarded fruit, a lengthening childhood, a backward maturity.

But once He ascended into heaven and sat at the right hand of the Father in the Glory which is His, then He could send His Spirit into our souls, so that He would be with us not as an external Person, but as a living Soul; then He would be not just a mere something mechanical to be copied, but something Vital to be reproduced, not something external to be portrayed in our lives, but something Living to be developed within us. His Ascension into heaven and His sending of His Spirit makes it possible for Him to unite Himself wholly with us, to take up His abode with us, body and blood, soul and divinity, and to be in the strictest sense of the term "Christ in us." It was expedient therefore that He go, otherwise He would have belonged to history and to a country. Now He belongs to all men.

We who live so much in the material world are apt to believe that the Spirit means a vague, indefinite and vacuous attitude or mood or subjective outlook, such as we understand when we speak of "the spirit of modern music," or the "spirit of a nation," or "school spirit." It cannot be too much emphasized that the Spirit which descends into the Body of the Church to make it one is no mere Divine influence, or outpouring of power, but a Person whose very essence is Love—the Person of God Himself.

This Spirit which is the soul of the Church is not something visible. Our Saviour said that His movements are like the wind (John 3:8). We do not see it, but we hear it sometimes as a gentle whisper, sometimes as a great rushing sound as the apostles heard it on Pentecost. The man who judges spiritual things as he judges gold, by weight, or the scientist who admits nothing real except the measurable, entirely miss the spirit, for as our Lord said, "the world seeth Him not, nor knoweth Him."

Thanks to His Invisible Spirit which He sends into His Mystical Body, Christ is living now on earth just as really and truly as He was living in Galilee nineteen centuries ago. In a certain sense He is closer to us now than then, for His very Body made Him external to us, but thanks to His Spirit, He can live in us as the very Soul of our souls, the very Spirit of our spirit, the Truth of our minds, the Love of our hearts, and the Desire of our wills. Thus the Life of Christ is transferred by the Spirit from the region of purely historical studies which we investigate with our reason, to the realm of spiritual experience where He speaks directly to our soul. It may have been a great consolation for the Canaanite woman to have touched the hem of His garment, for Magdalene to have kissed His feet, for John to have leaned on His breast the night of the Last Supper, but all these intimacies are external. They have great force and appeal because they are sensible, but none of them can even vaguely approximate the union, the intimacy, which comes by possessing Christ inwardly through His Holy Spirit. The greatest joys of life are those which come from unity—the unity of citizens in a nation, the unity of children and parents in a family, the unity of interests and ideals among friends, and the unity of two in one flesh in the Sacrament of matrimony. But even that last kind of unity, which is the deepest in the natural order because it bears fruit in a child, is still quite imperfect. The unity of the flesh need not always mean unity of soul. Sometimes the possession of another outwardly is the greatest obstacle to inward possession. We never reach the heights of unity until there is a fusion of love, of thought, and of desire, a unity so profound that we think with the one we love, love with the one we love, desire what he desires, and this unity is found in its perfection when the soul is made one with the Spirit of Christ which is the Spirit of God. The joys that come from human friendships, even the noblest, are but the shadows and reflections of the joy of a soul possessed of the Spirit of Christ. Elevate human happiness which comes from union with the one loved to the extremest point the heart can endure, and even that is but a spark compared to the flame of the Spirit of Christ burning in a soul that loves Him.

The great tragedy of history is not that men should fall, but that they should fail to rise to full realization of their vocation as children of God, in other words, that they should miss so much. All about us we see vast multitudes of men and women of refinement and culture, endowed with intelligence and possessed of every natural virtue and every now and then swept by noble emotions and ideals, but who are living second-rate, superficial, unimportant and morally insignificant lives, because they have never had their nature enkindled into flame by the Spirit of Christ. They may do much for the world in the material order, they may build bridges, harness waterfalls, accomplish great pieces of research, but they never sound the depths of their souls which can be filled only by God. The world of the supernatural has no more appeal to them than heroism has appeal to a coward. They have become so used to the dense atmosphere of the material, that they stifle in the more rarefied atmosphere of the supernatural.

And in this lies the danger of our whole civilization, which is gradually turning away from God. Nothing great, nothing really good was ever done in this world by any human life that had not a baptism of God's Holy Spirit. There is no escape from the words of Him who presided at Creation as the Word, and at the re-creation on the Cross as the Word-made flesh: "Without Me you can do nothing."

How differently do they live for whom our Lord is not just a figure in the past, but the very Spirit of their lives. The great facts of His earthly Life are re-lived not only in His Mystical Body which is the Church, but in every soul incorporated into that Body by baptism of the Holy Ghost. The details of His earthly Life do not belong only to distant history separated from us by nineteen hundred years. For the Catholic these centuries do not exist at all; the Gospel facts are perpetuated independently of their setting in time and space; His Life is not something which *was* lived; it is something which is *being lived* in us *now*. Nor is it just a mere copy in us of something lived before; rather is the Gospel Life the model of the new Catholic life; it is not a repetition but rather a prolonged Incarnation, for did He not say, speaking of His new way of living in us by His Spirit: "I will not leave you orphans: I will come to you. Yet a little while, and the world seeth Me no more. But you see Me: because I live and you shall live. In that day you shall know that I am in My Father, and you in Me, and I in you" (John 14:18–20).

These last words in which our Lord says that, thanks to His Holy Spirit, *we will live in Him*, and *He will live in us* are among the profoundest words ever heard by this sinful earth. Scripture is full of countless instances of how He lives in us by His Spirit. He is in those who are just (Matt. 10:41), who are poor (Matt. 10:42), who are sick, hungry, naked, thirsty, captive (Matt. 25:35–39), for we are all members one of another in His Mystical Body on earth. But more than that, He is in us as new human natures by which He prolongs His earthly Life. Thanks to His Spirit which He sends into our souls, He re-lives His earthly Life and death in each of us. In other words, we are other Christs; we do not merely imitate Him; we do not copy Him; we do not become His miniature, but we re-live Him, which is just another way of saying we are Christians.

Have you ever remarked how quickly the Creed passes over the earthly Life of our Lord? It begins with "born of the Virgin Mary," then immediately leaps to His Death: "suffered under Pontius Pilate, was crucified, died and was buried"; then comes His glorified Life: "He ascended into heaven, sitteth at the right hand of God, from whence He shall come to judge the living and the dead." Why so little stress on the earthly Life, if it is not to emphasize that it was just a preparation for His glorified Life in heaven and His mystical Life in our souls? The Incarnation, Passion, Death, Resurrection, Ascension, are not mere recorded events of history, they are acts in an enduring drama which is being acted *socially* in the Church and *individually* in every soul vivified by the Spirit of Christ. Christ is in us as the Spirit of our lives, and not outside us as an external example. Hence St. Paul recommends: "Let this mind be in you, which was also in Christ Jesus" (Phil. 2:5). Thanks to His possessing us by His Spirit we are sons of God. Bethlehem is not merely an historical event of a God "emptying Himself, taking the form of a servant"; it is also that great mystery by which we become by grace, what He is by nature, namely, the sons of God. The first filiation of a human nature in Christ is the beginning of a long line of progressive filiation which will endure until the end of time.

But He is in us not merely by sending His grace into our souls as children of God; He is also in us as we suffer (Acts 9:4), and thanks to us He completes His Passion in us: "I Paul ... now rejoice in my sufferings for you, and fill up those things that are wanting of the sufferings of Christ in my flesh, for His Body which is the Church" (Col. 1:24). He fights in us: "Wherein also I labour, striving according to His working which He worketh in Me in Power" (Col. 1:29). He dies in us, and He lives in us: "for we who live are always delivered unto death for Jesus' sake; that the Life of Jesus may be made manifest in our mortal flesh" (2 Cor. 4:11). And so it happens that as the Spirit of Christ lives in us and invades our soul, the human selfish self becomes less and less: "As therefore you have received Jesus Christ, the Lord, walk ye in Him; rooted and built up in Him, and confirmed in the faith, as also you have learned, abounding in Him in Thanksgiving" (Col. 2:6–7).

But not only does Christ live in us, but *we also live in Him.* We become so much one with Christ by possessing His spirit, that the union is a faint reflection of that hypostatic union by which His Divine and human natures were one in the unity of His Person. We are so much in Him that anything that has happened to Him must necessarily happen to us, but, of course, in a lesser way befitting our human natures. Our Lord spoke of the unity of the soul and Him as the unity of vine and branches; St. Paul speaks of it as unity of Head and Body. Whatever happens to the Head happens to the Body. But since He died, rose, ascended and enjoys glory, it follows that we who are one with Him must do the same. Because He died, we die . . . we die with Him, and prolong His crucifixion: "We suffer with Him, that we may be also glorified with Him" (Rom. 8:17). "Our old man is crucified with Him" (Rom. 6:6). "A faithful saying: for if we be dead with Him, we shall also live with Him" (2 Tim. 2:11). We are buried with Him: "For we are buried together with Him by baptism into death . . . for if we have been planted together in the likeness of His death, we shall be also in the likeness of His Resurrection" (Rom. 6:4–5). "Buried with Him in baptism, in whom also you are risen again by the faith of the operation of God, who hath raised Him up from the dead"(Col. 2:12). "Being made conformable to His death" (Phil. 3:10). *We rise with Him:* "Even when we were dead in sins, [God] hath quickened us together in Christ (by whose grace you are saved), and hath raised us up together" (Eph. 2:5–6). We share glory with Him: "And if sons, heirs also; heirs indeed of God and joint-heirs with Christ: yet so, if we suffer with Him that we may be also glorified with Him" (Rom. 8:17). We sit with Him in glory: "And hath made us sit together in heavenly places through Christ Jesus" (Eph. 2:6).

All this has been beautifully summarized by St. John: "In this we know that we abide in Him and He in us: because He hath given us His Spirit" (1 John 4:13). Thanks to that Spirit the Life of Christ becomes our Life in Christ. What He did in His own human nature in Galilee He is doing to-day in other human natures in New York, London, Paris and every city and hamlet of the world where there are souls vivified by His Spirit. He is still being born in other Bethlehems of the world outcasts; still coming into His own and His own receive Him not; still instructing the learned doctors of the law and answering their questions; still labouring at a carpenter's bench; still "going about doing good"; still preaching, governing, sanctifying, climbing other Calvarys and entering into the glory of His Father. There are poor people to-day in our bread queues, there are innocent men in our prisons, there are half-clothed families in our tenements who are as ragged and destitute on the outside as they are rich with the Spirit of Christ on the inside. Externally they appear to most of us like the ordinary poor who attack the rich, like the common captives who harangue against authority, like the selfishly needy who curse their lot, but the resemblance is only on the outside, and thus many are deceived. Some eyes are so filled with the dust of the world's traffic, that they cannot see the Divine grace in men's souls. The world classifies them in its social surveys as the poor, the dependent, the captive, but in the eyes of the Father in heaven, they are other Christs in other deserts, thirsty at other wells of Jacob, suffering on other crosses and captive in other prætoriums. The world sees them as so many economic problems; the heavenly Father sees them as beloved sons in whom He is well pleased.

This truth that the Spirit of Christ dwells in the just, escapes the world. We know our Lord said it, we confess it with our lips, we believe it in our heart, but do we seize it in all its reality? Not even just and saintly Christians realize it as they should, and on Judgment Day even they will be surprised that Christ walked the earth again in those who were filled with His Spirit. For when He shall say to them: "I was hungry, and you gave me to eat; I was thirsty, and you gave Me to drink; I was a stranger, and you took me in; naked, and you covered Me; sick, and you visited Me; I was in prison, and you came to Me" (Matt. 25:35–36), the just will answer Him saying, "Lord, when did we see Thee hungry and fed Thee; thirsty, and gave Thee to drink? And when did we see

THE MYSTICAL BODY OF CHRIST

Thee a stranger and took Thee in? Or naked, and covered Thee? Or when did we see Thee sick, or in prison, and came to Thee?" (Matt. 25:37–39). Then the Lord will answer and say to them: "Amen, I say to you, as long as you did it to one of these my least brethren, you did it to Me" (Matt. 25:40). What a waste! Even the social workers will have missed the glory of their vocation! They will think they fed a stomach, when lo! they broke bread for Christ and knew it not. They will think they gave a cup of water to a thirsty throat, when lo! Christ was sitting at their well. They will speak of the needy as Case 568, when lo! it was Christ who wore the clothes. Yes! Christ is still walking the earth in the souls of the just. The next time a beggar asks for bread, and you respond with a bitter word and closed door, enter into your heart and ask: "What if that man be Christ?"

## CHAPTER XI

# The Communion of Saints

As the earth is bigger than any nation, as the universe is bigger than the solar system, so too the Mystical Body is bigger than the Church on earth. Did not our Lord Himself tell us that it was a supernatural society[1] in which the members were bound together by love[2] of a common Father?[3] Did He not also say that it included the elect in heaven with whom the just on earth will one day be associated,[4] and that the communion between heaven and earth was such that the angels of heaven rejoiced at the conversion of a single sinner?[5] Because the Church is an organism made up of many members, a unity possessed of one Spirit,[6] it is possible for the members to share spiritual goods one with another, as the whole body shares the food which is taken into the stomach.[7] The Mystical Body in its entirety includes not only its members on earth who are still working out their salvation, but those who have died in God's favour but without payment of the last farthing of the debt of sin, and finally those who already have been received into eternal bliss and glory. In other words, there are three great divisions of the Mystical Body of Christ: (1) The Church Militant on Earth; (2) The Church Suffering in Purgatory; (3) The Church Triumphant in Heaven. The reciprocal relation and spiritual sharing of gifts and merits between these three who live the life of the same God, who worship the same Father who created them, the same Son who redeemed them, and the same Spirit who sanctified them is what tradition has called the Communion of Saints.

## (1) THE CHURCH MILITANT ON EARTH

We who live on earth and are incorporated in Christ actually by faith, hope and charity, but not *definitively*, constitute what is known as the Church militant. That which characterizes us is warfare, not a warfare against our brethren with the cold sword of steel, but against the powers of darkness with the warm, kindly spirit of charity. We are militant in the sense that we are yet in the process of working out our salvation, exposed to the weakness of will, the surprises of temptation, the attacks of the devil, and yet constantly striving to carry our treasure of grace in a frail vessel to the judgment seat of God. It was to the Church militant our Lord directed most of His gospel, that it might eventually become the Church triumphant in heaven. Its members, He said in His Sermon on the Mount, were to be "poor in spirit," "pure in heart," "meek," and "merciful," and were not to complain of their hard lot here below, for those who mourned would rejoice, and those who suffered persecution would receive a reward exceeding great. There was no promise to His Church militant of a material victory—not even a temporary one. His kingdom, He said, is not of the world; the cross is to be our daily portion; the earth is a place of trial and not a lasting paradise; there are enemies to combat, and these enemies must be conquered not by crushing them but by abnegation of self, by humility of heart and charity which would rather lose the world than endanger the salvation of an eternal soul. Such is the Church militant forever struggling that the Love of Christ the King may reign in men's hearts. But that such an ideal may be realized we must enter a warfare, for no one shall be crowned unless he has struggled. God hates peace in those whom He has destined for war. To the soldiers of the Church militant the order goes out from Paul:

Put you on the armour of God, that you may be able to stand
against the deceits of the devil. For our wrestling is not against
flesh and blood; but against principalities and powers, against
the rulers of the world of this darkness, against the spirits of
wickedness in the high places. Therefore take unto you the
armour of God, that you may be able to resist in the evil day,
and to stand in all things perfect. Stand therefore, having your
loins girt about with truth, and having on the breastplate of
justice, and your feet shod with the preparation of the gospel
of peace. In all things taking the shield of faith, wherewith
you may be able to extinguish all the fiery darts of the most
wicked one. And take unto you the helmet of salvation, and
the sword of the Spirit (which is the Word of God). By all prayer
and supplication, praying at all times in the spirit and in the
same watching with all instance and supplication for all the
saints. (Eph. 6:11–18)

## (2) THE CHURCH SUFFERING

Our Lord enjoined us to "work while it is day, for the night cometh
when no man can work" (John 9:4). That night when the season
of earthly merit has passed, is the moment of death. In the long
course of 1,900 years many soldiers of the Church militant have
served their allotted time, and reported to their Captain Christ.
Many of them served faithfully, but not perfectly; some of them
rested on their weapons when they might have struck more
heroically; others were timid, for they loved with a broken and
yet recovered loyalty; while still others, while never losing sight
of their great ideal, nevertheless fell short of being perfect as
the "heavenly Father is perfect." These soldiers well know they
are not to be immediately ushered before the Christ with the
same titles of glory as their fellow soldiers who died on the field
of battle or who burnt themselves out with love. Their King,
therefore, in His Mercy, has tempered His Justice and permitted

them further purgation in Purgatory, where they might wash the stains from their baptismal robes, and cleanse the rust from their confirmation armour so as to be pure and unspotted to stand in the majestic, august presence of the all Holy God.[8] These souls who are expiating the punishment due to their pardoned sins, form the Church suffering in Purgatory. They are the clients of the communion of saints, being incapable of meriting for themselves, and yet capable of sharing the merits of others. The Church suffering is not a place of mere punishment like hell, but a place of "urgent love, glad hope and sure expectation." There is a sacred rhythm of pain and joy in the lives of the poor souls, the pain of sin, the joy of their blessed hope. And by that they are essentially different from those who "have no further hope." "Yet a little while and your hearts will rejoice." A moment will come when Purgatory shall be no more, and give way to the blessedness of heaven. After all, Purgatory is only a thoroughfare to the Father, toilsome indeed and painful, but yet a thoroughfare to the land of eternal gladness. Every step of its road brings the Father nearer. Purgatory is like the beginning of spring. Warm rays commence to fall on the hard soil and here and there awaken timid life. Even so Christ our Head sends grace upon grace, strength upon strength, comfort upon comfort, in ever richer abundance unto His suffering members. The blessed light of glory spreads, and embraces an ever wider extent of the Church suffering. Countless souls are already awakening to the full day of eternal life, and singing the new song: "Salvation to our God who sitteth upon the Throne, and to the Lamb."[9]

### (3) THE CHURCH TRIUMPHANT

Finally, there is heaven, the place where the soldiers of earth who have fought the good fight, and kept the faith and have loved God, receive the reward of eternal happiness which is their due. Every second countless members of the Church militant and the Church suffering are passing into the joys of the Church triumphant, where the soul is set free to live in the depths of those things whose surface is but touched on earth: the fullness of Life, of Truth and of Love which is the Father, the Son and the Holy Ghost. There are only war veterans in heaven. No one enjoys its blessedness unless he has fought, for from the first day of creation the Divine command went out that no one should be crowned unless he had struggled. There in that glorious army of the all-conquering King will be the apostles[10] through communion with whose faith we entered into communion with God.[11] But in addition to this great white-robed body of martyrs, confessors, virgins, pontiffs and Holy Women with Peter and Paul at their head, all of whom drank the chalice of the Lord and ate the Bread of Life everlasting, there are also the angels who shared in creation and gave the Law to Moses,[12] who had their moment of trial when Michael fought against Satan. But above the angels and above men is that Mother of Soldiers, that Mother of heavenly Warriors, that Mother of the Captain of all who rode forth with Him to the Battle of Calvary, and who, too, was pierced by seven swords, Mary, the Mother of Jesus, Mary, the Mother of the Mystical Body, Mary, Queen of angels and saints. The number of the elect is not yet complete, but as the Church on earth grows, the Mystical Body of Christ grows to its fullness until it embraces that "great multitude which no man can number, of all nations, and tribes and peoples, and tongues, standing before the throne and in sight of the Lamb, clothed with robes and palms in hands, saying 'Benediction, and glory, and wisdom and thanksgiving, honour and power and strength to our God for ever and ever, Amen.'"[13]

These three divisions of the Mystical Body of Christ are not independent, but there is a constant flux and flow between each of them because all are filled by the same Spirit and all crowned by the same Christ.[14] The Mystical Body, like the universe, is "organic," and there is therefore bound to be the repercussion of merits throughout every part of it, on earth, in heaven, and in

Purgatory. If a stone is thrown into the ocean, it causes a ripple which widens in ever-broadening circles until it affects even the most distant shore. A toy dropped from the cradle of an infant disturbs in some way the distant stars. This is because each part of the universe is bound up with every other part as a physical whole. In like manner each part of the Church is bound up with every other part in a more vital and intimate way, because animated by the same charity and united in a mystical whole by the Holy Spirit of God. Great vital movements flow through its members on the field of battle, on earth or behind the lines in Purgatory or before the victorious King in heaven. The first stream flows between the Church triumphant and the Church militant on earth, for the angels and saints in heaven, in answer to our prayers, can intercede for us at the throne of God. They are not indifferent to our warfare, for the saints can never be indifferent to good; nor can they be indifferent to that other part of their body which we are; so eager are they for victory, so keen are they for enlistments in the army of the Lamb, so zealous are they for the cause of their Captain Christ, that they lend a most attentive ear to our prayers and supplications. As our Lord intercedes to the Father for us in virtue of His merits, so do they intercede to our Lord, not through their own merits, but through His merits, the source of our sanctification. The profoundest glory of the Redemption is that it raises man from his impotency to a co-operative share in the great work of the Redemption. The true kingdom whence comes all blessing is not God in His solitariness, but God and His own, Christ and His Mystical Body, Head and members, the King and His courtiers. The angels and saints, because they are one with God, and because they desire that His kingdom may come, present our petitions to Him, not because God does not know them, but because God has willed that we be actors with Him in the great drama of Redemption. The Body of Christ by its very nature implies communion of member with member, as the human body implies relation of cell with cell, and head with foot. Every love-force in the Body of Christ, whether on earth or in heaven, has its share in the world. This does not mean that God could not help us without the saints, for we know He could have preached to the world without the assistance of Peter and Paul. But in the very nature of things He has willed to help us through their co-operation, for it is the nature of God's love to be expansive and communicative. As in creation He communicated to artists and poets the power of being creative, so, too, in Redemption He communicated to angels and saints and to the members of His Mystical Body the power of prolonging His Redemption and dispensing its fruits. They know we are calling them through their face-to-face vision with God. The angels in heaven, Scripture tells us, see our actions, for we know the angel said to Tobias: "When thou didst pray with tears and didst bury the dead, and didst leave thy dinner . . . I offered thy prayers to the Lord" (Tob. 12:12). We know, furthermore, that when Abraham interceded with God on behalf of the wicked cities of Sodom and Gomorrah, God consented to spare the wicked cities if only ten just men could be found therein (Gen. 18). If Abraham had such influence with God while on earth, how much more must be this influence now that he is with Him in heaven. And above all the angels and saints, what shall we say of Mary's influence with Her Son in Heaven! She is still His Mother. And certainly just as He did not refuse Her request to change water into wine to relieve the embarrassment of Cana's wedding party, so He certainly will not refuse our requests when we ask that the water of our poor efforts be changed into the wine of Divine Love, so that She may be in the truest sense of the term our Mother.

And so the line of communication in the kingdom of God is between heaven and earth, above which we, the members of the Church militant, send our petitions to the members of the Church triumphant where the King reigns, and that Church in turn sends healing for our wounds, courage to our cowardly hearts, and the oil of strength for our weakness. How can the veteran soldiers at home be indifferent to the soldiers on the field of battle, since both are under the standard of the same Captain and the flag of His five wounds?"[15]

The second great line of communication exists between the Church militant on earth and the Church suffering in Purgatory. It is indeed one of the most consoling doctrines of the faith that we can still help our loved ones after death, if they stand in need of help, and by doing so perhaps make atonement for our ingratitude to them during life. Death does not break the bond, for our fundamental unity with them is not because they shared our flesh and blood or our common worldly interests, but rather because they live by the same Spirit and are members of the same Body under the Headship of Christ. The soul, which is the life of the body, must in the nature of things one day take leave of the body, but charity, which is the life of the soul, remains forever, unless we kill it by sin: "Charity never falleth away."[16] Now those members of the Mystical Body who died united to God in the centre of their being, but with the debt of sin unpaid and still stained with the imperfections of the world, pass for their final purification into Purgatory, that they may be cleansed from their sins to walk the holy way of God. These poor souls suffer from one great handicap: they cannot help themselves. This is only natural, for their time of merit is passed. A soldier carried from the battlefield can no longer fight the enemy. But they can be helped by us, as the wounded soldier behind the lines may be rehabilitated for the great day of victory. Unless we do help them they must endure the purifying purgation until the last tiny blemish of imperfection is burned away, and they are made ready "as by fire" to enter into the glory of the Church triumphant and the all-embracing love of God.

And so it is that from the earliest times the Church has zealously guarded the words of Sacred Scripture for those suffering members who have entered into the night "wherein no man can work." It is a holy and wholesome thought to pray for the dead that they may be loosed from their sins (2 Macc. 12:46). To these members of the Church suffering who are, we must not forget, members of the Mystical Body, the Church on earth applies the affectionate term the "poor souls." So conscious is the Church militant of her solidarity, so mindful is she of the communion of saints that in each Mass she prays to the Church triumphant for the poor souls of the Church suffering in these beautiful words, "Be mindful also, O Lord, of thy servants and handmaids ... who have gone before us with the sign of faith and rest in the sleep of peace."

Manifold are the means by which we may help the members of the Church suffering. A loaf of bread given to the poor, a visit to a hospital to bring solace to the sick, an alms to the beggar in the street, a glass of water to a friend, a kind word, a Hail Mary whispered softly as we go about our routine duties, a short indulgenced ejaculation in the midst of our pleasures, a slight mortification at table—any of these and each of them, if done out of love for God and for the intention of the souls in Purgatory, will hasten their release so that, like birds set free from a cage, they may fly to heaven to the very arms of the loving God. Surely if I may give physical help to my friends on earth who are bound to me by ties of earthly love, why cannot we who are members of the same Mystical Body and are bound by the immortal ties of the Charity of the Spirit of Christ, relieve the burdens of the souls in Purgatory? We are all one in Christ, and though our deeds be small, our alms be trivial, our mortifications be slight, they take in added virtue and efficacy when united in Holy Mass with the Sacrifice of Calvary, for then the Father in heaven sees not us but His Beloved Son offering the all-pleasing oblation for those who are beloved of us.[17]

Such is the communion of saints,[18] or the doctrine of the solidarity of the faithful in the Mystical Body of Christ. It transports us beyond the boundaries of nationality, beyond the confining limits of space and the servitude of time, into that eternal kingdom which has neither past nor future, where Abraham, Isaac, and Jacob live with Peter, Joan of Arc, and the Little Flower, where the soldiers on earth breathe the same atmosphere of charity as the souls in heaven, where the blood runs through every cell of the Mystical Body, whether in heaven, on earth, or in Purgatory because all are in Christ Jesus our Head.

What a relief to belong to another society where men's plans are not limited to tomorrow; where we can live, move and breathe in an infinite realm; where we may begin and break off; sow and let others reap; plan and let others complete; lay the foundation and let others build thereon, because Rome is eternal, because victory is assured, because Christ is King.

There are no limitations. The heart beating in the communion of saints takes in at once the timeless and spaceless charity when the Spirit brooded over the waters at the creation of the world, when the Spirit illumined the Virgin in the birth of Christ, and the apostles in the birth of the Church, and finally when with the fullness of the Mystical Christ God shall be all in all. From out of that remote past come the saintly souls, who, like Abraham, looked forward to Christ, to join hands with any son of Abraham to-day who sees in Him the Desired of the Nations. Never does the Catholic stand alone. Beneficent influences from the past, like the sun from another world, are pouring out upon his soul; powerful streams of living waters from the Eternal are renewing his spiritual youth like the eagle's; mysterious forces of invisible might issuing forth from his fellow soldiers in the Church militant are magnetizing him into greater zeal for the cause of Christ. Everywhere there is communion, traffic, exchange of prayers, merits, sacrifices, for we are all one in the communion of the saints of God.

## CHAPTER XII

# Reparation

The foundation of the science of sociology and the basis of all human relations is the solidarity of all men in Christ. The unity by which members of the Mystical Body are bound up one with another through the Spirit of Charity surpasses all the unities of earth. Blood unites the members of a family, common national interests unite the citizens of a country, but it is the Holy Spirit of God which binds the members of the Church into the unity of the Mystical Body of Christ.

Because of this close relation between member and member in the Church there is bound to be mutual influence. Even families and nations share this mutual influence to a lesser degree. A deed of heroism or a great scientific discovery by the father of a family, brings glory on all the members of that family. An outstanding act of service by a citizen of any nation sheds reflected lustre on the whole nation. In the biological order because of the close relationship between cell and cell in the human body, the food taken into the stomach affects to some extent every single part of the body. This vital unity in a living organism, because possessed of a soul, is a more fitting analogy for the solidarity of the Church than family or national unity. "We are members one of another," St. Paul is fond of repeating, and we are one because the Spirit of Christ which is the Spirit of Love makes us one. Like a mighty river that Spirit of Love swells and sweeps about the souls of men, breaking its secret of salvation, and whispering its wondrous message of healing for their wounds, and pardon for sins. That Love-stream which is the Life-stream, like the blood-plasm of the human body which carries life from within it, supplies the potency by which every unit in the organic Body of Christ is nourished and baptized with power. United as we are to our fellow men by our common life in Christ, there is reciprocity, mutual sympathy, and a sense of corporateness between us, for we are all parts of the same Body of Christ.

The two greatest sympathies are those of sorrow and joy. Firstly, consider sympathy with the sorrow of another. If the eye sees a blow about to be directed against the ear, the eye does not say: "It is not going to strike me, and therefore I am free from worry." As a matter of fact the eye does seek to prevent injury to the ear, for both are one because parts of the same organism. Now in the Mystical Body, the sorrow, the suffering, and the persecution of the Church in one part of the world should be felt by the Church in all parts of the world. As St. Paul says:

> For in one Spirit were we all baptized into one body, whether Jews or Gentiles, whether bond or free; and in one Spirit we have all been made to drink. For the body also is not one member, but many. If the foot should say, because I am not the hand, I am not of the body; is it therefore not of the body? And if the ear should say, because I am not the eye, I am not of the body; is it therefore not of the body? If the whole body were the eye, where would be the hearing? If the whole were hearing, where would be the smelling? But now God hath set the members every one of them in the body as it hath pleased him. And if they all were one member, where would be the body? But now *there are* many members indeed, yet one body. And the eye cannot say to the hand: I need not thy help; nor again the head to the feet: I have no need of you. Yea, much more those that seem to be the more feeble members of the body, are more necessary. And such as we think to be the less

honourable members of the body, about these we put more
abundant honour; and those that are our uncomely parts,
have more abundant comeliness. But our comely parts have no
need: but God hath tempered the body together, giving to that
which wanted the more abundant honour, that there might
be no schism in the body; but the members might be mutually
careful one for another. (1 Cor. 12:13–25)

On this logic the Church in Mexico, for example, is part of the
Mystical Body as much as the arm is part of the human body.
What it suffers the whole Church should therefore feel as its
*own*. Or to express the same idea in the language of St. Paul: "If
one member suffer anything, all the members suffer with it" (1
Cor. 12:13–26).

Do the members of the Church understand to its full extent
this oneness with one another through the Spirit? Do those
who retain their faith feel sad at the loss of that faith by those
who once possessed it? Do those who love God grieve at sinners
leaving the paths of peace? Do those who are wealthy realize
that the poor of the Church have need of their superfluities?
Do national boundaries blind our vision to that wider outlook,
that supranationalism which is the fatherhood of God and the
brotherhood in Christ? When the Church is being persecuted
in one part of the world, when Churches are pillaged, bishops
exiled, the faithful martyred, do we feel that their pain and their
sorrow are ours, as much as the pain in the arm is the pain in
the whole body? Those who are insensitive to these sorrows of
the Church in other parts of the world are insensitive to their
dignity as Christians. The interaction of the moon and the tides,
the sympathy between a baby's cry and the vibration of a distant
star, is as naught compared to that finer interaction and sympathy
between Christian and Christian in the Body of Christ which is
His Church.

What is true of sorrow and pain in the Mystical Body is true also of its joy. In the human body if the tongue tastes something sweet the whole body rejoices. In like manner, in the Church, St. Paul tells us "if one member glory, all the members rejoice with it" (1 Cor. 12:26). When therefore the Church canonizes a saint, when there is an increase of communions in the Church in Germany or France, when sinners return to the faith and do penance which makes even the angels rejoice, when the spirit of prayer and contemplation grows in the souls of men as worldliness decreases, all this should make us rejoice, for it is part of one Body.

Christianity then is social. Isolation and individualism is its enemy, fellowship is its strength. Once the nature of the solidarity of the Mystical Body is understood, one is prepared to understand not merely the *sympathy* we must have for its joys and sorrows, but also the *reparation* we can offer for those members who stand in need of it.

The analogy of the human body makes clear this idea of reparation. It is a well-established fact that all its members run up and find their keyboard in the brain. The connection between the right hand and the left is not direct, but mediate, i.e., it is established through the central nervous system. In the event of perfectly established and harmonious relations between the centres and its members, there is a perfect unanimity and reciprocity between the members themselves which guarantees mutual help and assistance. For example, let a speck of dust enter the eye and at once the hand flies up to minister. Let a man slip in the street and sprain his foot and the other foot will do double duty all the way home. If a person burn his face doctors will graft skin from another part of his body and apply it to his face. If a man is suffering from anæmia doctors will transfuse blood from another member of society to that weak individual to cure him of his anæmic condition. This fine fellowship and fealty springs out of perfectly sustained relations with the head.

In the Mystical Body then all members, who are one by obedience to the same head, can be of service one to the other. If one member slip another runs to help him up; if it is possible to graft skin, is it not also possible to graft prayer; if it is possible to transfuse blood, is it not also possible to transfuse sacrifice? This process of atoning, and sacrificing ourselves for other members of the Mystical Body, is what is known as reparation. Such is the meaning of the words of St. Paul: "Bear ye one another's burdens; so you also shall fulfill the law of Christ."

Such is the reason for the communities in the Church, such as the Carmelites and Poor Clares, the Trappists and the Carthusians, and many others whose supreme business in life it is to repair the harm done by others, and to bring succour to those who cannot help themselves. The world is full of those who sin and atone not; who offend God and never repent; who have their sins forgiven but who never do penance. These poor, burnt, anæmic, wounded members of the Mystical Body of Christ may yet be saved by those who out of their superfluities expend spiritual wealth for the salvation of souls. The world which asks of such saintly mortified souls hidden away in cloisters and convents, "What good do you do?" fails to understand that in the order of Divine Life they are doing for the wounded on the spiritual battlefields of the Church what, in the order of human life, nurses and doctors are doing on the battlefields of the world. And the saving of a soul is immeasurably more important than the saving of a body.

In these days when the world regards sin as a lesser evil than a headache, the value of reparation in the Mystical Body is apt to be overlooked. It needs to be repeated that reparation exists because there is sin. In every sin there is a double element: the joy of a forbidden fruit and the act of disobedience against God. Equilibrium can be established therefore only by a commensurate pain to atone for the forbidden joy, and a compensating repentance to atone for the act of disobedience. Of these two elements the latter is more important, for it gives to the first its moral significance. Otherwise pain would be pain for the sake of pain and not sacrifice. Then we would be like the Hindu mystics who glorify suffering as an end in itself. It is the sorrow, the contrition, and the desire to love God which changes pain into sacrifice, for what is pain but sacrifice without love? But it is not enough to be sorry for our sins. Sin involves a debt, and the debt must be paid. It is not sufficient for a man who has run into great debts to say to his creditor: "I am very sorry I have contracted these debts. I will not run up any more in the future." He must *pay the debts* in addition to being contrite. So likewise with sin. It is not enough to tell God we are sorry for our sins; we must pay the debts contracted by them, and if there was fun in running them up, there must be pain in tracking them down. If we take a hundred steps in the wrong direction we must put our foot down one hundred times to get back in the right direction. Where there was forbidden joy, there must now be willing sacrifice. There is no pardon without reparation. That is why beneath all the liturgical differences of all peoples there has always been sacrifice. They have testified with Paul that "without the shedding of blood there is no remission of sin."[1]

Simply because there are millions of souls who sin and are sorry, and who do no adequate penance for their sins this side of Purgatory, because there are members of the Mystical Body dead in sin who can be brought back to life only by God's grace through the intercession of pious souls, there have always been and there will always be in the Church mortified souls who burn themselves out that others may be saved on the day of the judgment of the Lord. They are daily putting into the spiritual treasury of the Church the common store of merits whence the spiritually poverty-stricken may draw in their hour of need.

The Church thus presents herself to the world as a copy of the society of persons within the Godhead itself, Father, Son, and Holy Ghost, who share the fullness of the nature of God.

Did not our Lord say: "O Father, all My things are Thine, and Thine are Mine"? (John 17:10) "All things which Thou hast given Me are from Thee. The words which Thou gavest Me, I have given to them" (John 17:7–8). And is not the Church a picture of the Trinity in its community of goods and attributes? What her members possess they possess in common. If her members no longer share temporal goods in common, as they did in the early Church, yet they share in common the infinitely more precious spiritual goods such as prayers, sacrifices, and merits. It is this high type of Spiritual Communion which makes it possible for the saintly souls to share their goods with the unsaintly, and for the saints to crucify themselves in union with Christ to bring other penitent thieves into the kingdom of God.[2]

These foregoing analogies set in relief the great redemptive work of our Divine Lord. Some Christians labour under the illusion that since they have been redeemed by Christ there is naught for them to do. Nothing could be further from the truth. Our Lord has redeemed us, but His redemption must be *applied* to our souls. He has filled the heavenly reservoir with Divine grace, but we must let that grace pour into our souls. But how can we do this except by becoming incorporated into His Life and His Death? What He has done to His own individual human nature, He wills that through Him we do to our own, namely, prove our love by death to the world and sin, as a prelude to an everlasting Easter.[3] His own physical Body has suffered and entered into its glory. He wills now that His Mystical Body made up of all the human natures incorporated to Him should enter into its glory by travelling the same paths even to Golgotha and the Cross. What the Head has done the Body must do, and since Christ has passed through His Good Friday to His Easter Sunday, so must every Christian in His Mystical Body imitate Him by taking up the same cross and rising from the same tomb. Christ in His own human nature has obeyed the law of creation that "no one shall be crowned unless he has struggled," but His Mystical Body has not yet fulfilled the last detail of that law. It is precisely this St. Paul means when he says that we must "fill up those things that are wanting of the sufferings of Christ in the flesh, for His Body, which is the Church" (Col. 1:24).

The redemption of Christ's Mystical Body can become complete only as we, through the influence of His grace, reproduce His own life in ours. "In all things," writes St. Paul, "we suffer tribulation, but are not distressed; we are straitened but not destitute; we suffer persecution, but are not forsaken; we are cast down, but we perish not; always bearing about in our body the mortification of Jesus, that the Life also of Jesus may be made manifest in our bodies. For we who live are always delivered unto death for Jesus' sake; that the Life also of Jesus may be made manifest in our bodies" (2 Cor. 4:8–10). There is therefore a mystical identity between Christ and us so that "if we be dead with Him, we shall also live with Him. If we suffer, we shall also reign with Him" (2 Tim. 2:11–12). We prolong the redemption of Christ in our own lives, and make it possible for the Divine Life of the Head to flow into the Mystical Body because conformed to His Life by dying to the world. That is why St. Paul told the Romans "to present your bodies a living sacrifice, holy, pleasing unto God, your reasonable service" (Rom. 12:1).

The redemption is reciprocal. Our Lord does not do everything and we nothing. The truth is between these extremes. The Oriental philosophy generally makes God do everything and man nothing. Our modern Western humanism makes man do everything and God nothing. Christianity reveals that we are called in some way to prolong His Life, Death, and Resurrection in our lives, because of our solidarity with Him. It is evident then that faith alone in the redemption of our Lord is not sufficient to save us. Faith is important because it marks our first disposition toward salvation. But "faith without good works is dead." Man must respond to the first steps God has taken, for which God justifies him, binding him to do good works in His name. The death of our Lord on the Cross, then, instead of dispensing us from dying, obliges us to do so. As was pointed out in an earlier chapter, we are not merely to copy the example of Christ as we might copy the example of a great man, for that would touch only the surface of the soul. Rather are we to "put on Christ" and be possessed of His Spirit (Rom. 13:14; Col. 3:12–13). "For let this mind be in you, which was also in Christ Jesus. Who being in the form of God, thought it not robbery to be equal with God, but emptied Himself taking the form of a servant, being made in the likeness of men, and in habit found as man. He humbled Himself, becoming obedient unto death, even to the death of the Cross" (Phil. 2:5–8). "For as the sufferings of Christ abound in us, so also by Christ doth our comfort abound" (2 Cor. 1:5).

Putting on Christ or living His mind is a long cry from any sentimental or external imitation. We are called to be conformed to Christ in all the details of His Life (Phil. 2:1–11; Gal. 3:5; 2 Cor. 5:4; Col. 2:12; Eph. 4:9). He is our Saviour, but our Saviour by Sacrifice. But His Mystical Body can have no other law than His, for He is its Head. Therefore it is incumbent upon every Christian to share in His Sacrifice; to realize in time what is implied on the Cross; to actualize in our own day what was procured for us on Good Friday. He, the glorious Christ reigning at the right hand of the Father, can never again suffer in His own human nature "knowing that Christ rising again from the dead, dieth no more" (Rom. 6:9). He therefore has willed to prolong His loving Passion unto the end of the world by perpetuating it in the members of His Mystical Body who if they suffer with Him will reign with Him. Thus every true Christian should say with Paul: "With Christ I am nailed to the Cross, and I live, now not I; but Christ liveth in me. And that I live now in the flesh: I live in the faith of the Son of God who loved me and delivered Himself for me" (Gal. 2:19–20) . . . "in nothing shall I be confounded, but with all confidence, as always, so now also shall Christ be magnified in my body, whether it be by life or by death. For to me, to live is Christ; and to die is gain" (Phil. 1:20–21).

This law of Sacrifice by which the Mystical Body works out its salvation and the salvation of others by reparation, is not the hard law of pain, though it seems to be that on the surface. God does not delight in pain as such. The inspiration of all Sacrifice is love, for love by its very nature tends to an incarnation, and an incarnation by its very nature tends to a crucifixion. Love tends to an incarnation in the family where the love of husband and wife coalesce in the production of their incarnate life—a child. Love tends to a crucifixion when rather than see any harm befall the one we love, we suffer and if need be die, that harm may be spared him.

This idea of love being the soul of Sacrifice is too often forgotten in these days, when love is measured in terms of what we receive rather than in terms of what we give. As long as there is a hierarchy of values, as long as one thing is better than another thing, as long as there are levels of goodness, the possessing of the higher must mean surrender of the lower, and that means sacrifice. Mortification, penance, reparation are not positive things, but only means to an end which is charity and love. Saints do not crucify their flesh and its concupiscences because crucifixion is an ideal. They see *through* the Cross: they love something beyond the Cross, and for that they are willing to suffer pain.

It was Love that made God incarnate: it is that same Love which led Him to the Cross to pour forth the crushed-out sweetness of His heart. Evil has never been able to stop the Flame of Love from shooting sparks into the souls of saints, firing them to love our Lord unto death even as our Lord loved them unto death, that the world might witness not only God loving man but man loving God. Many souls there would be who would not respond to it, but in the scales of His Judgment the love of a John upon His breast outweighed the treachery of Judas. God's love shines through the world despite its sin, its evil, its hate, just as the sun's rays pierce the interstellar cold, without ever warming it, and yet come warm to us.

The Cross then is the focal point of all creation. The fact of creation was only a prelude to the drama of Calvary. And Calvary was the perfection of love.

CHAPTER XIII

# The Expansion of the
# Mystical Body

The great characteristic of life is growth. Youth and growth, age and decay are inseparable. The law of growth was imposed on creation when God told man and the lower creatures of which he was the Master: "Increase and multiply." The same law of growth was imposed on the Church when our Lord told His apostles: "Preach the gospel to every creature." The Church was thus ordered to reproduce, to generate new life, to fill up the kingdom of God, to make conquests from the outside, to increase progeny from within, for the Church that does not reproduce, that is not missionary, is weaving its own shroud. "You have not chosen Me," said our Lord, "but I have chosen you, and have appointed you, that you should go and bring forth fruit; and your fruit shall remain" (John 15:16).

But how is this Mystical Body of Christ to grow from a mustard seed into a great tree? Is it to grow by God pouring out His grace on the souls of men, while we the members remain inactive? Or is it to grow by members co-operating with the grace of God? The laws of nature suggest the answer. The human body develops from infancy to perfection, thanks principally to food and drink. The food and drink would not aid the growth of the body, unless the body already possessed a soul, which is the principle of life. Corpses do not grow however much nourishment is poured into

176

them. Neither does the soul alone suffice for life. The food which the living body must have comes into the body through the other members of the body: the feet which walk to the tables and the hands which touch the food and take it into the organism. Thus two factors combine for growth: the living soul, and the food given to the body through the help of the members of the body itself.

The Church is the Mystical Body of Christ. Its soul is the Spirit of Christ, without which the Church would not be an organism, but only an organization. Its body is made up of all who have been incorporated by baptism. But the Body and Soul are not enough for the growth of the Church. The growth of the Church, like the growth of the Body, depends not only on its Spirit, but also on the activity of the members of the Mystical Body itself. The fact that we share His life does not dispense us from the obligation of working with Him for the increase of His Mystical Body. Do not the branches reach out to absorb the sunlight; do not the hands reach out to grasp the food? Why, then, should not our Lord, in like manner, make the growth of His Church dependent upon its members? He might have done otherwise. But since Mary was called to share in the redemption, since apostles were called to preach what Christ had preached, since Peter was called to be the rock of His Church, aye! since the call of Abraham and the endowing of Adam with free will, it is by means of men that God deals with men. As the diamond is polished only by the diamond, so it is by and through human natures that Christ spreads the kingdom of His Father. The zealous souls, the apostles, the missionaries in far countries, the saintly souls in our own land, the sisters in our schools, the priests in our parishes, all the Christ-loving men and women whose hearts are on fire with the love of God, are the eyes, the feet and the hands of Christ which reach out to the pagan, the dejected, the forlorn, the sinners, to lift them into that Body where they may be quickened again into Life and Love and Truth by the vivifying Power of the Spirit of Christ.

What nobler passion could there be than zeal for souls? What finer way to spend oneself and be spent than in drawing souls to the love of their Lord and their God? The world holds in high repute the physicians who restore health to the diseased, the teachers who bring learning to the illiterate, the social workers who mend broken human lives, and the scientists who extend the frontiers of our knowledge. All this is noble, but since there is a Life beyond this, let it be remembered that in the Book of Life they are written in letters of gold who do for souls what others have done for the body. The Heart of Christ holds in eternal love those spiritual physicians and surgeons who restore grace to diseased sinners, who root out the cancer of error that Truth may grow, those teachers who bring a knowledge of grace to the learned, those sisters of charity who make saints out of Magdalenes, and those missionaries who extend the frontiers of Christ's kingdom.

The responsibility to extend the Mystical Body of Christ falls upon each of its members. Any member who refuses it is guilty of a breach of trust. The privilege of being a cell in the Mystical Body is the privilege of stewardship and service and propagation. Through loyalty to this missionary imperative each member may pay his debt of thanks for the gift of faith. Every living unit thus stands between the past and the future with obligations to both which it cannot cast off. What we have received, we must pass on and not pocket; what has been given to us must not be confined, but cradled for growth. As guardians of the Divine Life which has come down to us since Pentecost, we must answer to God for misappropriation and impounding His gifts to our own ends. Every talent received must bear interest, and every grace received must furnish a highway along which the gospel of Christ shall have a straight and unimpeded path for propagation.

The barren fig tree is the fruitless Christian: the member of the Mystical Body who is not apostolic, who keeps the knowledge of God for himself, who refuses to enthuse over Divine possessions and who rebels against being an instrument of God's missionary activity. And so his commission is cancelled, and even the little he had is taken away.

"The harvest is great; the labourers are few." And they are few, not because those who are not incorporated into Christ's Mystical Body outnumber those who are, but because zeal is wanting. If there is any great characteristic of our age it is want of zeal for truth. Instead of strong passions steering the hearts of men, and making them brave enough to lead on erring mankind, there is only a weak, timid inactivity. There are no great loves, as there are no great hates. There are no great loyalties arousing souls, preparing them to sacrifice the seen for the unseen, the visible for the eternal. There are few causes espoused with readiness to die for them rather than surrender them. Each man to-day, in the language of Paul, is seeking his own, and not what is Christ's. In fact the world to-day considers it a fault to be zealous. There is no fire in our hearts, but only dying embers. There is need of reviving the missionary spirit with its consciousness that every member of the Mystical Body is like the tree planted by the fountain of living waters. The tree has its roots hidden in the soil of the Christian tradition of nineteen centuries; its branches move in the living present, passing on to the future, the promise and potency of the spiritual forests that are yet to be.

God has implanted in nature a tremendous enthusiasm for new life. The Holy Spirit has implanted in the Church even a greater enthusiasm for new life which only perverse human wills can quench. In the nature of things all life is aglow with the missionary spirit. Look to the trees in the springtime. The gold and silver of their blossoming is the beautiful and fragrant expression of life's loyalty to new life. They are making life's supreme effort to fulfil their stewardship. Every blossom is a declaration of trust, a cradle for the slowly forming fruit, and a token of how in the supernatural order every member of the

Church militant should sow the seed of God's truth in every soul he meets. We are commanded to love our neighbour, but there is no higher way to love him than to help him to love the Father and the Son whom He has sent. We do not know how to save our soul alone, but only in conjunction with others.

Occasionally missionary effort demands sacrifice. We may be sent to foreign lands to preach the Gospel to the pagans; we may be called upon to offer generously for those who do go, or to pray for them; but in each instance the sacrifice will be a joy, for its inspiration will be love. If there ever came a time when we had to choose between preserving our own goods or even our own physical life, or losing it to pass on to future generations the spiritual life of the Church, then we should have to surrender the lower values. If there is not sufficient vitality for life and fruit, and the tree must choose between living its life and being disloyal to the law of reproduction, it will always choose to die. Horticulturists have taken advantage of this fact in treating vines that are not doing their best. By cutting the bark, they practically scare a dilatory vine into believing it is about to die, and immediately it hurries and even doubles its output in fruit. Here we see the secret of the lavish output of blossom, bud and fruit. It is the sacrificial principle at work. Victim and priest in one, the fruit in bloom lays out its best upon the altar, literally pouring out its life that it may redeem the earth from future barrenness and make the solitary places glad. And while the sacrificial act for future generations is going on, Nature puts on her beautiful garments, flooding over with fragrance from her myriad censers, amidst the stately ritual of springtime and the music of singing birds. In like manner, the Church cannot be missionary unless it is sacrificial and happy in that sacrifice. As He who hung on the tree of Life has His heart pierced by a spear, only to pour forth the reproductive blood and waters of the Eucharist and Baptism, so too the Church, a product of that sacrificial act, must in virtue of the law of inheritance be sacrificed too, that the Lord's Prayer may be fulfilled, that His kingdom may come, and that the mustard seed may grow into the Tree of Life.

The deaths of the martyrs, the priests and nuns in the foreign missions of the world, the alms of the poor given until it hurts, are not separate and unconnected incidents in a world of space and time. To all the members of the Mystical Body, then, there goes out the command to increase and multiply. The gold of our prayers and our example, the frankincense of our alms and the myrrh of sacrifice are the means by which we fulfil our steward-ship. Thus may the day come when India's absolute renunciation of personality will be transformed into a renunciation wherein personality is not extinguished but perfected in Christ; when Hindu monasteries will be surmounted by the Cross; when the Orient learns from the West not only how to use our machinery, but also how to say our prayers; schools of contemplation arise in thoughtful Asia; the islands of the Pacific be caught in the fisherman's net and pay veneration to Peter; heathen lands take from us not only our electricity but also our sanctuary lamp; the vast army of those who have lived on the fringe of Christianity learn its true meaning, that all the world may know the love of the Heart of Christ.

## CHAPTER XIV

# The Mother of the Mystical Body

Thus far we have considered how Christ prolongs His Incarnation in the Mystical Body: the Church. But little or nothing has been said of the role played by His Blessed Mother in that new Body. This is because her importance is such that it deserves a special consideration.

Some dim suggestion and hint of the part Mary plays in the regeneration of the human race is to be found in the part Eve played in its fall. Sacred Scripture tells us that Christ is the second Adam, who by His obedience on the tree of the cross undid the wrong of the first and disobedient Adam under the tree of the knowledge of good and evil. If Christ is the spiritual counterpart of Adam and the new head of the human race, then Mary, the Mother of those who live in Christ, is the counterpart of Eve, the mother of those who die in Adam. A fitting parallel indeed, for if a woman played such an important role in the fall of the human race, then it is fitting that she be assigned no less eminence in its redemption. Mary is the Mother of the Mystical Body of Christ: the Church.

In order to understand how literal and real this truth is, dwell for a moment on the primary fact that Mary is the Mother of Christ. He who from all eternity was begotten of the Father, is generated in time of the Blessed Mother without man but by the overshadowing of the Holy Spirit. Her life from that point on is inseparably bound up with His; never does Scripture mention her apart from Him. She is with Her Divine Son in the flight to Egypt; she is with Him in the Temple praying the perfect prayer to the heavenly Father; she is with Him during His labours as a carpenter and years of obedience in the humble Nazarene home; she is with Him in His preaching and stands at the foot of the Cross as He dies for the redemption of the world.

Such beautiful devotion makes her the loveliest of all the lovely mothers of the world, the paragon of maternity and the prototype of motherhood. But this does not tell the whole truth concerning Mary. She was more than the mother of the historical Christ. If her Divine Son were only a man, then her maternity might be purely a corporal one. But recall that her Son is the Son of God as well as the son of man. Recall, furthermore, that during His earthly Life He promised to assume a new body after His Ascension into heaven, a body which would be made up of the countless faithful who believed in Him; recall, too, that through this Body would flow His Life and Truth and Love as the sap of the vine flows through the branches. Once He ascended into heaven it was no longer possible for His physical Body to grow and develop, for it possessed the fruits of glory. But the other Body which He assumed on Pentecost, which is His Church, could grow. He said it would grow like the mustard seed, and St. Paul, building on that thought, speaks of it as the "increase of God" (Col. 2:19).

This means that in addition to the physical Christ whose Life began at Bethlehem and ended with the Ascension, there is also the Mystical Christ which began with Pentecost and which will endure through all eternity. Now if the fullness of Christ embraces not only His historical Life in Galilee but also His Mystical Life in the Church, then should not Mary be not only the Mother of the physical Christ, but also the Mother of the fullness of Christ or the Mother of the Church? The Mother of Jesus should therefore be our Mother, otherwise the whole Christ would not be entirely the Son of Mary. She would be His Mother in the physical sense, but she would not be His Mother in the mystical sense. She would be the Mother of the Head, but she would not be the Mother of His Body. This could hardly be, for the sun which shines on the vine to give it strength, also gives strength to the branches; she who is the Mother of the Vine which is the historical Christ, must also be the Mother of the Branches which is the Church. As the Mystical Body is the complement and fullness of the natural Body of Christ, so too the Divine Motherhood of the Head should have its fullness in the Motherhood of the Mystical Body. Since she co-operated in the Incarnation by her consent, she should also co-operate in the prolongation of the Incarnation or the Church.

Would there not have been a great lacuna in what we received from our Divine Saviour if He had not given His Mother to us as our Mother? Think of all the other heavenly benefits He gave us, and then ask yourself why He should stop short of giving us as Mother the woman whom He chose above all the women of the earth, through whom He came to us in the form and image of man. He gave us His heavenly Father and taught us to pray to Him as "our Father"; He gave us His Body and His Blood in the Eucharist as the pledge of everlasting life; He gave us His Spirit to "teach us all truth" (John 16:13); He gave us the fruits of His Resurrection and Ascension, raising us to "sit together in the heavenly places" (Eph. 2:6); He gave us His victory over sin by making us heirs of heaven (Rom. 8:17); He gave us His Sonship by calling us to be adopted sons as He is the natural Son; He gave us His Life that we might live in Him (Gal. 2:20).

Now if His Mother was not given, then He is not the Perfect Lover who gives all. If His testament does not include the gift of His Mother, then has He a right to exclaim from the Cross "It is finished"? Can all be finished if there is yet one omission? Did He not say He would not leave us orphans, but would we not be orphans without a Mother? If He emptied His generous heart by giving us His Father, His Life, His Spirit, then why should His arm be shortened in holding back His Mother? He called us to be His brothers, and adopted sons of the heavenly Father. But if He has a Mother, should not we who are His brothers, also have the same Mother? Grace is the perfection of nature, and if in the natural order we receive natural life through a woman, why should we not also receive supernatural life? Once granted He has given us His Mother as our Mother, then how true ring His words: "And all My things are Thine, and Thine are Mine" (John 17:10).

What we would expect Him to do as fitting His Divine love, He has actually done. Note how Sacred Scripture first implicitly and then explicitly reveals how Mary is the Mother of Christians. St. Luke, in recounting the birth of our Lord, says that Mary brought forth her "first-born." Certain critics have argued that this meant our Lady had other children according to the flesh, although in fact the Scriptures clearly indicate she was a virgin. The statement "first-born" may indeed mean that Mary was to have other children, not by the flesh, but by the Spirit. It suggests that she was to have a spiritual progeny which would make up the Mystical Body of her Divine Son, just as Eve is called the "mother of all living" (Gen. 3:20) or the mother of men in the natural order. Sara gave only one son to the father of believers, Abraham, and yet she is called the mother of all Israel (see Gal. 4:26; Gen. 17:15–16). There is a clear suggestion in the words "first-born" that she who begot corporally the Head of the Church, was also to beget spiritually the members of the Church. Since the Head and the Body are inseparable, it is therefore true to say that as Mary bore Christ in her womb she was virtually carrying the whole Mystical Body. The mother earth that bears the vine also bears the branches.

When finally the Word is made flesh and she brings Him to the temple on the fortieth day for purification Mary's role in the Redemption becomes even clearer. Joseph was with her on that day, but the aged Simeon spoke only to her and reminded her that she was pierced by the sword of sorrow. Simeon, full of the prophetic spirit, was looking forward to the day when this Babe, the new Adam, would atone for sin on the Cross, as the Man of Sorrows, and where she as the new Eve would co-operate in that Redemption as the Woman of sorrows. Simeon was practically telling her that Eden would become Calvary, the tree would be the Cross, and she would be the Mother of the Redeemer. But if she is the Mother of the Redeemer, then was she not called to be the Mother of the Redeemed? And if Christ was her first-born, would not the Redeemed be her other-born, brothers of Christ and sons of the heavenly Father?

All this became clearer when our Lord began to preach. One day as He was breaking the bread of truth to the multitude someone in the crowd announced that His Blessed Mother was seeking Him: "But He answering said: Who is My Mother? . . . and stretching forth His hand towards His disciples He said: Behold My Mother and My brethren. For whosoever shall do the will of My Father, that is in heaven, he is My brother, and sister and Mother" (Matt. 12:46–50). These words did not mean a denial of His Blessed Mother whom He loved next to His own heavenly Father; rather did they mean that there are other ties than those of the flesh, and that in the spiritual order, she who is my Mother may be like Eve, "mother of all the living." The world was being prepared for the fuller and deeper significance of the words "first-born." That day came on the Friday called Good and on a hill called Calvary. Our Lord had already given His garments to His executioners. Later on He was to give His Body to the grave, and His Spirit to His Father. But He has two precious gifts yet to be conferred: His beloved disciple John and His sorrowful Mother, Mary. To whom could He give such gifts except to each other? And so to John, as representative of beloved redeemed humanity, He says: "Behold thy Mother." Then looking to His Mother He said: not "Mother," but "Woman," to remind her of her universal relation to the race of the Redeemer, "Woman, behold thy son"—"Behold thy son"—She had one Son already—He was hanging on the tree of ignominy. Now she was to have another; a son of Zebedee. John then was her second-born! All becomes clear. Her Son told her there was another Motherhood than that of the flesh; now she realizes how literally true it was. She brought forth her first-born in Bethlehem, and His name is Jesus; she brings forth her second-born on Calvary. Mary was destined to have other children than Jesus, but they were to be born not of her flesh but of her heart. Mother of Christ was she at the Cross. Her first-born in Bethlehem was brought forth in joy, but the curse of Eve hung about her labours at the Cross, for she was now, like Eve, bringing forth her children in sorrow. At that moment Mary suffered the pangs of spiritual childbirth for the millions of souls who would ever be called to the adoptive sonship of the Father, the brotherhood of Christ and the joy of calling her Mother. The cup of her sorrow at the Cross, like her Son's, was filled to the brim, and no one knows how much she suffered to become our spiritual Mother or the Mother of the Mystical Body of her Divine Son. We only know that the millions of martyrs throughout all Christian ages consider their pains as insignificant compared to hers and scruple not to address her as the Queen of Martyrs.

But even that tragic day when the angel's sword which guarded the gate of Paradise was thrust into Mary's heart did not mark the end of her vocation as Mother of the Church, as it did not mark the end of her Son's relation with His Church. He was yet to apply the merits of His Redemption by sending His Spirit upon the apostles to make them His new Body of which He, at the right hand of the Father, would be the glorious Head. But even this new Body our Lord would not assume without the co-operation of His Blessed Mother. If our poor intellects thought out the Redemption and the sanctification of the world, we would have planned to have our Lord take His Mother with Him to heaven on Ascension Thursday; we would have thought it becoming that her work was done once Easter gave victory of life over death. But not so with Divine Wisdom. *Her Divine Son willed that since she was the nurse and Mother of the Physical Body with which He redeemed the world, so she should be left behind to be the nurse and Mother of His Mystical Body with which He would pour forth the fruits of the redemption upon the souls of men.* As she had been the Mother of the Head, so she should be the Mother of the Body.

Ten days after the Ascension we find the apostles "persevering with one mind in prayer with Mary the Mother of Jesus"; awaiting the descent of the Holy Spirit. He had descended upon her at Nazareth to make her the Mother of Jesus; now He descends upon the apostles to make them His new Body and her the Mother of that Body. Virgin in the flesh she brought forth her first-born Christ; virgin by the purity of her faith she brings forth the other-born, the Church, and in both instances it is the Holy Spirit which renders her fruitful.

Such was God's reason for leaving the Blessed Mother on earth for a time after Her Son had ascended into heaven. Called to the sublime vocation of being the Mother of Christ in His redemptive work, it was her duty not only to cradle the Head of the Church in Bethlehem, but also to cradle the Body in Jerusalem. The Mystical Christ of Pentecost, like the physical Christ of Bethlehem, was small, and delicate, and frail like any new-born thing. Its members were small; its organs were in the process of formation, and though life was there it was yet to grow in "age and grace and wisdom before God and men." But that growth and development would not be without the menace of hatred and persecution, for new Herods would arise to attack the Church as the other Herod had attacked its Head. It was necessary therefore that the Mother of the infant Mystical Christ be there to bestow her loving care on it as thirty-three years before she had watched over the infant Christ. Every infant needs a mother's care, even an infant Church. The mystery of Jesus did not begin without her, neither could it finish without her. Our Blessed Lord had kept His promise: He did not leave us orphans. He gave us His Father as our Father, His Spirit as our Spirit, and His Mother as our Mother.[1]

Not only was it fitting that Mary be present as Mother at the birth of the Mystical Christ, but it was also fitting that she be present as Queen of the apostles on the solemn day when the Church begins preaching the Gospel to the world.

From the very beginning she was the apostle *par excellence* of her Divine Son. She it was who first made Jesus known to His precursor John the Baptist on the occasion of her visit to Elizabeth; she it was who first made Jesus known to the Jews in the person of the shepherds, and to the Gentiles in the person of the Wise Men. It was therefore in keeping with her vocation that she be with the apostles on Pentecost, to make the Mystical Christ known to the world, as she had made known the physical Christ to Judea and Galilee. She brought into the world apostolicity itself—He who came to cast fire on earth and willed that it be enkindled. Her role would now have been incomplete if she had not been in the very centre of the tongues of fire which the Spirit of her Son sent upon the apostles to make them burn with His message even to the consummation of the world. Pentecost was Mary's spiritual Bethlehem, her new Epiphany, in which, as Mother standing by the crib of the Mystic Christ, she makes Him known once again to other shepherds and other kings.

Finally, when in the Providence of God the Church had grown to its full stature and began its "public life" as her Son began His when He left the maternal home at Nazareth, Mary was called home to her reward. Her Divine Son had His Crucifixion and His Resurrection and then His Ascension. Mary had her crucifixion as the sword of sorrow pierced her heart on Calvary. But she was now to have the counterpart of His Ascension, and that was her Assumption into heaven. She had begotten Eternal Life; how then could she be subject to the corruption of the tomb? The Assumption of Mary into heaven was the natural consequence of her Divine Maternity, the counterpart of her Son's Ascension and the beginning of another world wherein we live by faith, hope and charity. In that state of glory for which we labour here below, Christ, the Head of the Mystical Body, lives to intercede for us before the heavenly Father (Heb. 7:25–27). Associated with Him in glory as she had been associated with Him in His earthly pilgrimage is His Mother, the Queen of angels and saints. Inseparably united at the Cross when the reservoirs of redemption were filled, Jesus and Mary are now inseparably united in heaven as those same merits are poured out upon all who believe in Him as Brother, in her as Mother, and in God as Father.

Called to co-operate with Him in the acquisition of graces on Calvary, she is now called to co-operate with Him in the dispensation of those same graces to the Mystical Body. There is every reason to believe that we who are members of the Mystical Body now receive the Divine Life of her Son through her, just as we first received the Divine Life of her Son in Bethlehem.

He is the Redeemer; Mary is the co-Redemptrix.[2] "Christ is the Head of the Church; Mary the channel therein of Christ's graces. All benefits, all graces, all heavenly favours come from Christ as from a Head. All descend into the Body of the Church through Mary, as through the neck of the human body the head vivifies the members." "Every grace given to the world comes by three steps in perfect order; from the Father to Christ; from Christ to the Virgin; from the Virgin to us."[3] The role of Mary in the Church is therefore just as active as her role in the Incarnation.

Mary's Motherhood embraces more than the bare fact that the Word took human nature in her womb. Her glory is more profound than that of the woman who hearing her Son preach, shouted: "Blessed is the womb that bore Thee and the paps that gave Thee suck" (Luke 11:27). Rather, as He answered: "Blessed are they that hear the word of God and keep it," Mary is the Mother of the Mystical Body. The Sacraments which vivify the members of the Church draw their efficacy from the Blood of her Divine Son, but it was she overshadowed by the Holy Spirit who gave

Him that Blood. The Eucharist continues His Presence in the Tabernacles of the Church, but it was Mary who gave Him the Body which He gives us. Christ is the Head of the Mystical Body, but within that Body Mary is the channel between Christ and the members, bringing to them the favours and efficacious powers of Christ.[4] This does not mean that Mary is equal to Christ; it does not mean that the Church adores Mary; it does not mean that Mary is Divine, but it does mean that we could never have Christ without His Mother; it does mean that as a woman shared in our fall, so a woman should share in our redemption, and that as it was through Mary that God came to us, it is fitting that through Mary we should go back again to Him.

How could we fail to love her whom our Lord loved so much? It is impossible to love Christ adequately without also loving the Mother who gave Him to us. Those who begin by ignoring her soon end by ignoring Him, for the two are inseparable in the great drama of redemption. Hence the Church from the day of Pentecost has been most zealous in defending her honour and her purity, praising her for giving a Saviour to the world. During Advent and Christmas season the Church says in her office: "Fruitful Mother of the Redeemer; thou hast to the astonishment of nature given birth to thy Creator; Virgin in thy Conception, thou didst after child-bearing remain a Virgin; Mother of God intercede for us." During the penitential season of Lent we sing to her as "the root of which Christ is the flower, and the gate through which Light has arisen upon the world." Then at Eastertide there is the hymn of gladness: "Queen of heaven, rejoice, He whom thou didst bear, hath arisen: yea, rejoice and exult, O Virgin, for Christ the Lord hath truly arisen, glorious and living from the tomb." And every day during the year the Church at Vespers chants the Magnificat which the Blessed Mother said when she visited her cousin Elizabeth, thus fulfilling the prophetic word of that very day: "All nations shall call me blessed, for He that is mighty hath done great things in me."

Not only does the Mystical Body as a whole honour Mary, but each member honours her as Mother, for she is the Mother of all only because she is the Mother of each of us. It is absolutely impossible to convey to anyone outside the Church the filial devotion we bear that sweet Mother of Mothers. As children who wish to influence their father go to their mother to intercede for them, so do we go to Mary.

When the wine of life is failing and our faith is weak, and our charity growing cold, we go to her who at Cana's feast interceded with her Divine Son for the replenishing of the wine of gladness (John 2:1 ff); when our whole frame racks beneath the tempter we fly to the patronage of Her Immaculate Heart whose heel crushes the head of the serpent (Gen. 3:15); when the cold hand of death is laid upon those whom we loved and our heart seems torn in twain because one with those who are gone, then we climb the Hill of Calvary to be consoled by the Mother of Sorrows who is also the Cause of our Joy. When through sin we have lost God, then we have recourse to Mary the Refuge of Sinners, for she, the sinless one, knows what sin is, for she, too, had lost her God. When the sweet inspirations of the Holy Spirit call us away from passing earthly joys to the life of sanctity we pray to His Mother that we may learn from her to love her Divine Son, "Whatsoever He shall say to you, do ye." Never was it known that anyone who fled to her protection, or asked her help was left unaided. She is our advocate before the Father. By her Virginal Conception Mary presided at our Christian birth in her Divine Son. By her Annunciation she conceives us anew each instant in Christ; and by her Visitation and Presentation she continues to bring Christ to us, and to present us to Christ, and by her Assumption into heaven she presides at our last end to bring us unto the glory of Him who is her Son, our Redeemer, and our Lord. And until that day comes we who live in the hope of that Eternal Union with the Daughter of the Father, the Mother of the Son, and the Spouse of the Holy Ghost, we pray from the bottom of our hearts that prayer which is the counterpart of the "Our Father"; the prayer of the children of Mary, and we say to her:

"Hail Mary, full of grace, the Lord is with thee. Blessed art thou amongst women, and blessed is the fruit of thy womb, Jesus.

"Holy Mary, Mother of God, pray for us sinners, now and at the hour of our death. Amen."

## CHAPTER XV

# The Sacrifice of the
# Mystical Body

In the heart of the world is the beautiful instinct to remember
those who died in sacrifice. Every nation has its memorial day
consecrated to the heroes of its battles and its wars. Now if there
be such a remembered gratitude for those who died for a nation,
why should there not be a memorial for Him who died for the
world? If we revere the memory of those who sacrificed themselves
for others, why should we not remember Him from whose death
all sacrifice has received its inspiration and its seal? Calvary is too
beautiful to be lost! The Cross bearing the burden of the Saviour
of men is too holy to be forgotten! "Greater love than this no man
hath, that he lay down his life for his friends." Such love deserves
to be perpetuated.

Lest men should forget—and how quickly they do—our Lord
resolved to institute a memorial of His Sacrifice. Most men at the
approach of death prepare their last will and testament, in which
they dispose of their property. On the eve of His death, our Lord
made His last will and testament, but, unlike men, He left that
which no man when dying ever left, namely, Himself.

This He could do, being God. He would leave Himself not in
any indifferent act of His Life, but in that supreme act where Love
reached its peak in the Sacrifice of Good Friday. The particular
means He chose to represent the awful separation of His Blood

from His Body on the Cross were the symbols of bread and wine. Gathering His apostles about Him in the Upper Room on the night that has since been called Holy Thursday, He anticipated the Sacrifice of the Cross which would follow in less than eighteen hours. By the separate consecration of first the bread and then the wine He symbolically represented His future Crucifixion in which His Body as Bread of heaven, and His Blood as the Wine of Life were to be separated one from the other for the redemption of the world. He was thus offering up what was in store for Him; anticipating, as it were, His Baptism of Blood by pledging Himself to death in the sight of His Father and men. Everyone knows the circumstances of that evening. He took bread in His hand and blessed and broke and gave to His disciples, and said: "Take ye and eat; This is My Body." And taking the chalice, He gave thanks and gave to them saying: "Drink ye all of this, for this is My Blood of the New Testament, which shall be shed for many unto the remission of sins."[1]

Then looking forward to all ages and all times, and to all hearts who would ever crave a memorial of the death which gave us everlasting life, He said: "Do this in commemoration of Me" (Luke 22:19).

The next afternoon at three o'clock that which He anticipated and foreshadowed and mystically represented in the Last Supper came to pass: His Body was delivered to executioners; His Blood was poured forth.

Now, here we are 1,900 years removed from that Last Supper and from the Cross of Golgotha. Keeping both in mind, and the fact that He the God-man begged us to remember His last will and testament, cast your eyes about the world and ask yourself these questions: Who have done that which He asked us to do the night of the Last Supper in commemoration of Him? Who have taken bread and wine into their hands and by the mystical sword of the words of consecration symbolically represented the separation of both on a Cross when Love sunk to the depths and arose as Sacrifice? Who has a daily Memorial Ceremony in which there is re-enacted in an unbloody manner the tragedy of Calvary?

For an answer enter into any Catholic church in the world and during the early morning hours you will see a priest, whose heritage is one with those of the Upper Room, mount an altar, take bread and wine in his hands, breathe over them the very words of our Lord Himself, and as a bell tinkles, and hundreds of heads in the church bow in prayer, you will see the priest kneel in adoration of the Bread which is the Body, and the Wine which is the Blood of our Lord and Saviour. As both are lifted above the head of the priest, as the Cross was lifted above the earth, you will understand how that same Lord erects Calvary once again amidst hearts who love and hands that crucify. Someone has remembered His words! The command, "Do this in commemoration of Me" has not fallen on deaf ears. Calvary was too beautiful to be forgotten. It is remembered! It is commemorated! It is re-enacted! It is represented; it is prolonged through space and time and its memorial is the Mass.[2]

There is grave danger that we may believe the Mass to be only a memorial ceremony such as we have on Memorial Day for our hero soldiers; or a kind of imitation of the Last Supper on the stage of the altar in which we are passive spectators, or a prayer in which there is only a repetition of the beautiful words of the Last Supper. No! The Mass is none of these things. *The Mass is the Sacrifice of the Body of Christ.*[3]

The Mass, in other words, is a supratemporal reality, by which the glorified Christ in Heaven prolongs His Sacrifice on the Cross by and through us. The Mass, according to the Council of Trent, is therefore a veritable sacrifice: "That by means of it that bloody Sacrifice, which He once offered on the Cross, may ever be represented and its remembrance be preserved until the end of the world, and its healing power be applied and spent for the remission of those sins daily committed by us."[4] In both the Cross and the Mass there is the same Priest and Victim which is

Christ, but the way of offering the sacrifice differs. On the Cross He was alone; in the Mass He is with us. On the Cross He offered up His Life for all who would one day be incorporated into His Mystical Body; in the Mass He renews the Sacrifice for all who are actually incorporated into that Mystical Body. On the Cross the "Historical" Christ offered Himself, in the Mass the "Mystical" Christ which is Christ and us, are associated in the offering. The Cross was in Jerusalem as space, and 1,900 years ago as time; the Mass is the same Cross made actual throughout space and time. There is no time nor space between Calvary and now. The Mass is the tremendous experience of the reality of Golgotha with its forgiveness and its love, its power and its pardon extended and prolonged even unto this hour.

The Mass, I say, is not only the sacrifice of the physical Body of Christ, but also the sacrifice of the Mystical Body the Church. It is not a mere empty symbolism of Calvary. Let us try and understand this tremendous mystery.

On the Cross, our Lord took the human nature which He assumed from His Mother in the unity of His Person and as Priest on the Cross offered it to His Father in reparation for the sins of men. That human nature after the Resurrection and Ascension was elevated to the glory of heaven. The human nature of Jesus can therefore never suffer again. It has entered into its reward beyond crucifixion and death. "Christ rising again from the dead dieth no more, death shall no more have dominion over Him" (Rom. 6:9). *He can therefore add nothing to His priestly office except by and through us*, and it is this He has chosen to do. He wills to do with other human natures scattered throughout the world, what He did with His own human nature taken from His Virgin Mother. As Head of the Mystical Body in heaven He calls others to Himself, other Peters, Pauls, Johns, Marthas, Marys, Theresas, Augustines, Cyrils—in a word, the millions of baptized men and women who have been incorporated into Him by baptism as His new Mystical Body. He asks them to give Him their human natures in love, that He may continue His Redemptive Priesthood by and through them, so that not only He in His own human nature, but *He in ours,* may offer us anew to His heavenly Father in an unending act of Priestly Sacrifice. As a great patriot in time of national crisis seeks not only to offer his own life for the sake of his country, but also strives to rally others to himself, that through their corporate selflessness the whole nation might be preserved, so He, the glorified Christ in heaven, seeks the enlistment of you and me—all of us—under His headship, that we may offer ourselves with His offering on the Cross to win the triumphs of other Loving Calvaries, even as He.

It is precisely this thought St. Paul had in mind when he wrote to the Romans. "I beseech you therefore, brethren, by the mercy of God, that you present your bodies a living sacrifice, holy, pleasing to God, your reasonable service" (Rom. 12:1). That means that we positively co-operate with Christ in the Mass so that His Sacrifice and ours are one in a certain sense. But if we add something to the Sacrifice of our Lord, does it mean that His Sacrifice on the Cross was incomplete? No! The Sacrifice of the Cross was complete and perfect in itself. It is not complete as regards us; the merits of that great redemptive act have to flow unto us. The heroic deaths of soldiers who die to defend the liberties of their country must be applied to the citizens that they may enjoy that liberty; so, too, the death on the Cross for all mankind must be applied to every individual. But how can the merits of the Cross be applied unless we incorporate ourselves in some way to His Priestly act and "complete" it as regards ourselves? How can Calvary be effective unless we become incorporated to Calvary, and how can we become incorporated to Calvary except by becoming like the Christ who died there? For as the Church in the language of St. Paul is the "fullness" of the historical Christ, so the Mass is the "fullness" of Calvary. This is the meaning behind the pregnant words of that great apostle: "I fill up those things that are wanting of the sufferings of Christ in my flesh, for His Body, which is the Church" (Col. 1:24). As Head, therefore, our Lord has endured every possible pain and sorrow. As regards the "Whole Christ," that is the Head and His Mystical Body, the sufferings are not yet completed. The members of that body, which we are, must still work out our salvation by "crucifying the flesh and its concupiscences." In this way do we "fill up those things that are wanting of the sufferings" of the Mystical Christ, which is the Church. He in His glory can Sacrifice Himself no more, unless we give Him a new Body with which to undergo another Calvary. His Calvary is localized in Jerusalem unless He can prolong it; His death is past unless we renew it in our own devoted and consecrated lives. It is the Mystical Body of Christ therefore which makes Calvary as actual now as then. Thanks to His new Body He can offer an unending Sacrifice to His heavenly Father for the Redemption of that Body.[5]

If this doctrine seems strange and novel, it is because we have forgotten that the glorified Christ in heaven has incorporated unto Himself a Mystical Body, which is His Church and in whom we are, not as fish are in water, but as branches are in a vine. The relation between Christ and the Church, we have been insisting throughout these pages, is not a periodical nor affective external relation, but a truly vital, internal union—a living prolongation of Christ through space and time. What He has done in His physical Body, He now does in His Mystical Body of which He is the Head.[6]

Calvary was the Sacrifice of the Head who is now Christ in His Glory; the Mass is Calvary or the Sacrifice of the Head and the Mystical Body which we are.

How beautifully the liturgy of the Church brings out this extension of Calvary to all the members of the Mystical Body. It was said above, that since His Ascension, our Lord seeks out new human natures with which He may "fill up" the Calvary of His Mystical Body. He asks for your human nature and for mine, and asks that we take all the sufferings and pains attendant upon our natures and unite them with His Supreme Sacrifice on the Cross.

Our sorrows and tears, our mortifications and our promises have no intrinsic merit in themselves, for sufferings of themselves are valueless. They are like bank cheques without a signature. Suppose now we unite them with our Lord, so that they are made part of the infinite merit of Calvary; suppose we offer them to our Lord so that they are His, and His name is stamped on them, then they become precious because part of the very Sacrifice of Christ. Only when they are "massed" in Calvary's sacrifice do they become acceptable Sacrifices; only when they are one with the Cross do they become as redeeming as the Cross; only when they are crucified with Christ do they hold the pledge of an everlasting Easter.

Our Lord in instituting the Holy Sacrifice of the Mass willed that we should present our sacrificed lives to Him under the symbols of bread and wine. Hence it was the custom in the early Church for those who assisted at the Mass to bring an offering of both bread and wine.[7] But why should our Lord out of all creation choose these two particular substances to represent His Body and Blood? First of all, I suppose, to represent our unity one with another in His Mystical Body. Just as bread is made only from a multiplicity of grains of wheat, and wine only from a multiplicity of grapes, so, too, are we, the individual members of the Mystical Body, made one with Christ in the re-offering of Calvary to the heavenly Father. The second reason, probably, was to remind us that our part in the Mass was a sacrificial part, and that we assisted at it not as spectators, but as co-operators. For just as grapes become wine only by passing through the Calvary of a wine press, so too we become one with Christ only by reproducing in our lives the Cross which He lived in His own.[8]

When, then, the priest at the altar offers the bread and wine to the heavenly Father, he is offering also individual members of the Mystical Body. But the offering is not merely our physical presence at the tremendous mystery of the Mass, but rather the offering of the very substance of our being represented by bread and wine, the substantial nutriments of life! aye, more, the very Sacrifice of our lives as bread and wine are themselves begotten of the sacrifice of wheat and grapes. Possibly few Catholics understand the full implications of the offertory of the Mass. They say they "assist" at the Mass, as if they were passive watchers of the drama. They really do not "assist"; they "participate"; they share; they co-offer themselves with Christ.[9] And if there is any picture to adequately represent the part of the faithful in the offertory of the Mass, it is the picture of our Lord standing on the hill of Calvary before His great Cross. Crowded about Him on the same hill we stand with our little crosses stretched on the ground alongside of His great model Cross. The very moment He makes the offertory of His Life and walks to His Cross to prove His love for us is stronger than death, we walk to our little crosses, make the offertory of our lives in union with His, to prove that our love of Righteousness, of Justice, of Truth, of Love and of God is stronger than our love of that life which quickly passes away.

A few minutes later comes the awful mystery of the consecration, in which the priest, by the separate consecration of bread and wine, renews in an unbloody manner the immolation of Christ on His Cross. When the priest, in obedience to the command of our Lord at the Last Supper to "Do this in commemoration of Me," pronounces the words over the bread, "This is My Body," and over the wine, "This is My Blood," the primary significance of the words is that the substance of the Bread is changed into the substance of the Body of our Lord and the substance of the wine is changed into the substance of His Blood. Mystically divided by the separate consecration, our Lord thus renews the Sacrifice of Calvary. But our Lord is not alone. The Vine Sacrificed Himself on the Cross; the Vine and Branches now Sacrifice themselves in the Mass. The primary meaning of the words of consecration then refer to the Vine: This is the Body and This is the Blood of Christ renewing the Sacrifice of Calvary. But the secondary meaning refers to the Branches united to the Vine to form the

Mystical Body, in which Peter and Paul, Mary and Anne, and each one of us who are members of the Church say: "This is my Body; this is my Blood. I offered myself with Thee at the offertory; now I immolate myself with Thee at the consecration. Take my Body and my Blood with Thee to the Cross; take my Body and Blood with all the pains, sorrows, agonies; with their capacities for love, for service and for repentance; take them with Thee to the Cross, that they may be united with Thy Sacrifice which alone makes them acceptable to Thy heavenly Father; that Thou mayest purchase me to Thyself in *act*, as Thou didst purchase me in *Hope* at Calvary; take not merely my possessions, my titles, my apostolate, my zeal, my energy, but take all that I am—the very substance of my life—my Body; my Blood. Take them, make them one with Thy Sacrifice as the drop of water becomes one with the wine. Possess them so that what is mine is Thine; so that the heavenly Father, in looking down upon Thy renewed Calvary, may find that there is but one Body and one Blood, which is that of Thee, His Beloved Son, in whom the Father is well pleased."

If, then, the offertory of the Mass is the co-offering of Christ and us, then the consecration is the co-crucifixion of Christ and us. In both we so completely surrender our human natures to Him, that when the heavenly Father looks down from heaven He sees but one Priest, but one Victim, and but one Calvary.[10] The Mass is the one thing in the world which makes it possible for us who live in the twentieth century to share in the sacrifice of Calvary. And our share, be it noted, is not merely that of a witness at a theatrical representation of events which are past; rather, we are *contemporaries of Calvary*. Like Mary, John and Magdalene, we gather at the foot of the Cross in this day and hour, with our souls filled with the spirit of sacrifice, such as animated their own, and with our arms strong as Samson's we lift the cross from the rocks, even unto the very Father in heaven, in propitiation for our sins and the sins of the world.

Calvary, then, is the source of Divine Life; the altar is the canal. Calvary is the Treasury of merit; the Mass is its application; Calvary is the reservoir of Grace; the Mass is the open floodgates pouring it into our souls. Calvary was the Sacrifice for the nameless millions who might one day share its redemption. The Mass is the singling out by name of those millions who actually do share that great act of redemption. On Calvary He was the Active Victim and we the possible ones in the order of time; in the Mass He is the Victim who does not suffer and we the victims who do." The Mass, then, is Calvary *recalled, renewed and applied*—the only thing in this world which makes it possible for us to follow His command, "Take up your cross daily and follow Me." In no other act of His Mystical Life does He come so close to us. Bethlehem is with us in the Real Presence; His voice is with us in the Church; His hands are with us in the Sacraments, but His love unto death is with us in the continued Sacrifice of the Mass. Why do so few appreciate and love this gift? I suppose because so few loved and appreciated the death on the Cross. If Calvary and the Mass are one Sacrifice, then naturally enough the proportion of those who mount the Calvary of the Sacrifice of the Mystical Christ will be just as small as the number who mounted the Calvary of the Sacrifice of the natural Christ. In the eyes of God the Father there are no divisions of people into nations and nationalities; there are only two classes of souls: the crucified and the crucifiers; the Christ on the Cross and those who hung Him there. And until the end of time there will be only two battle-cries rallying supporters to either cause; one, the cry of Christ bidding us climb His Cross: "And I, if I be lifted up from the earth, will draw all things to Myself." The other, the cry of the earthly: "Come down from the Cross and we will believe." That latter group we leave to the judgment of God.

Thanks to this truth Calvary is set up in our midst. Thanks to it we need not go back twenty centuries to the material Cross, for our glory is not in the *material* Cross on which our Lord suffered;

rather it is the Spirit of that Sacrifice coming in power to him who has faith in Christ. The Mass is Calvary realized, made present, contemporized, lifted out of the limit of space and time, living in the members of the Mystical Body, sealing us, separating us from the world, sacrificing us, changing our crosses into crucifixes and making us so much one with Christ that the heavenly Father sees but Him whose Sacrifice alone is acceptable and whose prayers alone are heard.

There are little children, fresh from their first Communion, old men and women looking forward to Eternal youth, young maidens, pure as the Mother of their Saviour, young seminarians looking forward to their first Mass, penitent sinners as late season flowers offering the best that is left in their lives, and yet all these losing their individuality for the time being to be one with the Mystical Christ, who, at the moment after the consecration, prays in the name of the priest at the Mass:

> We humbly beseech Thee, Almighty God, to command that these things [Christ's Body and Blood, as well as ourselves, our vows and prayers] be borne by the hands of Thy Holy Angel to *Thine Altar on High*, in sight of Thy Divine Majesty, that so many of us as at this Altar shall partake of and receive the Most Holy Body and Blood of Thy Divine Son, may be filled with every heavenly blessing and grace. Through Christ Our Lord, Amen.

## CHAPTER XVI

# The Eucharist and the Unity
# of the Mystical Body

"The Eucharist is the consummation of the spiritual life and
the end of all the Sacraments.¹ Baptism is the condition of its
reception, but Baptism looks to the Eucharist at least by desire."
"Baptism," says St. Thomas, "is a Sacrament of the Death and
Passion of our Lord, inasmuch as by it, man through the power
of Christ's Passion, is regenerated in Christ. The Eucharist is
a Sacrament of the Passion of Christ, inasmuch as by it man
is *perfected in union* with Christ who has suffered."² Baptism is
fundamentally a death, and the incorporation into the Mystical
Body is its secondary and derived effects. The Eucharist is fundamentally a Life, and is therefore necessary to salvation—though
not with the same necessity as Baptism. "Although the actual
reception of the Holy Eucharist is not necessary for salvation, as
is Baptism, nevertheless so far as the 'reality' itself is concerned
(that is to say, the fruit of the Sacrament), which is the *unity of the
Mystical Body*, the Sacrament of the Holy Eucharist is necessary
for salvation."³ There must be at least an implicit desire for the
Eucharist, then, during the reception of the Sacrament of Baptism. That is one reason why the Church has sponsors. "From the
fact that children are baptized, they are destined by the Church
for the Eucharist; and just as they believe through the Church's

THE MYSTICAL BODY OF CHRIST

faith, so they desire the Eucharist through the Church's intention, and as a result, receive its reality."[4]

Confirmation, in like manner, finds its perfection in the Eucharist. The purpose of Confirmation is to make the baptized member of the Mystical Body a defender of the faith. In Baptism man receives the power of securing his own eternal salvation; in Confirmation he is called upon to defend it against enemies. Because this Sacrament gives great permanence to the soul's union with Christ, it prepares for increased intimacy with Him which becomes possible in the Eucharist, its end and consummation. That is why there are sponsors in Confirmation as well as in Baptism, and that is why the Holy See has asked the Church to return to the custom of administering Confirmation before the Eucharist.

Holy Orders is the Third Sacrament which impresses an indelible mark upon the soul. Baptism incorporates us to Christ the King, Confirmation to Christ the Teacher, and Holy Orders to Christ the Priest. "Holy Order is instituted primarily," says St. Thomas, "for the sake of the Sacrament of the Holy Eucharist; all the other purposes are secondary. And the other sacraments exist because in this Sacrament of the Holy Eucharist, they love their foundations."[5] So intimate is the relation between Holy Orders and the Holy Eucharist that they were instituted at the same time, and almost in the same act. It is worth emphasizing at this point that all the priest's powers over the Mystical Body of Christ, derive from his power over the True Body of Christ or the Eucharist.

A priest has the power to forgive sins, to baptize, to administer the last rites, to witness a marriage, only because he has the power to celebrate Mass. "Every priest performs two acts: the principal one is over the True Body of Christ; the other, which is secondary, is over the Mystical Body of Christ, but the second act depends on the first, and not the first on the second."[6] This is the point where Anglicanism breaks down, even though it does imitate the Church in externals. It repudiated the Mass as a "superstition"; it denied the Real Presence in the "Black Rubric"; it left out of its Ordinal for over a hundred years all mention of the sacrificial power of the priest. Hence its clergyman can no more forgive sins than a government clerk. Having no power over the Eucharist, they have none over the Mystical Body of Christ.

Penance also looks to the Eucharist. Like Baptism, it puts us on the way to complete incorporation to Christ in the Sacrament of His Body and Blood. There is this difference, however, between the two Sacraments: In Baptism, the sinful man receives the remission of every punishment. But that is not true of Penance, for there the Person of Christ always operates, but its power depends on the sorrow and acts of the penitent.[7] The penances performed by the penitent are the expression of his desire to be once again with Christ. In the Sacrament of Penance the priest is the representative not only of Christ, *but also of the faithful.* The latter point is seldom thought of, but it must be recalled that Divine Life flows through the Mystical Body. When one member sins, he hurts and weakens all the others. He therefore needs *their* forgiveness along with the forgiveness of Christ. When that is given he may then receive the fullness of Divine Life in the Eucharist.

Extreme Unction eliminates the traces of sin from the soul, and disposes the soul for Eternal Communion in the Kingdom of Heaven. Just as the whole Mystical Body was in some way involved in the Sacrament of Penance, so it is likewise here involved. The liturgy asks that several priests assist at the administration of this Sacrament, so that "the whole Church co-operate in producing the effect of this Sacrament." But if but one priest is present the Sacrament is still administered "in virtue of the entire Church of which this one priest is the minister and the representative."[8]

Finally, the Sacrament of Matrimony is intelligible only in terms of the Eucharist, of which it is a kind of fleshly symbol. "By this Sacrament, husband and wife receive the grace to be

associated in the union of Christ and His Church."⁹ The Church
therefore asks the bride and groom to be married at the Mass
where is consummated the unity of Christ and His Church, which
they symbolize in the unity of the flesh. It must not be thought
that Matrimony is a greater Sacrament than the Eucharist, because it is ordained to the common good, namely, the procreation
of the human species, while the Eucharist is ordained only to the
private good of the recipient. St. Thomas considers that objection
and answers it as follows: "Matrimony is ordained to the common
good as regards the body. But the common spiritual good of the
whole Church is contained substantially in the Eucharist."¹⁰

In conclusion, the Eucharist is the term and efficient cause of
all the other sacraments.¹¹ "Absolutely speaking, the Sacrament
of the Eucharist is the greatest of all the Sacraments, because it
contains Christ Himself substantially; whereas the other Sacraments contain a certain instrumental power, which is a share of
Christ's Power. Now, that which is essentially is always of more
account than that which is such by participation."¹²

From this consideration we pass on more directly to the
Eucharist as the source of the unity of the Mystical Body. The
Church is one, not only because it is governed by one Head, Christ,
and His one Vicar on earth; not only because all its members
are vivified by the same soul, which is the Holy Ghost; but also
because we are all nourished by some Divine Life in the Eucharist.
The unity flowing from this Divine Sacrament is two-fold: (*a*)
the unity of Christ and of His Mystical Body; (*b*) the unity of the
members of the Mystical Body with one another.

## I. THE UNITY OF CHRIST AND THE MYSTICAL BODY

If there is any bad guess about the secret of the Church's strength
and unity during 1,900 years, it is the guess that "organization"
is its explanation. This, simply, is not the fact. Governments
have been more strongly organized, but they have perished. The
secret must be sought in the interior of the Church's life, and in

particular in the Eucharist. An example will make this clear. Some years ago, Timiriazeff, a Russian botanist, planted a willow wand weighing five pounds in a pot containing exactly two hundred pounds of soil. He watered and watched the willow for five years, after which time he took it out, shook off every adhering particle of soil, weighed the tree and found it now weighed 169 pounds 3 ounces. He then weighed the soil, and found that the soil, which originally weighed 200 pounds, had lost only 2 ounces. How account for the difference in the weight of the tree? Its increase was certainly not to be explained by anything exclusively material or external, but rather by the fact that the leaves were in contact with the great invisible world of solar energy, the leaf is the one and only medium where solar energy becomes translated into vital force.

The Church is the great Tree of Life. The secret of her Life is not to be sought in anything external or earthly, though it has roots in the earth. The real source of its energy is something invisible and spiritual. What the solar energy is to the tree, that the Eucharist is to the Mystical Body; what the leaf is to the tree, that each individual Catholic is to the Church. As each leaf draws force from the great invisible solar energy, so does each Catholic draw life through Communion with Divinity in the Eucharist. Without the sun, the tree could not live; without the Eucharist, the Church could not live. The more Catholic leaves there are on the tree of Life or the Church, the greater her strength and her unity; and as the tree is one though made up of a multiplicity of leaves because all nourished by the same sun, so the Mystical Body is one though made up of many Catholics because all nourished by the same Eucharist. Such is the secret of Catholic unity—the communion of man with God. "If any man eat of this bread he shall live forever; and the bread that I will give is My flesh for the life of the world" (John 6:52).

Another example will reveal in even a clearer way, the unity achieved by the Eucharist. In the human body is the blood plasma, the richest fluid known. This lymph flows through all the alleys of the body carrying in its stream an untold wealth of provisions, which is tapped by each cell or group of cells for nourishment. The flowing tide of sustenance passes by every door, displaying and offering its goods, and each cell takes delivery of what it needs, not only for its life, but also for the repairing of its wasted parts.

Now, the Eucharist is to the Mystical Body what the blood plasma is to the human body, though in a far superior way. This great Spiritual Plasma, the Eucharist, flows and streams through the Mystical Body in every part of the world wherever a Mass is celebrated. It offers itself first to this Catholic and then to that; dips the Chalice of its Life to one, for the increase of its Divine Life; breaks its Bread of Life to another, for the remission of sin and its punishment, and in general strengthening every soul with its Christ-Love. And just as the human body is one, though composed of many cells, because nourished by the same plasma, so the Mystical Body is one, though composed of many Catholics, because nourished by the same Eucharist. This is the meaning of those beautiful words of St. Paul: "We being many, are one Bread, one Body, all that partake of One Bread" (1 Cor. 10:17). In the world outside there is no great unity because each man has a different nourishment. One is fed by science, another by humanism, another by philosophy; hence there is divergence of opinion and even conflict. But in the Church all the members are nourished by the same Bread of Divine Life, and are therefore compacted into one Body.

The unity of Christ and His Mystical Body through communion is the perfection of a law which runs through nature; or perhaps, it would be truer to say, the natural law is its reflection. All nature witnesses the fact of communion with a higher life. The oxygen, hydrogen, carbon, and other chemicals which exist in the mineral order can enter into the realm of life only on condition that they commune with plant life, are taken up into its body, and begin to live by its vital principle. A plant can transcend its plant existence, only on condition that it commune with the animal, surrender its lower life and enter into the higher life of a sentient creature. Animals, too, can become more than animals, if they die to themselves and enter into the life of man, so that they become an inseparable part of his rational life and live by his immortal soul. In like manner man can become more than "mere man" or a partaker of Divine Life, on condition that he "die" to his lower self by Baptism, and commune with the Eucharistic Life of Christ. Because He is a person, Communion with Christ does not rob Him of His identity and personal rights, as a plant is robbed of its identity by communion with an animal. Rather it is the perfection of his personality, for now man becomes all that he was destined to become by God, His adopted son and heir of the Kingdom of Heaven. If the plant could speak, it would say to the sunlight: "Unless you are reborn, you cannot live in my Kingdom"; if the animal could speak, it would say to the plant: "Unless you are reborn, you cannot live in my Kingdom"; man can speak and say to all three: "Unless you are reborn, you cannot live in my Kingdom." With perfect justice, then, does Christ say to us: "Unless you are reborn, you cannot enter into My Kingdom." Communion is thus the condition of entering into a higher Life, even the Life of Christ.

Thus far we have been speaking of our incorporation into the Life of Christ through the Eucharist. It is principally in the sixth chapter of St. John that we find the idea most clearly developed. Unfortunately, however, this is about the only aspect of the Eucharist we hear dwelt on. There is also another side of it, which is developed by St. Paul in his First Epistle to the Corinthians—that the Eucharist is not only an incorporation into the *Life* of Christ, it is also an incorporation into His Death: for "as often as you eat this bread or drink this chalice you show forth the Death of the Lord until He comes" (1 Cor. 11:26). Natural life has two sides: the anabolic and the katabolic. Supernatural life also has two sides: the building of the Christ-pattern and the tearing down of the old Adam. The first aspect is never forgotten; in fact, it is so much stressed that we continually speak of "receiving" Communion, as if there could be a "receiving" without a "giving," or an ascent into a higher life without a death to a lower one. Does not an Easter Sunday presuppose a Good Friday? Is not all love reciprocal? Does it not imply mutual self-giving which ends in self-recovery? Then should not the Communion rail be a place of exchange, instead of a place of exclusive receiving? Is all the Life to pass from Christ to us, and nothing to go back in return? Are we to drain the chalice and contribute nothing to its filling; are we to receive the bread and give no wheat to be ground? To receive the wine and give no grapes to be crushed? If all we did during our lives was to go to Communion, and receive Divine Life, to take it away, and leave nothing behind, we would be *parasites* on the Mystical Body of Christ.

The Pauline injunction bids us "to fill up in our body the sufferings wanting to the Passion of Christ": We must therefore bring a spirit of sacrifice to the Eucharistic rail; we must bring the mortification of our lower self, the crosses patiently borne, the crucifixion of our egotism, the death of our concupiscences and even the very difficulty of coming to Communion. Then does Communion become what it was always intended to become, namely, a commerce between Christ and the soul, in which we give His Death shown forth in our lives, and He gives His Life to show forth in our intimacy with Him. We give Him our time, He gives us His Eternity; we give Him our humanity, He gives us His Divinity; we give Him our nothingness, and He gives us His All.

Thus do we fill up what is wanting in the Passion of Christ— not the Passion of the historical Christ Who is enjoying bliss at the right hand of the Father, but the Passion of the Mystical Body which is His Church. Thus are indulgences built up; thus are merits accumulated, from which the spiritually indigent may draw; thus are the poor fed from our superfluities. The Spiritual State of the Church at any one given period of history thus varies in direct ratio and proportion with the way the members incorporate themselves, not only into the Life of Christ, but also into His Death. The more they die to themselves, the greater the effect of the Life they receive from Him. The amount of Divine Life we receive depends upon our capacity. The fuller we are of ourselves, the less room there is for Christ; the more empty we are of ourselves by crucifying our flesh, the more He can pour forth the torrents of His Love. There is such a thing in the spiritual order as indigestion, i.e., when the soul receives more Divine Life than it can assimilate. There is only one way to remedy this, and that is to enlarge the capacity for assimilation, and that implies mortification or "showing forth the Death of the Lord until He comes." The Eucharist, then, is the bread of Christ and His Mystical Body, not only because we are all made one in His Life, but also because we are all made one previously in His Death.

## 2. THE UNITY OF THE MEMBERS OF THE MYSTICAL BODY WITH ONE ANOTHER

Now we touch on the second effect of the Eucharist, namely, it con-corporates us to one another as brothers in Christ. The dominant religious error from the sixteenth century to the present day has been to believe that religion is a purely personal matter between God and man. Any attempt to regulate the social and economic actions of men by the application of moral and religious principles was regarded as an encroachment of religion on the domains of business. The Church, on the contrary, has insisted that religion is not only a personal relation between man and God, but also a social relation, for how could a million men love one God without loving one another? Religion involves mutual relations between men who love God. We cannot love God without loving our neighbour, nor can we love our neighbour without loving God (Matt. 22:37–39; 1 John 3:10; 1 John 3:14, 23; 1 John 4:8, 11, 21). From the supernatural point of view, the common love of God the Father implies mutual relations between adopted sons, and this fellowship of adopted sons constitutes the Mystical Body of Christ.

The Eucharist is the perfection and guarantee of that solidarity and the seal upon the social character of religion. The Council of Trent expressly declared that Christ willed to make the Eucharist: "the symbol of this one Body of which He is the Head, to which He would have us united as members by the close bonds of faith, hope and charity, even to the point where among ourselves we would speak the same mind and know not divisions."[13]

The Eucharist establishes the holy fellowship of its members not by anything external, but by the interior nourishment of souls. The Fatherhood of God is not a vague title by which creatures address their Creator. If the Fatherhood of God means anything, it means that He has called us to be His sons and partakers of His Divine Nature. But we can be sons of God only by sharing a common Body and a common Blood. This has been made possible by the Heavenly Father sending His own Divine Son into this world, through whose Spirit we receive the gift of Divine adoption. The Communion rail is therefore the most democratic institution on the face of the earth, for there all men are made equal because all sons of God. The modern world tries to unite men on the basis of economic equality, namely, by sharing wealth, as is done in Communism. The Eucharist, on the contrary, unites men on the basis of brotherhood. Men are not brothers because they share equally; otherwise thieves who share loot would be brothers. But brothers may share the Eucharist, because it starts with brotherhood, makes all men equal, because it makes them all infinitely precious as sons of God. The Communion rail admits of no fundamental differences; there the employer must take the paten from the employee; the professor must eat the same Bread as the student, and the Greek must be nourished from the same tabernacle as the barbarian, for all are one Body, because they eat the same Bread. The Eucharist is a greater Leveller than

Death; it dissolves all boundaries, nationalities and races into a supernatural fellowship where all men are brothers of the Divine Son and adopted sons of the Heavenly Father.

This important truth concerning the Eucharist is too often forgotten. Just as Communion with the death of Christ is neglected in our spiritual life, so also is Communion with one another neglected in our social life. The full truth is that at the Communion rail we not only receive communion with Christ, but we also receive Communion with one another. The law to love God and love our neighbour here finds its supernatural counterpart. The basis of the supernatural unity is LOVE, as the basis of natural unity is BEING. What *Being* is to Metaphysics, that *Love* is to Theology—though we have not yet built our manuals around that central truth.

When the Catholic in New York receives Communion he is more one with his brother, the Catholic convert in Africa, than he is one with his fellow countryman and best friend who has never received Christ into his soul. There is no greater reason for charity than this profound truth that we are "members one of another." All who receive Christ are one Body, and since no man hateth his own flesh, so neither should anyone hate those who are his brothers in the Mystical Body of Christ. This brotherhood through the Eucharist was intended by our Lord to be the basis of all international agreements as well as the relations between Capital and Labour.

Nationalism is the assertion of a particular blood against a common Divine Blood, and therefore is the raw material for wars and conflicts. Even in the natural order, the nations of the world have a link of fellowship in their common origin, for "God hath made one, all mankind, to dwell upon the whole face of the earth" (Acts 17:26). But this common blood or nature has never sufficed to draw them together. Nations have always forgotten their common origin in the antagonism of a narrower clanship.

In order to restore that unity, God, in His Mercy, willed to draw all nations into the fellowship of the Blood of Christ. The fore-heralding of these triumphs came when it broke down the exclusiveness of the Jew. The Jews of old kept all other nations at arm's length. The "middle partition" or marble balustrade which divided the inner and outer courts in the temple at Jerusalem characterized their attitude toward other nations. An inscription upon it ran thus: "No alien to pass within the balustrade around the temple of the enclosure. Whosoever shall be caught so doing must blame himself for the penalty of death which he will incur." When they thought St. Paul had broken this rule, by bringing Trophimus within the partition, the Jews sought to kill him. The middle partition Christ broke down forever. "For which cause be mindful that you being heretofore Gentiles in the flesh . . . were at that time without Christ, being aliens from the conversation of Israel, and strangers to the testament, having no hope of the promise, and without God in this world. But now in Christ Jesus, you who sometime were afar off, are made nigh by the blood of Christ. For He is our peace, Who hath made both one, and breaking down the middle wall of partition, the enmities in His Flesh: making void the law of commandments contained in decrees, that He might make the two in Himself into one new man, making peace; and might reconcile both to God in one body, by the Cross, killing the enmities in Himself" (Eph. 2:11–16).

This welding of all nations into one vast fellowship with God is the only possible basis of international peace. Take away the supernatural foundation for amity among nations and peoples, and there is no other standard than that of utility. And what is true of international relation is true of those between Capital and Labour. The Eucharist puts a high value on Labour in the Scriptural sense of work, for the very elements of sacrifice, bread and wine, are the produce of labour. Months of toil have gone into the production of both the bread and the wine. Labourers, farmers, machinists, millers and bakers have all toiled to make the bread destined to be man's offering to God. In the same way, wine is the produce of all those who labour in pruning, gathering and pressing, which has enabled the vineyard to bring forth grapes. Certainly the Son of God in choosing bread and wine had in mind not only the unity symbolized by these elements, but also the great dignity they set upon work.

But all this is as nothing compared with the higher unity achieved when all workers unite at a Communion rail to receive the common Food of Him Who Himself worked to the Death of the Cross for the salvation of the world. Capital and Labour both *work*, though they work in different ways. But over and above that common thing, there is the supernatural fellowship established through the Eucharist, which intensifies their union as members of the Mystical Body of Christ. It was this sublime truth of the unity of the members of the Mystical Body of Christ, which con-stitutes the background of the complaint Leo XIII brought against those "who live in luxury and call themselves the *brethren* of the multitudes whom in the depths of their hearts they despise." The Rev. Dr. Francis J. Haas, commenting on this passage, writes: "Of course, an argument resting on an appeal to the Mystical Body of Christ could never have been expected to affect the average non-Catholic employer. Yet one may ask, to what extent during these forty-seven years has it influenced Catholic employers and Catholics in positions of influence? And one may answer that it has touched them only slightly, if at all." In the eyes of Christ, a Catholic employer and a Catholic employee are more brothers in the sense of blood relationship than a non-Catholic capitalist of a steel company and his brother-in-the-flesh-capitalist of a holding company. The first two have God as a common Father; the latter have only a common human father. Hence the greater crime for social injustice on the part of the Catholic than the non-Catholic.

If Catholic employers and employees *acted* their faith as brothers in the Mystical Body of Christ, they would give an ex-ample to the rest of the world, and that is what the Mystical Body of Christ was intended to be. It was never intended to embrace every soul born into it, for men would exercise their freedom and stay away from its blessings; furthermore, we were sent out even unto the end as "sheep among wolves." But the example must be given nevertheless, for the Church was planned by God to be the "leaven in the mass." Industrially and economically, Catholics have done little so far to be the leaven in the mass, they have not attempted to apply the doctrine of Eucharistic brotherhood to their non-Sunday work-a-day business lives. In plain simple language, it is the failure to *live* our Communions which is partly responsible for the woes of the day. Communism, in that sense, is a reproach to our faulty understanding of the Eucharist. It is a cancer on society which reminds us of our unfulfilled duty as Catholics who should be *one* in economic and social justice, because we are already one in Him Who is Justice Incarnate.

There are many other possible applications of the Doctrine of Brotherhood with one another through Communion—such as fellowship with the faithful departed, fellowship with the saints triumphant in heaven, fellowship with the penitent, the suffering, and even fellowship with nature from which the elements of the Eucharist have been extracted. Suffice here to conclude with the consoling reflection that this Sacrament which is the end and perfection of all the others, is by its very nature intrinsically bound up with sacrifice. The real error of the Anglican schism which broke them off from the Church in all but an imitation of its externals even to this day was to retain communion of symbols, without the Sacrifice of the Mass. As a matter of fact, the Sacrifice is first and then the Sacrament, for it was the Cross which made the Eucharist, and it is its prolongation or the Mass which makes the Communion. Sacrifice leads to Sacrament even in the natural order. Is it not a profound truth of the natural order, that we live by what we slay? Must not the plant be sacrificed or slain before it can enter into communion with the animal and thereby become its sacrament? Must not the animal be sacrificed or slain before it can enter into communion with man and become his sacrament? Now by a wonderful paradox of God's love, the human race which crucified Christ is the same race which has been nourished by the very life they slew. He might have ended His life by Sacrifice, but to let us take His Life away, and then to take it up again from the grave, in order to give it to us, as *our LIFE*—that is a love which is beyond all human comprehension. To be willing to die for us, was much; but to be willing to live for us all over again, was everything. Truly indeed, our sin was a *felix culpa*. We love by what we slew; Communion flows from Sacrifice; there is no Communion rail without an altar; there is no Bread of Life without a Consecration; Sacrifice leads to the Sacrament.

## CHAPTER XVII

# The Fullness of Christ

Good Friday and Easter Sunday are related as the Cross to the Crown, or the struggle to the triumph. Good Friday is the seed falling to the ground to die, Easter Sunday is that same seed springing forth unto the freshness of life. What happened to the individual human nature of our Lord during those three days is the figure of what happens to His Mystical Body in the fullness of time. The law of His Physical Body is also the law of His Mystical Body. In both there is a death to a lower life, and in both there is a resurrection to the higher life of union with God.

This great mystery is developed in two Greek words found in the Epistles of St. Paul: one, Kenosis, meaning an "emptying," the other, Pleroma, meaning a "filling." "Let the mind be in you which was also in Christ Jesus: who . . . *emptied* Himself, taking the form of a servant, being made in the likeness of men, and in habit found as man" (Phil. 2:5, 7). "That you may be filled unto all the *fullness* of God. . . ." "Until we all meet unto the unity of faith, and of the knowledge of the Son of God, unto a perfect man, unto the measure of the age of the fullness of Christ" (Eph. 3:19, 4:13). "Because in Him it both well pleased the Father that all fullness should dwell" (Col. 1:19).

There is no history more enchanting, there are no events more amazing, than the story of these two words. First of all, the history of God emptying Himself. All goodness empties itself in the sense that it tends to diffuse and to communicate itself. The sun is good, and it empties itself in light and heat; the flowers are good, and they empty themselves in the riotous colours of their petals and the perfume of their silken chalices; animals are good, and they empty themselves in the generation of their young; man is good, and he empties himself by the communication of ideas, by the sharing of his wisdom, his power and his wealth, and above all else by sacrifice, born and begotten of unselfish love. Now God is Perfect Goodness, for He possesses within Himself the fullness of Life, of Truth and Love in the society of the Father, Son and Holy Ghost. God therefore needs nothing to complete His happiness, for what is happiness but the possession of Life and Truth and Love? If, then, God willed to call creatures into existence, it was not because they could add to the joy of His Life, or the knowledge of His Truth, or the thrill of His Love. There could be only one reason why God should call creatures into existence; that is, because He willed that others should drink of His everlasting Fountains of Joy and Happiness.

That process by which Divine Love opened the Fountains of the Godhead and poured out the Goodness is called by St. Paul the Kenosis—the emptying of God—not an emptying in the sense that He lost what He gave, for He no more lost His Perfection by giving than we lose anything in loving our friends, or by looking at our image in a mirror. Rather, He emptied Himself in the sense that others began to share that which before was unshared.

Divine Love did not empty itself all at once. Only progressively through the ages did Love pour itself out in ever-increasing draughts until He had given all. He permitted creatures but glances behind the curtain of His Divinity, for the complete vision, if given all at once, would have been too great for man, as a bright light sometimes blinds rather than illumines. The first outpouring of the chalice of Divine Love was at the beginning of time. Love did not contain the torrents of its Power and Goodness, but He emptied Himself of them and told them to nothingness. That was Creation, in which the universe as a masterpiece reflected the Divine Artist, so that all who looked upon the canvas might detect the Hand that held the brush and the Mind that guided its delicate shadings. Love did not keep the secrets of His heart, but He emptied Himself of them and told them to men: that was Revelation. Thus did men come to learn of God not through His works, but through His revealed words spoken to the prophets; not through the masterpiece of His hand, but through the revelation of His mind. Love tends to become like the one loved; God loved man, and so He emptied Himself and was found in the form and habit of man: that was the Incarnation. Thus did men see Love in the flesh walk the earth, teaching them how to love God and how to love their neighbour. Love also gives itself to the one loved, and if need be suffers and dies, for greater love than this no man hath, that he lay down his Life for his friends. That was Redemption: in which Incarnate Love emptied Himself of His Life on the Cross, and poured it out from a riven side in the form of water, the symbol of our regeneration, and blood, the price of our redemption.

Love by its very nature tends to unity, not only in the flesh but in the spirit. Unity in the flesh was the Incarnation. The final emptying of Divine Love came when He poured out, not His Blood on the Cross, but His Spirit on the Church on the day of Pentecost. Thus did He become the Life of our life, the Soul of our souls, the Spirit of our spirits.

There was nothing more that Divine Love could do. He had emptied Himself of His Power and Wisdom in Creation, of His Secrets in Revelation, of His Majesty in the Incarnation, of His Body and Blood in the Redemption, and of His Spirit in the Church. Well, indeed, might Love say: What more can I do for My vineyard than I have done? The Chalice of My Love I have poured forth, even the last drop. I have kept back nothing. I have given you all that is Mine as God. Truly, indeed, might St. Paul say: *He emptied Himself.*

But now let us look at the other side of the picture. All love
is reciprocal. I love, but I am loved. The love which spends itself
is to be loved in return, for every emptying implies a filling.
The emptying of the river calls for the filling of the ocean; the
emptying of the seed in the grave of the earth means the fullness
of life in the cluster of fruit; the emptying of the light and heat
of the sun cries out for the filling of the earth with its radiant
energy; the emptying of the strength, youth and lifeblood of
parents is filled by the charms and radiance of their children.
Everywhere the story is the same. The humiliation of the Cross
calls out to the exaltation of the Resurrection; Good Friday to
Easter Sunday. The reason is obvious: Love is not sterile, but a
patient usurer who gets back his own in time. If, then, Love is
fecund and productive, if Love by its very nature cries out for love
in return, then surely the Divine Love that empties Itself must
be filled; the downward course of His Love striking the mirror of
our hearts must be reflected back again to heaven. Then, like the
planets which travel in orbits, the Divine Love that was sent out to
the circle of this universe would once more return to its starting
point, filled with the myriad loves of creatures it met on the way.
If God has emptied Himself of Divine Life, then He should be
filled with it in the hearts of men; if He has poured forth, then
He should be replenished; if He has drained His Chalice, then
it should be filled again. And at this point begins the history
of the filling; or the story of how man loved God, because God
first loved man. If the story of the "emptying" of God stretches
in history from the Creation to the Descent of the Holy Ghost,
then the story of the filling reaches from the Descent of the Holy
Ghost to the final glorification of the kingdom of Heaven, or the
return of Prodigal Love back again to the Father's House. In a
word, the growth of the Mystical Body of Christ is the story of the
"filling up" of Christ to His full stature in the glory of the celestial
Jerusalem. And these are the stages of the "filling."

The Love of God that emptied itself in Creation is filled as the Church lays hold of material things, breathes over them the words "Praise ye the Lord," and thus makes them pay tribute to the Creator. The gold in the bowels of the earth, the wheat in the field, the grapes in the vineyard, the trees of the forest, cannot of themselves thank God, but the Church by putting gold in the chalice, wheat and grapes in her Mass, wood in the crucifixes, thus "fills up" unto God the very Love that He once poured out in the creation.

The Love of God that emptied Himself of His secrets in Revelation is filled up by the faith of the Church in the 300,000,000 Catholics throughout the world, who chant her Credo and profess unto death that they believe every truth Christ teaches, because He can neither deceive nor be deceived.

The Love that emptied itself in the Incarnation by God becoming the Son of man is now filled by man becoming an adopted son of God, a brother of Christ, and heir of the kingdom of heaven. The Love that emptied itself in the Redemption is now filled in the Mass, where we share His death on the Cross, that we may also share in His Resurrection.

The Love that emptied itself in the outpouring of the Spirit of God on the day of Pentecost is now filled up by the Church, which incorporates to itself millions and millions of souls who for twenty centuries have lived the Life of the One Body, been vivified by the same Spirit and been obedient to the One Head.

If you would know the extent of the growth of the fullness of Christ in His Mystical Body, then think of how much a human organism grows from the moment of conception. In the course of its life millions and millions of cells have been unified and vivified by the soul. But even that is an inadequate picture of the growth of the Mystical Body of Christ, for the soul of man leaves the body, but the Holy Ghost never leaves the Church. Think, then, of the growth of the States from the few settlers which came to these shores from foreign lands 400 years ago up to the present,

THE FULLNESS OF CHRIST

where we present the spectacle of 120,000,000 people united
under one flag and one common cause. But even that is imperfect,
for the Spirit of a nation is not a unifying soul as the Spirit of the
Church. There is no adequate human analogy for what St. Paul
calls the fullness of Christ which is the Church. There is no way
of adequately measuring the amount of faith, of hope and of love
that has been returned by the Church to God since the day of
Pentecost. But since the Church is a living personality because
she has the same Soul, the same Head, the same Mind, the same
Heart, the same Life now that she had 1,900 years ago, she can
tell us of her growth and fullness in the First Person. And these
are the words of the Church as the fullness of Christ:

On the day of Pentecost there were twelve cells in my Body
beside the Blessed Mother, who was left by her Son to be my
mother and nurse during infancy. My Body first began to
grow within the nursery of Judaism where I had my birth;
but within a few short years, I had incorporated unto myself
even the Gentiles, who knew no God but Caesar. My Spouse,
Christ, had told me that I would be hated as He was hated,
and while still an infant there were other Herods would have
slain me in Rome, as they would have slain Him in Bethlehem.
I have had but few moments of peace. From the outside, I was
attacked by the sword; from the inside, I was abused by false
brethren. And yet neither persecution nor error has stopped
my growth. The sword strengthened my courage, and error
sharpened my intellect. In a century I had grown until I filled
the Roman empire, and then, beyond its outposts, I sent forth
missionaries to the barbarians, who helped me to grow unto
that fullness I had when I crowned Charlemagne in the year
800. My Body grew in age and grace and strength and in the
twelfth century of my existence, like Christ in His twelfth
year, I was instructing the doctors of the world in the temples
of the mediaeval universities which I founded throughout

the world. In the sixteenth century I lost some cells of my Body, as I had lost some centuries before in the errors of the Gnostics and the Pelagians. And yet after each loss there came new strength, for my lot, like my Spouse Christ, is to be ever rising from the tomb where men leave me as dead. Heresy taught me again how much Christ was living His new Life in my Mystical Body, for I found myself recalling that at Capharnaum some of the disciples left Him and walked with Him no more. And so I chastised myself at the Council of Trent and brought myself into subjection, and now at this very hour the twelve cells whom I numbered in my Body on Pentecost now number 300 million souls in every corner of the globe. In the course of my life of 1,900 years, as in the life of a human body, some of my cells have died and been replaced by others, but I have remained the same, because my soul is the abiding Spirit of God. Some of my members have been gathered into the Church triumphant, where they enjoy blessedness with my Spouse Christ; others of my members who while they were with me in the Church militant, sinned, and atoned not, are now gathered in Purgatory, which is the Church suffering, where they wash their baptismal robes clean enough to appear before the Spotless King in the glory of heaven. How much longer I shall live on this earth; how much time awaits the consummation I know not. But when the number of the elect is completed, when the seats vacated by the fallen angels are filled, when I shall have grown to my full stature, then shall the end come; then shall the Church militant on earth and the Church suffering in Purgatory be gathered into the unity of the Church triumphant in heaven on the glorious Easter that shall never end, because there is no time with God, but only Eternal Love.

While struggling here below, I console my children with the vision of that great Easter Day when I shall have grown to my fullness, when shall be fulfilled the words of our Lord addressed to His heavenly Father the night before He died: "Father, I will that where I am, they also whom Thou hast given Me may be with Me; that they may see my glory which Thou hast given Me, because Thou hast loved Me before the Creation of the world" (John 17:24).

In moments when my children despair of the struggle, fear the hatred and sins of the world, I recall to their minds that as the physical Body of Christ suffered to enter into its glory, so must His Mystical Body, with all the members who are part of me suffer in order to enter our glory. "To him that shall overcome I will give to sit with Me on My Throne; as I also have overcome and am set down with My Father on His Throne" (Rev. 3:21). I console my members by telling them that here there is faith, but in my fullness in heaven there will be vision; that while my Body is growing there is Hope, but when it shall have reached maturity there shall be possession; that now there is struggle and shadows, but in my Easter Sunday there shall be only Triumph and Light. I am impatient for my full growth; that is why I am so zealous of truth; why I am so zealous in apostolate, that is why I am so prayerful in my life.

Like a spouse separated from his Spouse, I yearn to be eternally one with my Head, Christ. I have been adding living stones for centuries to the foundation stone of my Spiritual edifice which is Peter, but the coping stone is not yet completed. Perhaps I must yet pass through the Golgotha of the world's persecution, as my Head in His physical Body passed through the Golgotha of His Crucifixion. But I shall be ready for death, for death is the portal to life. I yearn for transformation[1] when Time shall be no more,[2] when He who called Christ to rise from the dead shall call me to life, because of the Spirit which is in Me.[3] A vision of that Eternal Easter wherein Christ and I are united as Spirit and Spouse has been accorded me, and through John I have set it down in the Apocalypse: "I saw a new heaven and a new earth. And I saw the holy city, the new

Jerusalem coming down out of heaven from God, prepared as a bride adorned for her husband. And I heard a great voice from the Throne saying: Behold the tabernacle of God with men, and He will dwell with them. And they shall be His people; and God Himself with them shall be their God. And God shall wipe away all tears from their eyes; and death shall be no more, nor mourning, nor crying, nor sorrow shall be any more, for the former things are passed away. And He showed me the holy city Jerusalem coming down out of heaven from God, having the glory of God, and the light thereof was like to a precious stone as to the jasper stone, even as crystal. And it had a wall great and high, having twelve gates, and in the gates twelve angels, and the names written thereon, which are the names of the twelve tribes of the children of Israel. On the East, three gates; and on the North, three gates; and on the South, three gates; and on the West, three gates. And the wall of the city had twelve foundations, and in them the twelve names of the twelve apostles of the Lamb. . . . And the building of the wall thereof was of jasper stone: but the city itself pure gold, like to clear glass. And the foundations of the walls of the city were adorned with all manner of precious stones. . . . And the twelve gates are twelve pearls, one to each . . . and the street of the city was pure gold as it were transparent glass. And I saw no temple therein. For the Lord God Almighty is the temple thereof and the Lamb. And the city hath no need of the sun, nor the moon, to shine in it. For the Glory of God hath enlightened it, and the Lamb is the lamp thereof" (Rev. 21). "And I saw a great multitude which no man can number of all nations, and tribes and peoples and tongues, standing before the throne, and in sight of the Lamb, clothed with white robes and palms in their hands: And they cried with a loud voice saying: Salvation to our God, who sitteth upon the Throne, and to the Lamb. And all the angels stood round about the throne, and the ancients, and the four living creatures: and they fell down on their faces,

THE FULLNESS OF CHRIST

and adored God, saying: Amen, Benediction and glory and
wisdom and thanksgiving, honour and power and strength
to our God for ever and ever. Amen" (Rev. 7:9–12).

Such is the end and destiny of the Church which St. Paul
describes as the fullness of Christ. It was born of the emptying
of God's love; it is filled by all the virgins and martyrs, confessors
and pontiffs, saintly mothers and fathers, devoted husbands
and wives, sacrificing missionaries and apostolic priests, simple
children who never grew wise with the false wisdom of the world,
all of whom filled up once again with love the Divine Chalice,
which God Himself drained in making and redeeming us. The
end is not yet. The Church, like her Spouse, may yet have to pass
through a terrible Calvary before attaining her glorious Easter.
But the end will come when the Mystical Body of Christ, which is
His Church, will have grown to its fullness, just as the glory of the
physical body of Christ came when it had reached its fullness on
Easter Sunday; the end of history will come at the moment when
Love which came down from heaven as Emmanuel disguised in
lowliness, becomes transfigured in its fullness as the Church, the
glory of the Great Original, the Lamb of God who taketh away
the sins of the world; the end will come when the number of the
elect is completed and when the last baptized soul, hewn from
the great quarry of humanity, shall be shaped and squared, cut
for service in the great Living Temple whose name is Love. And
that will be heaven!

## CHAPTER XVIII

# Catholic Action and the Mystical Body

What role does Catholic Action play in relation to the Church? The answer is: Catholic Action is organic to the Church, as much as a hand or foot is organic to the body. Such was the definition of the Holy Father, Pius XI: "Catholic Action is the participation of the laity in the hierarchical apostolate, for the defence of religious and moral principles, for the development of a healthy and helpful social action under the leadership of the Ecclesiastical Hierarchy, but outside and above all political parties, in order that Catholic life might be restored to the family and society."

Catholic Action, therefore, does not exist apart from the Church, and, in particular, apart from the Hierarchy who are successors of the Apostles. It is a *participation* in the organic life of the Church, and is just as meaningless apart from the Hierarchy as an eye is meaningless apart from the head. Catholic Action, consequently, is Catholicism in action. It is Catholic because of its nearness to Divinity; it is action because of its nearness to humanity. But there can be no divorce between the two. Action without the Church, or independent of it, is purposeless movement or agitation, for "without Me you can do nothing." Catholicism without Action is a buried talent, for the tree that beareth not fruit shall be cut down.

Catholic Action is not only organic with the Church because it is a participation in the Mystical Body under the leadership of the bishops; it is organic with the Church because of the motive the Head of the Church had in instituting it. Many members of the Church already had *juridical incorporation* into it—for example, the Religious (both men and women), diocesan clergy, and the like, all of whom had vows approved by the Holy See or were recognized by Canon Law. But the laity, while an organic part of the Body of Christ, were as yet not organized in any *official* capacity. The purpose of Catholic Action is to organize in the Church by a definite statute, or by Papal approval, that which before was not organized. To the incorporation by grace it adds a kind of *juridical incorporation*, and gives the laity an official capacity in the vital life of the Church. Through Catholic Action the Holy Father has done for the laity in general something akin to what he might do by approving a Third Order or a Confraternity of Prayer. He gives the laity an *official status*, deepens the consciousness of unity with the Church, strengthens their sense of solidarity with it, and above all integrates them to the unique end of all Catholic Action, namely, to make Christ reign in the souls of men. The laity, of course, are not subject to the Headship of the Church directly (as the Hierarchy, which is of divine institution), but indirectly, that is, through the Hierarchy. They are subordinate as regards their functions, without being *inferior* as regards the worth of their activity. "Careful to keep the unity of the Spirit in the bond of peace."

Catholic Action is immanent in the sense that it demands spiritual perfection in the laity, as members of the Mystical Body of Christ.

Action is of two kinds: immanent and transitive. Immanent action is the kind that remains within the subject to perfect it—for example, thinking and willing. Transitive action is the kind that passes out of the subject to perfect something external to itself—for example, the heat issuing from a radiator. Now, since the Church is a Mystical Body, it has this double kind of activity; and since Catholic Action is organic with the Mystical Body, it follows that Catholic Action must therefore manifest itself in two ways—by the development of spiritual life and by external apostolate. As the Holy Father has expressed it: "Catholic Action has for its object both the Christian perfection of its members and the Christian apostolate towards those on the outside." Here we wish to stress the immanent aspect of Catholic Activity, for too often it is assumed that Catholic Action refers exclusively to our neighbour but not to ourselves. This, of course, is contrary to the Catholic principle that apostolate is the result of zeal, that action must always follow contemplation, and that we can make others burn only on condition that we ourselves are already on fire with the love of God.

The inspiration for the immanent Catholic Action is the Sacrament of Confirmation. Confirmation is, in the strictest sense of the term, the Sacrament of Catholic Action. Unfortunately no Sacrament is more neglected by Christians than Confirmation. Catholic Action is an attempt to make the laity more conscious of their responsibility in virtue of their reception of that Sacrament. There are three Sacraments which imprint an indelible seal on the soul: Baptism, Confirmation, and Holy Orders. Baptism incorporates us into Christ the King, for it makes us citizens of His Kingdom. Confirmation incorporates us into Christ the Teacher, for it strengthens us as soldiers to fight for the truth of that Kingdom; Holy Orders incorporates us into Christ the Priest, for it makes us ministers of His Sacrifice. Of these three, Confirmation is ordained for Catholic Action because it represents the adult stage in the spiritual life, but more so because it prepares us spiritually for the defence of the Faith. Every baptized soul must defend his Faith, but Baptism does not give a special mission as Confirmation does. In the language of St. Thomas, the one confirmed *ex officio* is designated and consecrated for that function.

The obligation to preserve the faith and truth and holiness of the Mystical Body is to some extent a participation in the priesthood of our Lord. But the preservation of faith and defence of Divine Truth is unintelligible apart from the Holy Ghost, who is poured into our souls in the Sacrament. There is no apostolic zeal apart from the Spirit. Without the Spirit we may convince others, but we will never convert. Catholic Action, then, can be a very dangerous thing when the emphasis is placed on *action*, for how can we act unless we are acted upon, how can we give unless we receive, how can we enkindle others unless the Pentecostal fires already blaze in our own souls? Action alone, without the inner life vivified by the Holy Spirit, is mere *dissipation* and *agitation*, but it is not fruitfulness and growth. Confirmation emphasizes this very truth by reminding us that we are not qualified to be soldiers until we are sealed with the Holy Ghost. Communists are just as active as Catholics. They are sometimes more active. If activity alone is our goal, then how do Catholics differ from Communists? They differ in their inspiration: one is fired by the Spirit of Christ, the other by the fire of Antichrist.

Too much stress, then, cannot be laid upon the development of the spiritual life in every apostle of Catholic Action. True, a Catholic cannot receive the Sacrament again, but he can stir up its grace and excite its flame by prayer and contemplation, and above all by a deepening consciousness of what St. Peter has called the "royal priesthood" of the laity: "But you are a chosen generation, a kingly priesthood, a holy nation, a purchased people: that you may declare His virtues who hath called you out of darkness into His marvellous light. Be you also as living stones built up, a spiritual house, a holy priesthood, to offer up spiritual sacrifices, acceptable to God by Jesus Christ."

The priest who receives the third seal, or Holy Orders, is the official representative of Christ because given power over His Body in the Mass. But the layman shares that priesthood in virtue of the second seal, or Confirmation; that is why a layman is empowered in case of necessity to administer the first seal, or Baptism, which incorporates a soul into the Mystical Body of Christ. Catholic Action, then, in virtue of Confirmation is a lay priesthood. Its first activity is immanent, or the development of the spiritual life, and not a feverish, hectic humanitarian busy-body propaganda for the Church. The activity becomes external certainly, but only on condition that it be first internal. It is first God-ward, then man-ward; first the state of a victim, then the state of a combatant; first the office of a priest, then the office of a defender; first immanent, then transitive; first centred about the Mass, and only then about the masses.

Catholic Action is transitive, inasmuch as it applies the fruits of the Spirit to those inside and outside the Mystical Body of Christ.

Catholic Action is first *ad intra*, then *ad extra*. Since the Sacrament of Catholic Action is Confirmation, and since Confirmation is a Sacrament which makes souls organic with the Mystical Body, it follows then that they who receive it are one with the Mystical Body and can have no activity apart from it. The external activity of Catholic Action will, therefore, be the same as the activity of the Mystical Body in the world. But the activity of the Mystical Body in the world is the activity of a leaven in the mass: that is, it is not a rival political system or economic policy or international code set up in contrast with the world; it is rather the very soul of these activities. To make this clear, it is important to recall that the great characteristic of our Lord's teaching is what might be called *political* or *economic relativity*. He was totally indifferent to any worldly government, whether it be monarchical or democratic, parliamentarian or imperial. His economics was almost that of a hand-to-mouth existence, for He said of economic goods: "After these things do the Gentiles seek." He laid down no code for governments, said nothing about armaments, said nothing about slavery, and yet, *He did something for all these*. How? By choosing a corporate group whom He made the Mystical Body on

Pentecost, and by making them the leaven in the mass of society and directing them to seek first the Kingdom of God and its Justice and all these things would be added unto them. Catholic Action is not the earth, but the salt of the earth. It can therefore never identify itself with any explicit political party or economic system lest, when that perish, the Church seem to perish with it. Such was the guiding principle of Leo XIII's Encyclical *Graves de Communi*, and it is repeated again by Pius XI in his letter *Dilectissima Nobis*, in which he says that "Catholic Action is outside and beyond all political parties." This does not mean that Catholic Action must be indifferent to economics or politics. That would be an error in the other extreme. It would be wrong to be *immersed* in politics; so it would be wrong to be *separated* from politics, just as it is wrong to identify God with the universe as the Pantheists do, or separate Him from the universe as the Deists do. Catholic Action, says Pius XI, implies as "extensive a participation as possible in public life." It demands an interest in politics and economics, but not in politics as identical with modern political parties.

Being in public life does not mean teaching that Catholicism will perish if democracy perishes, or if aristocracy is defeated, or if any given system of economics is rejected. Leo XIII, it will be recalled, told the French Catholics that democracy was coming; hence, "Catholics would compromise their spiritual interests by opposing it." He asked them, therefore, not to oppose it in the name of the Church, but to give to it if not their "adhesion in principle, at least their adhesion in fact, and in any case, a positive adhesion." Catholic Action comes into direct conflict with politics and economics, and sets itself up against them, *only when* systems of *politics and economics touch the altar;* that is, when they attack the fundamental relations of man to God. When political parties and economic systems attack religion expressly, then the Catholic cannot be indifferent to them; he must oppose those systems and parties with all his force, not because they are politics and economics but because they are a *religion*—a religion which would destroy religion, an Antichrist which would destroy Christ. In the language of theology, such political and economic systems are politics only "materialiter," but they are a religion "formaliter," because they lay claim to the body and soul of man, and would subjugate even his conscience to the State, which would recognize no power except its own.

In treating of the Mystical Body St. Paul tells us that the hand cannot dispense with the services of the foot. This is because the Church is made up of a multiplicity of members, as the body is formed of a multiplicity of cells. The Church fails, therefore, in those parts where its members fail. Hence the importance of each member of the Church doing the work assigned to him in his particular state of life. Catholic Action means precisely this: it does not mean that a hand should be a foot, but that the hand should be a good hand, and the foot a good foot. This idea can be clarified by recalling that the Holy Father recognizes as an ideal in the conversion of pagan peoples, not the apostolate of foreign missionaries among them, but the developing of *native* apostles, so that the Japanese may be converted by the Japanese, the Chinese by the Chinese, and so forth. This is also the ideal of Catholic Action. Too often we think of Catholic Action as zealous laymen going into "foreign" fields to evangelize them—for example, doctors labouring to purify the stage, lawyers working to spiritualize the trade unions. Catholic Action does not mean this *in ideal*. It means, if we follow through the logic of the Holy Father, that different groups and classes will be Catholicized by and through the Catholics *in those groups*—that is, that the stage will be cleansed by and through Catholicism on the stage, that the medical profession will be made moral by and through Catholic doctors, that law will be made honest by and through Catholic lawyers, that the working classes will be saved from Communism for the Communion of Saints by and through Catholic workers themselves. The Bishop labours in his diocese, the priest in his parish, and the layman in his trade; and if every Catholic played his role well in his particular profession, the world would soon be a better place in which to live.

In summary Catholic Action is something clear and distinct as long as it is understood in terms of the Church as the Mystical Body of Christ.

(*a*) Catholic Action is organic with the Mystical Body of Christ, and is juridically incorporated into its Apostolic life through the appeal of the Vicar of Christ, who subjects the laity to Him through the Bishops, the successors of the Apostles.

(*b*) Catholic Action is first immanent activity or the development of the spiritual life infused in the soul through Baptism and, in particular, through Confirmation, the Sacrament of Catholic Action.

(*c*) Catholic Action is the external action of giving others to drink of the fountains of everlasting Truth, after we ourselves have drunk deeply of their refreshing draughts. It is independent of all political parties and economic systems, but not independent of politics and economics inasmuch as they look to the common good and the salvation of souls.

(*d*) Catholic Action is not essentially a "foreign" missionary activity, but a domestic activity in the fields where God has placed us through His holy will.

The laity will become increasingly conscious of their role as they understand the role of the Church as the Mystical Body of Christ. Christ in His Life in the Church has no other hands with which to give bread to the poor than our hands; He has no other feet with which to visit the sick than our feet; He has no other lips with which to speak truth than our lips; He is therefore *incomplete* without us, in the sense that St. Paul says the Church is "His fullness." What would happen to our human bodies if our hands and feet and lips refused to co-operate with the other parts of our bodies? Something analogously sad and tragic happens to the Mystical Body when some of its members fail. Hand-action and foot-action help to keep the physical body alive; Catholic Action keeps the Mystical Body alive, healthy and growing.

# Notes

## FOREWORD

1. Matthias Scheeben, *The Glories of Divine Grace*, vol. 2, trans. Patrick Shaughnessy (Rockford, IL: Tan Books, 2000), 72.

2. Scheeben, 138.

3. See Athanasius, *On the Incarnation of the Word* 54, trans. Archibald Robertson, in Nicene and Post-Nicene Fathers, Second Series, vol. 4, ed. Philip Schaff and Henry Wace (Buffalo, NY: Christian Literature, 1892), newadvent.org. See also *Catechism of the Catholic Church* 460.

## INTRODUCTION

1. Fulton J. Sheen, *Treasure in Clay: The Autobiography of Fulton J. Sheen* (New York: Doubleday, 2008), 14.

2. "Archbishop Dolan promises not to sidestep controversial issues," Catholic News Agency, April 15, 2009, https://www.catholicnewsagency.com/news/15684 /archbishop-dolan-promises-not-to-sidestep-controversial-issues.

3. See page 35.

4. See page 39.

5. See page 3.

6. Fulton J. Sheen, preface to Leslie Rumble and Charles Carty, *Radio Replies*, vol. 1 (Rockford, IL: Tan Books, 2001), ix.

7. See pages 86–87.

8. See page 42.

9. See page 212.

10. See page 8.

## CHAPTER 1

1. According to St. Thomas, Christ bears a triple relation to us: (a) He is the exemplary cause of our satisfaction and the model of our perfection (Matt. 11:29; John 13:15; John 14:6). (b) He is the author of our redemption and the infinite treasure of grace. Because He is God as well as man, He merited for us every grace of pardon, salvation, and sanctification (Rom. 3:24; 1 Tim. 2:5; Acts 4:12; Rom. 5:15–20; Heb. 7:25; Heb. 4:14–16; Eph. 1:7). (c) He is the cause of our sanctification (John 15:5; Eph.

3:17). "Since Christ's humanity is the instrument of the Godhead, therefore all Christ's actions and sufferings operate instrumentally in virtue of His Godhead for the salvation of the world." For since He is our head, then, by the Passion which He endured from love and obedience, He delivered us as His members from our sins. . . . "For just as the natural body is one, though made up of diverse members, so the whole Church, Christ's Mystical Body, is reckoned as one person with its Head who is Christ." *Sum. Theol.*, 3, q. 48, art. 6.

## CHAPTER 11

1. Since Christ's Personality was not limited to a human nature, it was in a certain sense a symbol of the human race; it was possible for Christ to incorporate under His Divine Personality all the human beings that would ever be. This potentiality becomes an actuality in the Church or the Mystical Body which is the "filling up" of the possibility of the Incarnation.

2. Cf. Anscar Vonier, O.S.B., *The Personality of Christ*, pp. 70 ff.

3. These correspond to the three causes: Christ was formal cause of the salvation of men, because He taught as a Prophet. He was efficient cause, since He founded a Kingdom of which He remains the Head. He was final cause, since the end and purpose of life was sanctification and He redeemed as Priest. Cf. Sheen, *The Eternal Galilean*, for a treatment of these three offices. . . . "In the Jewish religion there were three types of Mediators: Kings, Prophets, and Priests. The prophet brought to man the message of God; the priest in the name of God administered to men the things of God; the theocratic king was the lieutenant of God." F. Prat, *St. Paul*, vol. 2, p. 198. In the Old Testament these offices were divided among different individuals; in Christ they are united. For the application of the threefold causes to the Passion, cf. *Sum. Theol.*, 3, q. 48.

4. In the New Testament a prophet signifies one who speaks to men in the name of God: 2 Pet. 1:21. Cf. John 1:8, 3:34, 8:12, 13:13, 14:16, 18:37; Matt. 23:10. "The source and fountain of knowledge is the Word of God, namely Christ. From His knowledge as the Word, which is the fount and source, is derived all knowledge of the faithful." St. Thomas on *Gospel of St. John*, 27:25. Cf. *Sum. Theol.*, 3, q. 42, art. 4, for the reasons why our Lord did not write, but taught. The power of teaching belonged to Christ in virtue of the hypostatic union. Suarez, *De Myst. Vitae Christi*, disp. 30, sect. 1, n. 2, p. 458, vol. 19. Cf. St. Thomas, *Sum. Theol.*, 3, q. 3, art. 8.

5. John 18:37; Matt. 4:17; Mark 1:15; Luke 4:23. This kingship of Christ was legislative, judicial, and executive, the fullness of power:
    (1) Legislative. Cf. the Sermon on the Mount where there constantly recurs the phrase, "But I say unto you." Matt. 5; John 14:15; John 15:10; Matt. 28:10.
    (2) Judicial. John 5:22. Cf. *Sum. Theol.*, 3, q. 59, art. 1 and 2; art. 2, 3, and 4.
    (3) Executive. Matt. 25:31, 34, 41, 46; John 14:2, 3.
    "The dominion of the Redeemer embraces, therefore, all men, as was said in the words of our predecessor of lasting memory, Leo XIII, which we make our own: 'The empire of Christ extends not only over Catholic people and over those who, reborn in the fount of Baptism, belong by right to the Church, even though error has driven them far and dissension has separated them from the bond of love; it embraces even those who do not enjoy the Christian faith, so that all mankind

is under the power of Jesus Christ.'" Encyclical, *Quas Primas*, of the Holy Father Pius XI.

Christ is not only Spiritual King of souls; He is also Temporal King of the nations. "It would be a grave mistake," says the same Encyclical, "to refuse to Christ as man temporal royalty over the entire universe." All government derives its power from God (Rom. 13:1), and all power has been given to Him by His Father on earth and in heaven (Matt. 28:18). Cf. *Sum. Theol.*, 3, q. 59, art. 1, ad. 2; 3, q. 59, art. 1; 3 q. 59, art. 4.

6. Heb. 5. Every priest has a double function: to give God to man and to give man to God. Our Lord gave God to man by giving us Himself; He gave men to God by wiping out sin and renovating our natures. The Incarnation was the priestly anointing of Christ. Cf. *Sum. Theol.*, 3, q. 22, art. 1-6.

7. "Going therefore, teach ye all nations; baptizing them in the name of the Father, and of the Son, and of the Holy Ghost: Teaching them to observe all things whatsoever I have commanded you: and behold I am with you all days, even to the consummation of the world" (Matt. 28:19, 20).

8. Every person may be considered from a double point of view: (a) as an individual and (b) as a member of society, and under both aspects acts may be attributed to him. Cf. St. Thomas, *De Malo*, q. 4, art. 1. For example, the president of the United States has an individual personal existence as a private citizen, but he is also a member of society, or better still, the head of a society in the political order. In this latter capacity, his acts have a social significance. His executive acts bind the citizens even without any explicit declaration on their part.

The human race has had a double head: Adam and Christ. Each was a person, but each was also the head of a society, one in the order of the flesh, the other in the order of the spirit. All who are united with them as heads, constitute one body with the head. "Omnes homines computantur unus homo per participationem naturae communis" (*Contra Gent.*, lib. 4, cap. 52). "Tota multitudo hominum a primo parente humanam naturam accipientium quasi unum collegium, vel potius unum corpus unius hominis consideranda est" (*De Malo*, q. 4, art. 1). When therefore Adam declared war against God we declared war, without any explicit declaration on our part. We are one body with the head of the human race in the order of nature. "By one man sin entered into this world, and by sin death; and so death passed upon all men, in whom all have sinned" (Rom. 5:12). The Redemption of the human race by Christ has the same repercussion for good as the sin of Adam has for evil. "As by the offence of one, unto all men to condemnation: so also by the justice of one, unto all men to justification of life, for as by the disobedience of one man, many were made sinners; so also by the obedience of one, many shall be made just" (Rom. 5:18, 19). "For you are all one in Christ Jesus" (Gal. 3:28; 1 Cor. 15:21, 22). There is solidarity therefore in the natural as well as in the supernatural order. If there were no Adam, there would be no human race; if there were no Christ, there would be no regenerated humanity.

Our relation to Adam and Christ is not the same in all respects. (1) We are in Adam as regards our natures, though not in our persons. Original sin which passes on to us from Adam is a sin of nature, not a personal sin. "The first Adam was made into a living soul; the last Adam into a quickening spirit" (1 Cor. 15:45). "Peccatum originale est peccatum naturae principaliter, et personae consequenter; sed donum gratiae converso se habet" (*Sum. Theol.*, 2, d. 20, q. 2, art. 4; 2, d. 30, q. 1, art. 2; *De Malo*, q. 4, art. 1; 7). (2) We are one with Adam by the fact of our nature; we are one with Christ by the act of our persons—voluntarily. We must know Christ in order to become what Christ is; it is not necessary to know Adam personally in order to be what Adam is. (3) In Adam we are subject to our nature; in Christ our nature is made subject to us; i.e., freedom and personality are brought to their proper dominion over natural impulse and sensibility.

How do we become incorporated to these two heads of the human race, Adam and Christ? Inasmuch as one has to do with natural life and the other the supernatural life, it is only to be expected that the initiation into their "bodies" or corporate societies will be like the initiation into all life, namely, by a birth. We become incorporated to Adam by being born of the flesh; we become incorporated to Christ by being born of the spirit. By the mere fact that we are born of woman through carnal propagation we are of the race of Adam; by the fact we are born of waters of the Holy Ghost in baptism we are of the race of Christ (John 3:5). This will be discussed later.

9. "The first man Adam was made into a living soul; the last Adam into a quickening spirit" (1 Cor. 15:45).

10. "Not by the works of justice, which we have done, but according to His mercy, He saved us, by the laver of regeneration, and renovation of the Holy Ghost" (Titus 3:5).

11. "Abide in Me, and I in you. As the branch cannot bear fruit of itself, unless it abide in the vine, so neither can you, unless you abide in Me. I am the vine; you the branches; he that abideth in Me, and I in him, the same beareth much fruit; for without Me you can do nothing" (John 15:4, 5).

12. "And He said: So is the kingdom of God, as if a man should cast seed into the earth, and should sleep, and rise, night and day, and the seed should spring, and grow up whilst he knoweth not. For the earth of itself bringeth forth fruit, first the blade, then the ear, afterwards the full corn in the ear. And when the fruit is brought forth, immediately He putteth in the sickle because the harvest is come" (Mark 4:26, 29).

13. "And He said: To what shall we liken the kingdom of God, or to what parable shall we compare it? It is as a grain of mustard seed: which when it is sown in the earth, is less than all the seeds that are in the earth: And when it is sown, it groweth up, and becometh greater than all herbs, and shooteth out great branches, so that the birds of the air may dwell under the shadow thereof. And with many such parables, He spoke to them the word, according as they were able to hear" (Mark 4:30, 33).

14. "But when He, the Spirit of truth, is come, He will teach you all truth. For He shall not speak of Himself; but what things soever He shall hear, He shall speak, and the things that are to come, He shall show you" (John 16:13).

15. "If the world hate you, know ye that it hath hated Me before you. If you had been of the world, the world would love its own: but because you are not of the world, but I have chosen you out of the world, therefore the world hateth you. Remember My word that I said to you: The servant is not greater than his master. If they have persecuted Me, they will also persecute you: if they have kept My word, they will keep yours also" (John 15:18-20).

16. "As thou hast sent Me into the world, I also have sent them into the world. And for them do I sanctify Myself, that they also may be sanctified in truth. That they all may be one, as Thou, Father, in Me, and I in Thee; that they also may be one in Us; that the world may believe that thou hast sent Me. I in them, and Thou in Me; that they may be made perfect in one: and the world may know that Thou hast loved them, as Thou hast also loved Me" (John 17:18, 19, 21, 23).

17. "I came forth from the Father, and am come into the world: again I leave the world, and I go to the Father" (John 16:28).

18. "While I was with them, I kept them in Thy name, Those whom Thou gavest Me have I kept; and none of them is lost, but the son of perdition, that the scripture may be fulfilled" (John 17:12).

19. *Lectures on Justification*, pp. 216–219.

20. Cf. Eph. 4:3–4; Col. 3:15–16; Rom. 5:5; 1 Cor. 12:11; Eph. 4:7, 12; 1 Cor. 12:18, 19, 28; 1 Cor. 12:24, 26; Col. 1:4, 9, 12; 2 Tim. 2:10; Eph. 5:25, 4:12.

21. Cf. Mura, *Le Corps Mystique*, vol. 1, p. 108. In a human body the members have existence only in the whole and form one physical being of which no part can exist outside of the whole. In the Mystical Body, on the contrary, the members which make it up are living beings, complete in themselves, numerically distinct, already existing antecedent to their incorporation with Christ. In like manner, in the natural body, the soul is a principle of being essentially incomplete and ordained to the body as its necessary complement, to form one substance. But in the supernatural order, the soul of the Mystical Body is a Divine Person, subsistent, self-sufficient, and contracting no substantial union with the divine organism which is animated by its life.

22. "Mystical" is not opposed to "real," for there are other realities besides those which we touch and see. The Mystical Body is a reality which expresses itself by a metaphor, like all immaterial and suprasensible objects. It is not a mere abstraction, but a veritable reality because it is the subject of attribution, properties, and rights. Prat, op. cit., p. 360.

"Mystical" is therefore differentiated both from the unreal and the ideal. This supernatural reality is thus distinguished from the physical Body of Christ, and also from a purely natural society. The body whose soul is the Holy Ghost is real in a higher order than the real of the concrete. Cf. M. d'Herbigny, S.J., *De Ecclesia*, vol. 1, p. 119: "Haec societas, quamvis ex hominibus constet non secus ac civilis communitas, tamen propter finem sibi constitutum atque instrumenta quibus ad finem contendit supernaturalis est et spiritualis, atque idcirco distinguitur ac differt a societate civili." Cf. Leo XIII, *Immortale Dei*.

The Mystical Union is definitely not a hypostatic union, for despite it we still retain our nature and independent personality with full responsibilities for our acts. Mura enumerates seven bonds of unity (op. cit., vol. 1, p. 110).

23. In the Synoptic Gospels the term "Kingdom" is most often used to describe the union of Christ and regenerated humanity; this was because the Jews were already familiar with the Kingdom of God. In Paul, the union is spoken of as the "Mystery." The Mystery, as the Kingdom, appeals to all men, Gentiles as well as Jews, and incorporates them to Christ. St. John speaks of the union most often as "Life"—the Life which Christ received from the Father and which He passes on to

us. Emile Mersch, S.J., in his profound work entitled *Le Corps Mystique du Christ* (vol. 1, p. 216), after a study of the Synoptics, Paul, and John, concludes that at first sight, "Kingdom," "Mystery," and "Life" seem to signify three different things. But in reality it is the same rich, unique gift, under different aspects. The first, that of "Kingdom," expressed the economy of salvation in terms of the prophecies and the expectation of the people. It was a way of speaking which was necessary at the beginning, and the one which our Blessed Lord and the apostles most habitually employed before their audiences in Palestine.

The second idea, that of "Mystery," is a theology, and almost a polemic. It opposes the splendour of the divine decrees to the narrowness of our thoughts and our exclusiveness, and was of a style eminently befitting an apostle who had to assert the transcendence of divine mercy against the nationalism of Israel, and the limited wisdom of the Gentiles.

The third life, that of "Life," is something more psychological, and at the same time the most metaphysical. It shows Christianity in its essence and as it affects our internal life.

All these ideas, despite their shades of meaning, express the same thing. "Kingdom" implies a subjection, a conservation; "Mystery" a hidden sanctification and unity; "Life" a regeneration which bestows a new existence. They all come to us; we are incorporated in Christ, and this "incorporation suffices to make of us children of the kingdom, beneficiaries of the mystery, and sons of adoption. These three notions summarize: (1) The Synoptic Gospels and the Acts, (2) The Epistles of St. Paul, (3) The writings of St. John; i.e., all of the New Testament. The New Testament is in its turn the manifestation of the Old Testament. In other words, they end in Christ, for it is in Christ that the Kingdom is inaugurated, the Mystery revealed, and the Life communicated" (Mersch., op. cit., p. 218).

24. The incorporation with the Mystical Body takes place through baptism. Just as a man becomes a member of the society of Adam, or the human race, by being born of the flesh, so too He becomes a member of the Society of Christ, or the Church, by being born of the spirit, or the waters of the Holy Ghost. Such was the message of our Lord to Nicodemus. Baptism constitutes our "naturalization" into the Mystical Body of Christ. "For you are all the children of God by faith, in Christ Jesus. For as many of you as have been baptized in Christ, have put on Christ. There is neither Jew nor Greek; there is neither bond nor free; there is neither male nor female. For you are all one in Christ Jesus" (Gal. 3:26, 28).

The baptism in the early Church was administered by immersion, the plunging into the waters symbolizing our burial and death, the rising from the waters our resurrection. This makes clear the words of St. Paul to the Romans: "Know you not that all we, who are baptized in Christ Jesus, are baptized in His death? For we are buried together with Him by baptism into death; that as Christ is risen from the dead by the glory of the Father, so we also may walk in newness of life. For if we have been planted together in the likeness of His death, we shall be also in the likeness of His resurrection" (Rom. 6:3, 5).

There are various grades of incorporation, more or less perfect. (1) Baptism of water which effects a *real, juridical*, and *total* incorporation. (2) Baptism of blood; e.g., a martyr who dies for the faith before receiving baptism of water, becomes incorporated in the Church by that very fact. The incorporation is *real* and *juridical*, though not total, because the martyr could not efficaciously receive the other sacraments, as Eucharist or confirmation, without baptism by water. (3) Baptism of desire; e.g., a person who is receiving instruction for the Church or who has the desire to be received into the Church, becomes incorporated into the Church really but not juridically. "*Nondum* quidem per sacrum Baptismum *renati* estis, sed per signum crucis in utero sanctae matris ecclesiac jam *concepti* estis." (Ps. Aug. *de Symbols* 1, 2, cap. 1, P.L. 40, 637.) Cf. St. Thomas, *Sum. Theol.*, 3, q. 68, art. 2; art. 2, 69; art. 4.—Catechumeni, qui nulla sua culpa sinc baptismo moriantur, baptizati accensendi sunt (*Canon Law*, 1239, 2).

25. "But doing the truth in charity, we may in all things grow up in Him who is the head, even Christ: From whom the whole body, being compacted and fitly joined together, by what every joint supplieth, according to the operation in the measure of every part, maketh increase of the body, unto the edifying of itself in charity" (Eph. 4:15, 16).

26. "For we are God's coadjutors: you are God's husbandry; you are God's building. According to the grace of God that is given to me, as a wise architect, I have laid the foundation; and another buildeth thereon. But let every man take heed how he buildeth thereupon. For other foundation no man can lay, but that which is laid; which is Christ Jesus. Now if any man build upon this foundation, gold, silver, precious stones, wood, hay, stubble: Every man's work shall be manifest; for the day of the Lord shall declare it, because it shall be revealed in fire; and the fire shall try every man's work, of what sort it is. If any man's work abide, which he hath built thereupon, he shall receive a reward. If any man's work burn, he shall suffer loss; but he himself shall be saved, yet so as by fire. Know you not, that you are the temple of God, and that the Spirit of God dwelleth in you?" (1 Cor. 3:9–16).

"Now therefore you are no more strangers and foreigners; but you are fellow-citizens with the saints, and the domestics of God, built upon the foundation of the apostles and prophets, Jesus Christ himself being the chief corner stone: In whom all the building, being framed together, groweth up into an holy temple in the Lord. In whom you also are built together into a habitation of God in the Spirit" (Eph. 2:19–22).

27. "Being subject one to another, in the fear of Christ. Let women be subject to their husbands, as to the Lord: Because the husband is the head of the wife, as Christ is the head of the church. He is the saviour of his body. Therefore as the church is subject to Christ, so also let the wives be to their husbands in all things. Husbands, love your wives, as Christ also loved the church, and delivered Himself up for it; that He might sanctify it, cleansing it by the laver of water in the word of life: That He might present it to Himself a glorious church, not having spot or wrinkle, or any such thing, but that it should be holy, and without blemish. So also ought men to love their wives as their own bodies. He that loveth his wife, loveth himself. For no man ever hated his own flesh; but nourisheth and cherisheth it, as also Christ doth the church: Because we are members of His body, of His flesh, and of His bones. For this cause shall a man leave his father and mother, and shall cleave to his wife, and they shall be two in one flesh. This is a great sacrament; but I speak in Christ and in the church" (Eph. 5:21–32).

28. "The Natural Christ redeems us; the Mystical Christ sanctifies us. The Natural Christ died for our sins; the Mystical Christ lives in us; the Natural Christ reconciles us to His Father; the Mystical Christ unites us to Him" (Prat, op. cit., t. 1, p. 359).

29. St. Paul speaks of the Church as Christ's Body in two senses: (1) Christ is often spoken of as "the Head of the Body, the Church" (Col. 1:18), and (2) Christ and the Church are one and the same, or even one person "for you are one in Christ" (1 Cor. 12:12). This latter is the interpretation of his phrase "in Christ Jesus," which is repeated 164 times. There is no opposition between these two ideas; one is really complementary of the other. They mean that Christ is in the Church as its Head and the Church is Christ or the *totus Christus* because He is the source of its Life. Hence Christ lives in Christians (Gal. 2:20) and Christians live in Christ (Rom. 6:11). The power of Christ is in Christians (2 Cor. 12:9) and Christians are powerful in Him (Eph. 6:10). Christ grows in them (Gal. 4:19) and they grow in Him (Eph. 4:15). The difference between the two is then merely a question of vocabulary. The thought has not changed. In St. Paul's first epistles, the role of the Head is given to Christ. He is the foundation of the edifice, although as Head of the organism He is interior to it (1 Cor. 10:17). He animates and vivifies it; it is His plenitude. His superiority as Head is therefore like the superiority which characterizes a soul as it puts life in a living thing. For a full treatment, cf. Mersch, op. cit., Vol. I, pp. 128 ff.

"Nomen ecclesiae dupliciter accipitur. Quandoque enim nominat tantummodo corpus quod Christo conjungitur sicut capiti; . . . sic vero Christus non est ecclesiae membrum, sed est caput influens omnibus ecclesiae membris. Alio modo accipitur ecclesia secundum quod nominat caput, et membrum ecclesiae" (*Sum. Theol.*, 4 d. 49, q. 4, act. 3, ad. 4).

30. "Above all principality, and power, and virtue, and dominion, and every name that is named, not only in this world, but also in that which is to come. And He hath subjected all things under His feet, and hath made Him head over all the church, which is His body, and the fullness of Him who is filled all in all" (Eph. 1:21–23).

"But doing the truth in charity, we may in all things grow up in Him who is the head, even Christ: From whom the whole body, being compacted and fitly joined together, by what every joint supplieth, according to the operation in the measure of every part, maketh increase of the body, unto the edifying of itself in charity" (Eph. 4:15, 16).

St. Paul uses the analogy of matrimony to bring out the Headship of Christ. As a man is the head of a woman so Christ is the Head of the Church: "Because the husband is the head of the wife, as Christ is the head of the church. He is the saviour of his body" (Eph. 5:23).

31. There are three kinds of Grace or Divine Life in Christ: (1) The Grace of Union constituting the personality of the Word Incarnate (*Sum. Theol.*, 3 q. 7, art. 12). (2) Sanctifying Grace constituting His individual life in the supernatural order. (3) The Grace of the Head constituting His Social Life in the Mystical Body. These three kinds of life are mentioned in the beginning of the Gospel of St. John. (1) "And the Word was made flesh and dwelt amongst us" (1:14). (2) "We saw His Glory, the Glory as it were of the only begotten of the Father, full of grace and truth" (ibid.). (3) "And of His fullness we have all received, and grace for grace" (1:16). The first two refer to Christ in His individual human nature, the last as Head of the Mystical Body. It is this that concerns us here. Cf. *Sum. Theol.*, 3, q. 6, art. 6; 3 q., art. 10; q. 6, art. 6; q. 7, arts. 11 and 13. St. Thomas says that the grace of a member of the Mystical Body is compared to the grace of Christ, as a particular potency may be referred to a universal power (ibid., 3, q, 7, art. 12). The building up of the Mystical Body by the incorporation of souls into it, does not pertain to the perfection of Christ because He is perfect in His glory, but inasmuch as it brings

others to share in His Perfection (ibid., 3, q. 7, art. 4). Being the principle of divine life in the supernatural order according to His Humanity, as God is the principle of all being in the natural order, so as in like manner as all perfections of being are found in God, all perfections of grace are found in the Head, Christ (*De Veritate*, q. 20, art. 9). The night of the Last Supper our Lord said that He sanctified Himself, His Body; and from this sanctification there flows out grace to souls (*Sum. Theol.*, 3, q. 8, art. 2). For a treatment of how this Divine Life is poured out into humanity, see ibid., 3, q. 13, art. 2, where St. Thomas shows that in Christ there are two kinds of powers: (1) The power of His human nature, either in the limits of its own forces or with the help of grace. (2) The instrumental potency belonging to it in virtue of its union with the Person of the Word. From the second point of view, the human nature, as the instrument of the Word, has the power to operate all those miraculous transformations subordinate to the end of the Incarnation, and to restore all things in heaven and on earth. Just how the Mystical Body becomes the *instrumentum conjunctum* for the communication of the Life of the Head will be discussed presently.

32. "'Sacramentum magnum in Christo et in ecclesia.' Ita enim duo in carne una ut Sponsa jam mystice caro Christi corpusque fiat eiusque membra *theandrismum* ex illa incorporatione vere participent" (d'Herbigny, op. cit., Vol. II, p. 368).

33. In the Incarnation the human nature of Christ was without a human personality, but was subject to the Divine. In like manner, the members of the Mystical Body are without a human personality, not because they have none, but because by an act of their will and with the help of grace, they become identified with their Head—Christ. His Will is their will. His Person is their law: "I live, now not I, but Christ liveth in me," says St. Paul (Gal. 2:20). I have my human personality, and yet I have it not, because Christ is my life: such is the attitude of a Christian.

There is then a sense in which the axiom: *Actiones sunt suppositorum*, applies to the human instruments of Christ, who teach, govern, and sanctify in His name. They become the "*instrumenta conjuncta*" of Him, and through them He works as He once worked through His physical Body. This does not mean however that there is a Hypostatic union between Christ and His Mystical Body, as there was in the union of His Divine Nature and His human nature in the Person of the Word. "Unio enim hypostatics Dei et hominis in capite Ecclesiae Christo, per aliquam solum umbram seu analogiam producit sui imitationem in corpore, nempe per assimilationem *adoptivam* (1 John 3:2). Per Ecclesiam Spiritus Dei manifestat historicam sui in mundo activitatem cum ipse in ea vivat (2 Cor. 6:16); quae unio, hypostaticae absolute inferior, naturam tamen humanam simpliciter transcendit (1 Cor. 6:17)," d'Herbigny, op. cit., Vol. I, p. 166.

34. The obvious difficulty is that Christ's Body perfectly obeyed His Soul, while the organs of the Church do not always perfectly obey the Spirit. For a discussion of this, see Chapter V, "Scandals."

## CHAPTER III

1. Col. 1:16–18. "The whole church, which is the Mystical Body of Christ, is regarded as one Person with its Head which is Christ" (*Sum. Theol.*, 3, q. 39, art. 1, c.). Elsewhere St. Paul says, "All things are in Him, all things are by Him, all things are for Him." All things are *in* Him because He is the perfect image of the Father, and

therefore He comprises the ideal and the model of all things possible. All things are *by* Him as the efficient cause (by appropriation). All things are *for* Him, because He is author of nature and of grace.

2. 3, q. 8, art. 1. A similar treatment is to be found on Order, Perfection and Power in *De Veritate*, q. 24, art. 4. The triple influence mentioned in the *Summa* corresponds to the triple office of Christ as King, Prophet, and Priest. The manner in which Christ exercises the Headship of the Church since His Ascension into Heaven is treated in: 3, q. 48 and 49, and 3, q. 64, art. 4. "Though the passion of Christ be a bodily phenomenon, it has a spiritual power from the Divinity that is united with it, and therefore it has efficacy by means of spiritual contact, i.e., by faith and the sacraments." 3, q. 48, art. 6, ad. 2.

3. "Ecclesia una est constituta ex angelis et hominibus" (3 d, 13, q. 3, art. 2, s. 1, sed contra 2). "Ecclesia militans est hominum in praesenti viventium; ecclesia triumphans est ex hominibus et angelis in patria. In *Epist. ad Eph.*, cap. 1, lect. 8. Gratia capitis operata est a constitutione mundi, ex quo homines membra ejus esse coeperunt" (3 d, 13, q. 3, art. 2, s. 2, sed contra 2). "Christus ab initio mundi erat caput justorum" (4 d, 8, q. 1, art. 3, s. 2, ad. 1). "Sicut est una fides antiquorum et modernorum ita una ecclesia; unde illi qui tempore Synagogae Deo serviebant ad unitatem ecclesiae, in quo Deo servimus, pertinebant" (4 d, 27, q. 3, art. 1, s. 3, c.).

4. 3, q. 8, art. 3. "Those who are unbaptized, though not actually in the Church, are in the Church potentially. And this potentiality is rooted in two things—first and principally in the power of Christ which is sufficient for the salvation of the whole human race, and secondly in free will" (ibid., ad. 1).

"Ille qui est in peccato mortali est quasi membrum mortuum" (4 d, 20, q. 1, art. 5, qo. 1 s.c.; 3 d, 13, q. 2, art. 2, s. 2, ad. 6; 3, q. 8, art. 3, ad. 2). The faithful who belong to the Church but who are in mortal sin, are united only by a *material unity* (3, d 13, q. 2, art. 2, s. 2, c.).

5. The Church has not two heads: Christ and Peter. Christ is per se the Head; Peter is His visible representative or vicar, or as we say the Visible Head. Igitur ecclesiae unius et unicae unum corpus, unum caput, non duo capita quasi monstrum: Christus videlicet et Christi vicarius Petrus Petrique successor. Boniface VIII, *Unam Sanctam.*

"Christus est caput omnium eorum qui ad ecclesiam pertinent secundum omnem locum et tempus et statum; alii autem homines decuntur capita secundum quaedam spiritualia loca, secut episcopi suarum ecclesiarum; vel etiam secundum determinatum tempus, sicut Papa est caput totius ecclesiae, scilicet tempore sui pontificatus; et secundum determinatum statum, prout scilicet sunt in statu viatoris" (3, q. 8, art. 6).

6. In England, for example, the King is the head of the Anglican Church and the Parliament the supreme body which controls it. Hence before the Anglican Church can lawfully change its Prayer Book it must receive authority to do so from Parliament. National churches such as the Russian Church before the World War are typical also of the aristocratic form of church government. In America the aristocratic form of church government manifests itself in the Federation of Churches, in which the various sects pool their assets, melt away their dogmatic differences and agree not to disagree. On a still larger scale the great Church Conference at Stockholm in 1925 and Lausanne in 1927 where most Christian

sects met (not the Catholic Church, of course) with a few non-Christian bodies are representative of this form of government. At both these conferences a chairman presided at the discussion but he had no authority to bind the delegates in their decision. Representatives of the various sects were asked to give their opinions concerning the nature of the church, its social functions, methods of co-operation between the various churches, the liquor question, and the child and the adolescent in industry.

7. Peter's name was changed at the beginning of our Lord's public life. Originally, he was Simon. Our Lord told him he would be called Peter (John 1:42). The name Peter in its original and in its Latin form means rock. There can be no doubt therefore that he was the rock on which Christ founded His Church. In Sacred Scripture there are only three men who had their names changed by God, and in each instance they were lifted out of narrow individuality to headship over the elect. Abram was called Abraham, Jacob was called Israel and Simon was called Peter (Gen. 17:5, 32:38, 35:10).

The power of Primacy promised in Matt. 16:16 was conferred later on on Peter. Our Lord tells Peter: "I have prayed for THEE, that THY faith fail not: and *thou*, being once converted, confirm *thy* brethren" (Luke 22:32). These words were spoken *only* to Peter, that Satan might not sift him and his brethren as wheat (Luke 22:31). In other words, the faith of the Church was to be preserved *in Peter*. After the Resurrection Our Lord reaffirmed the Primacy by giving Peter authority over His lambs and His sheep (John 21:15–17). Peter exercised this authority after Pentecost (Acts 1:15–22, 2:37–40, 3:4–7, 5:15 ff., 15:11). The full development of Primacy can be found in d'Herbigny, *The Ecclesia*, Vol. I, pp. 258–309.

8. The distinction our Lord made between the man and his office was no doubt made because of the common human failures which he was to exhibit, and those also who were to follow him in his office. And this is to be noted because after his fall, when he was restored, the Lord asks him thrice: "Simon (not Peter), son of Jonas, lovest thou Me?" Anonymous, *A Spiritual Pilgrimage*, p. 26.

9. The origin of the word Pope or *Papa* has been said to be an abbreviation of the words *Pater Patrum*, Father of Fathers.

10. It has been held by some critics that the primacy of Peter was not recognized until the fourth century. This position is gradually giving way under the advance of historical study.

(1) There is the manifest primacy of jurisdiction in the Gospels. Cf. McNabb, *New Testament Witness to St. Peter*.

(2) Even non-Catholic scholars now admit that "the evidence of St. Paul is entirely in accord with the evidence of the Gospels as to the prerogative position assigned to St. Peter in relation to the rest of the Apostles." Cf. C.H. Turner: "St. Peter in the New Testament" in *Theology*, 1926, p. 194. The same evidence he finds in all the Gospels.

(3) The liturgical books of the Eastern Church prove that they believed the "Petrine" claims as expressed in the Gospels and the Acts, e.g., in the office of the Feast of St. Peter's chair are the words: "Supreme foundation of the Apostles, Thou didst also become first Bishop of Rome." And again:

Of Rome made first Bishop
There wert the praise and glory of the greatest of cities,
And of the Church, O Peter, the foundation,

And the gates of hell
Shall not prevail against it,
As Christ foretold.
(Passages found in Cardinal Pitra's *Hymnographie*, pp. 57, 137.)

(4) In the year 96 there is historical evidence of a very interesting nature to prove that the primate of the Roman Church had supreme doctrinal authority, and was conscious of having responsibility towards other Churches. The Bishop of Rome at that time was Clement. In the year 96 he wrote the most famous document of primitive Christianity outside the New Testament. In the early lists of Roman Bishops Clement follows Anacletus, who was preceded by Linus, who followed Peter. (Hegesippus of Syria, 160–175, is first authority for this succession. His statement is found in the *Ecclesiastical History of Eusebius*, IV, 22, 1–3.) Clement is probably the one mentioned by St. Paul in his letter to the Philippians, 4:3. The occasion of the famous letter of Clement to the Corinthians was that a dispute had broken out in the Church of Corinth which Clement wished to settle. What is remarkable about it is that Clement does not write as brother to brother, but as authority to one under obedience. "By reason of the sudden and repeated calamities and reverses which are befalling us brethren, we consider that we have been somewhat tardy in giving heed to the matters of dispute that have risen among you, dearly beloved, and to the detestable and unholy sedition . . . which a few headstrong and self-willed persons have kindled. . . . But if certain persons should be disobedient unto the *words spoken by Him through us* let them understand that they will entangle themselves in no slight transgression and danger. . . . Ye shall give us great joy and gladness if ye render obedience unto *the things written by us through the Holy Spirit*." This letter was written in the year 96. That means that the generation of men in their sixties were thirty years old when they heard Peter and Paul. We are, therefore, very close to apostolic times. Irenaeus tells us that Clement himself "both saw the Apostles themselves and conferred with them and had the preaching of the Apostles still resounding in his ears and their tradition before his eyes" (Eusebius, *Eccl. Hist.*, IV, 23).

When Clement wrote this letter to the Corinthians one of the Apostles was still living, i.e., St. John. Although the relations were more natural between Corinth and Ephesus, where John lived, than between Corinth and Rome, yet it is not an *Apostle* but the successor of Peter who wrote demanding that the seditious group submit their rebellious wills to Him. If Clement were overstepping his authority, the Corinthians would certainly have resented it, but Clement's right was not contested, for his letter was preserved by the Church of Corinth and publicly read as one of its most treasured possessions (Letter of Pope Clement, Eusebius, *Eccl. Hist.*, IV, 23).

(5) Within fifteen years we have the testimony of Ignatius, the martyr Bishop of Antioch, who "was sent from Syria to Rome and became food for wild beasts on account of his testimony to Christ." Ignatius wrote seven epistles, the most important of which was his letter to Rome. The form of address to the Church in Rome is different from the form of address in his other six letters. For example, he writes "to the Church which is in Ephesus," "to the holy Church which is in Trolles of Asia," "which is in Philadelphia of Asia," "which is in Smyrna in Asia," but when he comes to the Church of Rome he writes: "To the Church which presides in the region of the Romans." There follows another phrase, "which presides over the love," i.e., is pre-eminent in charity. Duschesne takes the whole phrase to mean that "the Roman Church presides over all the Churches." Lightfoot, the

Anglican scholar, says "he (Ignatius) assigns a primacy to Rome" (*St. Clement of Rome*, Vol. I, pp. 69–72). The letter to the Romans is inscribed "to the Church that hath mercy . . . that hath been beloved and enlightened by the Will of Him who willeth all things, and that are according to the love of Jesus Christ." Then it is lauded as "worthy of God, worthy of honour, worthy of felicitation, worthy of praise, worthy of success, worthy in purity." Harnack, who can be accused of no prejudice in favour of the Primacy, says: "Soften as we may all the extravagant expressions in the Epistle to the Romans, it is at least clear that Ignatius conceded to them a precedence in the circle of sister Churches" (*History of Dogma*, Vol. II, p. 156). Cardinal Newman has pointed out also that Ignatius in his letters to the other churches "warns them against heretics and exhorts them to unity. But in the case of the Roman Church he does nothing of the kind. He does not say a word about heresy or schism; he does not refer to its bishop or take him (as it were) under his wing" (*Essays: Critical and Historical*, Vol. I, p. 253).

(6) To this testimony might be added that of Irenaeus (130–200), Clement of Alexandria (190–215), Caius of Rome (199–217), Tertullian (160–235), and many others. Harnack admits that "at the end of the second century the working primacy of Rome cannot be denied" (*Entstehung und Entwicklung der Kirchenverfassung*, pp. 118, 119).

It is true the early documents are not replete with evidence for the Primacy of Peter, but because he and his immediate successors did not carve their names on every rock of the Coliseum did not mean Our Lord did not confer the primacy. It is indeed a remarkable thing that all the evidence we have for the few centuries is in favour of the primacy of Peter, but there is no evidence against. Nine hundred years later, when the primacy is denied in the East, it is denied not on *historical* or dogmatic grounds, but on political grounds. A collection of texts on the Primacy of Peter has been made by James T. Shotwell and Louise Loomis, entitled *The See of Peter*, 728 pp. The editors' notes on the texts, however, are not always accurate.

(7) The most remarkable study of the Primacy of Peter is one recently made by an Anglican minister, the Rev. S. Herbert Scott, entitled: *The Eastern Churches and the Papacy*. The rule of faith for the Anglican Church is not only the Bible (which was the rule of faith for the continental reformers), but also the three Creeds, Nicene, Athanasian, and the Apostles' Creed. This was an admission that tradition, in addition to the Scriptures, was the rule of faith. But the 8th article of the 89 is careful to add that the reason these three creeds were accepted is because their content and the content of the early Councils of the Church which defined them might "be proved by most certain warrants of Sacred Scripture."

Dr. Scott, in his study, makes a critical investigation of the Primacy in these very councils which the Anglican Church accepted as part of their rule of faith because in accordance with Sacred Scripture. The conclusion of Dr. Scott is that if the Anglicans are sincere in accepting the decisions of these councils, they must accept the Primacy of Peter. "If we take," he writes, "the evidence of Ecumenical Councils, as set out at length above, the records and documents of these assemblies show that the Easterns all along believed and accepted—

(1) The Primacy of the Bishops of Rome.

(2) That the Bishop of Rome had that primacy because he was the successor of St. Peter.

(3) That Christ had given the headship of the Church to Peter, i.e., that it was of 'Divine Right.'

(4) That the headship was passed on, and was in fact inherited by his successors in the Bishopric of Rome, so that the bishops of Rome held their headship, therefore, *de jure divino.*

(5) The documents of the Councils of Ephesus and Chalcedon (to take no others) show that these Eastern councils, by accepting and promulgating the judgment and sentence of Celestine on Nestorius, and the exposition of the Catholic faith, the Tome from Leo, acknowledged the power and right of the Roman Bishop to declare authoritatively to the Universal Church where the Catholic faith was" (p. 352).

All Seven Councils, which the Anglicans accept, Dr. Scott concludes, proclaimed "Peter ever lives in his successors and gives judgments."

## CHAPTER IV

1. "One Body and One Spirit" (Eph. 4:4.) "What the soul is to the body of man, that the Holy Ghost is to the body of Christ, which is the Church" (St. Augustine, P.L.T. 38, col. 1231). This is true in the sense that the soul unifies the activities of the body and gives the body life.

"Spiritus Sanctus est ultima perfectio et principalis totius corporis mystici, quasi anima in corpore naturali (3 d. 13, q. 2, art. 2, s. 2). Sicut constituitur unum corpus ex unitate animae, ita ecclesiae ex unitate Spiritus."

In *Epist. ad Coloss.*, cap. 1, lect. 5: "Ipse Spiritus Sanctus increatus idem numero est in capite et in membris, et aliquo modo a capite ad membra descendit, non divisus sed unus, Sed ipsum donum quod Spiritus Sanctus in nobis habitat, non traducitur de subjecto in subjectum" (3 d. 13, q. 2, art. 1, ad. 2; 3 d. 13, q. 2, art. 2, s. 2, ad 1). "Spiritus Sanctus unus et idem numero totam ecclesiam replet et unit" (*De Veritate*, q. 29, art. 4; 3 q. 8, art. 1, ad 3).

2. "The soul of the Mystical Body is the Holy Ghost.... Not only does the Holy Ghost dwell in the Church and in each of the just as in its temple, but it is as a principle of cohesion, of movement and life" (Prat, *St. Paul*, 1920 ed., vol. 1., p. 360). "Hoc affirmare sufficiat quod, cum Christus sit caput ecclesiae, Spiritus Sanctus sit ejus anima" (*Encyclical on the Holy Ghost*, Leo XIII).

See *St. Thomas*, 1 q. 76, art. 1, ad. 4. Vol. ii, d'Herbigny, p. 263.

"In the 'Mystical Christ' perfect accord existed between the office of the head and the office of the soul. Without such accord confusion would reign. Every vital activity of the 'Mystical Christ' whose end is the sanctification of souls, postulates not an identity but an accord in act, between the impulse coming from the Head and the impulse coming from the soul, who is the Holy Spirit.... But if there is an accord of action, a journey together towards the same end, there is no confusion of persons. Many differences distinguish the action in us of the Holy Spirit from the action in us of Christ. The most important is that the Holy Spirit comes to us through Christ" (Dugenay-Burke, *Christ in the Christian Life*, pp. 36, 37).

"Far from being a source of obscurity, the active interpenetration of the Son and Holy Spirit is for us a source of intense light. Thanks to it we better understand why Christ had to rise from the dead in order to send us the Holy Spirit and to become Himself a quickening Spirit. It also throws light upon the nature of the Mystical Body, which is not a fiction, a simple metaphor or a purely moral entity, but a composite of the supernatural order, receiving at the same time the vital influx from the head, the centre of the organism, and from the soul, the principle of life" (F. Prat, *The Theology of St. Paul*, vol. 2., p. 293).

3. *The Problem of Reunion*, p. 208. The Acts of the Apostles abound with references to the guidance of the Holy Spirit in the Church. It was the Spirit who accorded to Peter the order to receive the Gentiles into the Church in the person of Cornelius and his family as the first fruits of that vaster Apostolate (Acts 10:9 ff.). The Council of Jerusalem made its decision concerning conflict of Jew and Gentile in the words "It hath seemed good to the Holy Ghost and to us, to lay no further burden upon you" (Acts 15:28). Saul and Barnabas "being sent by the Holy Ghost, went to Seleucia" (Acts 13:4). Paul and Timothy "were forbidden by the Holy Ghost to preach the word in Asia" at a certain time in their journey (Acts 16:6). Paul declared himself "bound in Spirit" (Acts 20:22).

4. *Et unam, sanctam, catholicam et apostolicam ecclesiam*. These four notes are found in the fourth section of the Nicene Creed, which is read in the Mass. They come in the Creed immediately after the first three sections which treat of the Blessed Trinity. The four notes are therefore in some way the temporal extension of the Eternal Life and are bound up intrinsically with that Divine Life. In a certain sense, these marks of the Church are a reflection of the Trinity. The Trinity is one, because the Three Persons, Father, Son and Holy Ghost, have only the one nature which is the nature of God. The Trinity is holy, because holiness is fixity in goodness; whence the triple "Sanctus, Sanctus, Sanctus," addressed to each Holy Person. The Trinity is catholic because the Godhead is possessed by each Person in all its fullness. No Person is more God than another. Finally, the Trinity is apostolic, for apostolic means original, and the Trinity is the source, the origin and the fount and principle of all the life, truth and goodness in heaven and on earth.

5. "As the Body is one by the unity of the soul, so the Church is one by the unity of the Spirit" in *Cp. ad Col. I.*, lect. 5. "That they all may be one, as Thou, Father, in Me, and I in Thee" (John 17:21). The Father and Son are one in the Holy Ghost. We too are one with Christ by the same Spirit. The Holy Ghost is the effluent cause of our unity (see Mura, *Le Corps Mystique*, vol. 1, p. 146). "For as the body is one, and hath many members; and all the members of the body, whereas they are many, yet are one body, so also is Christ. For in one Spirit were we all baptized into one Body, whether Jews or Gentiles, whether bond or free; and in one Spirit we have all been made to drink" (1 Cor. 12:12, 13). "One Lord, one faith, one Baptism. One God and Father of all, who is above all, and through all, and in us all" (Eph. 4:4–6; 1 Cor. 12:4; Gal. 3:28).

6. On Pentecost the sign of the possession of the Holy Spirit was the infused power to speak all the languages, so to-day the sign of that same Spirit-infused Body is its power to speak the language of all peoples. St. Augustine, commenting on this fact, says that "A man when baptized receives the Holy Ghost, and even though he does not speak all tongues, he can be sure the Church does. The Church is the Body of Christ. I am a member of the Body which speaks all languages; I therefore speak all languages. United by the intimate bonds of charity, all the members of the body speak as if they were one man. The Church is their mouth; the Holy Ghost is their soul" (In *Joan. Tract. XXXII*, n. 7).

7. A.D. Sertillanges, *The Church*, p. 62. "For the temple of God is holy, which you are" (1 Cor. 3:17). "That He might present to Himself a glorious Church, not having

spot or wrinkle, or any such thing, but that it should be holy and without blemish"
(Eph. 5:27).

8. "The very works which I do bear witness to me that the Father hath sent Me"
(John 5:36).

9. "As My Father hath sent Me, I also send you."

10. "How shall they preach unless they be sent?" (Rom. 10:15). "Ye are built upon
the foundation of the Apostles and Prophets: Christ Jesus is the corner-stone. In
Him all the building is duly fitted together, and groweth into a temple holy in the
Lord" (Eph. 2:20, 21).

11. "The Apostles . . . in like manner founded churches in every city, from which
all other churches, one after another, derived the tradition of the faith and the
seeds of doctrine, and are every day deriving them that they may become churches.
Indeed, it is on this account only that they call themselves apostolic, as being the
offspring of apostolic churches. Every sort of thing must necessarily revert to its
origin for classification. Therefore the churches, although they are so many and
so great, comprise but the one primitive Church (founded) by the Apostles, from
which they all spring." Tertullian (160–235), *The Prescription of Heretics*, P.L., t.
11, col. 32. In this same work Tertullian states that Clement, who was Bishop of
Rome and successor of St. Peter as Vicar of Christ at the close of the first century,
was ordained priest by St. Peter. St. Cyprian wrote the following about the year
250, which gives the reverse side of the picture: "Novatian is not a Bishop in the
Church, nor can he be reckoned as such, because disregarding the Evangelical
and Apostolic tradition, he succeeded nobody, but started with himself." Ep. 69
ad Mag. 3. Ed. Hartel, vol. ii., col. 752.

Irenaeus (130–200) wrote in the same vein: "By this order and by that tradition
which is in the Church from the Apostles, the preaching of the truth has come
down to us; and this is a most complete demonstration that the life-giving faith
is one and the same which from the Apostles even until now has been preserved
in the Church, and transmitted in truthfulness." *Adv. Haereses*, III, c. 3.

### CHAPTER V

1. "All that the people fear in the Church, all that they hate in her, all against
which they harden their hearts and thicken their heads, all that has made peoples
consciously and unconsciously treat the Papacy as a peril, is the evidence that
there is something in it which cannot be looked at languidly, as we might look on
a Hottentot dancing at a new moon or a Chinaman burning papers in porcelain
temples. The measure of the madness with which men hate her is but their vain
attempt to despise." G.K. Chesterton.

### CHAPTER VI

1. "It is not you who speak, it is the Holy Ghost" (Mark 13:11).

2. Acts 9:4; "And falling on the ground, he heard a voice saying to him: Saul, Saul,
why persecutest thou Me?" Eph. 5:29, 30: "For no man ever hated his own flesh,
but nourisheth it and cherisheth it, as also Christ doth the Church: because we

are members of His body, of His flesh and of His bones." Rom. 12:6, 7: "And having different gifts, according to the grace that is given us, either prophecy, to be used according to the rule of faith; or ministry, in ministering; or he that teacheth, in doctrine." 1 Cor. 13:3: "And if I should distribute all my goods to feed the poor, and if I should deliver my body to be burned, and have not charity, it profiteth me nothing."

3. John 14:7: "If you had known me, you would without doubt have known my Father also: and from henceforth you shall know Him. And you have seen Him." 15:26: "But when the Paraclete cometh, whom I will send you from the Father, the Spirit of Truth, who proceedeth from the Father, He shall give testimony of Me." 16:13: "But when He, the Spirit of truth, is come, He will teach you all truth. For He shall not speak of Himself: but what things soever He shall hear, He shall speak. And the things that are to come, He shall shew you."

4. John 14:16: "And I will ask the Father: and He shall give you another Paraclete, that He may abide with you forever."

5. John 14:26: "But the Paraclete, the Holy Ghost, whom the Father will send in My name, He will teach you all things and bring all things to your mind, whatsoever I shall have said to you." John 16:13: "But when He, the Spirit of truth, is come, He will teach you all truth. For He shall not speak of Himself: but what things soever He shall hear, He shall speak. And the things that are to come, He shall shew you."

6. John 15:26: "But when the Paraclete cometh, whom I will send you from the Father, the Spirit of truth, who proceedeth from the Father, He shall give testimony of me." Acts 1:5 and 8: "For John indeed baptized with water; but you shall be baptized with the Holy Ghost, not many days hence." "But you shall receive the power of the Holy Ghost coming upon you, and you shall be witnesses unto Me in Jerusalem, and in all Judæa and Samaria, and even to the uttermost part of the earth."

7. Acts 2:4: "And they were all filled with the Holy Ghost: and they began to speak with diverse tongues, according as the Holy Ghost gave them to speak."

8. 1 Cor. 2:4, 5, 6, 7, 10, 12: "And my speech and my preaching was not in the persuasive words of human wisdom, but in shewing of the Spirit and power: That your faith might not stand on the wisdom of men, but on the power of God. Howbeit we speak wisdom among the perfect: yet not the wisdom of this world, neither of the princes of this world that come to nought. But we speak the wisdom of God in a mystery, a wisdom which is hidden, which God ordained before the world, unto our glory: But to us God hath revealed them by His Spirit. For the Spirit searcheth all things, yea, the deep things of God. For what man knoweth the things of a man, but the spirit of a man that is in him? So the things also that are of God, no man knoweth, but the Spirit of God."

9. "Actus sunt suppositorum," which may be translated, "It is the substance that acts."

10. Vincent McNabb, *Infallibility*, pp. 53, 54.

11. *Constitutio Dogmatica De Ecclesia Christi*, cap. IV.

12. 1 Pet. 5:4: "And when the prince of pastors shall appear, you shall receive a never fading crown of glory."

13. Vincent McNabb, *The New Testament Witness to Peter*, pp. 130, 131.

14. *Const. Dog. de Ecclesia Dei*, c. 4.

15. *Now I See*, p. 344.

## CHAPTER VII

1. What is indeed remarkable about our Lord communicating this power to the Apostles is the similarity between it and the conferring of infallibility on Peter. All the Apostles were present on that occasion, but our Lord addressed Peter in the singular, "And I say to thee: thou art Peter . . . and I will give to *thee* the keys of the kingdom of heaven . . . and whatsoever *thou* shalt bind upon earth, it shall be bound also in heaven: and whatsoever *thou* shalt loose on earth, it shall be loosed also in heaven" (Matt. 16:18, 19). The keys were given to Peter alone; Peter alone was to be the rock; he alone was to feed the lambs and shepherd the sheep; he alone would be preserved from errors of faith by the prayer of Christ, *but* the authority which Christ gave him as Head would be shared by the other apostles as long as they were with him and under his headship. And so it is that we find our Lord saying to the other apostles the plural of one of the injunctions to Peter alone: "Whatsoever *you* shall bind upon earth, shall be bound also in heaven: and whatsoever *you* shall loose upon earth, shall be loosed also in heaven" (Matt. 18:18). The same words, but they were first said to *Peter alone, apart* from the other apostles; then they were said to all the apostles, but *united to Peter*—hence the Vicar of Christ cannot be separated from the Bishops, neither can the Bishops be separated from the Vicar of Christ. They are united and dependent. Such is the meaning of the hierarchy of the Church. Peter was chosen and then the Church built upon him. The Church was not founded and then Peter taken from it. The foundation rock is first, then the edifice. It is in union with Peter that the Church derives its visible unity. The principle of unity precedes the things to be unified; the subject of a painting is chosen before the colours; the idea comes before the words to express it, and the plan before the building. The other apostles were one with Peter. The mission of all of them was the same; they were all divinely chosen, but they were not all of equal authority.

2. The apostles accordingly acted in His name (Acts 2:23, 8:12–16; Eph. 4:7–11). More particularly they exercised the triple power: legislative, judicial, and executive in His name. Legislative: "For it hath seemed good to the Holy Ghost and to us, to lay no further burdens upon you" (Acts 15:28; see Matt. 28:18–20). Judicial: "And Jesus said to them: Amen I say to you, that you who have followed Me, in the regeneration, when the Son of Man shall sit on the seat of His Majesty, you also shall sit on twelve seats, judging the twelve tribes of Israel" (Matt. 19:28). Executive: "I have told before, and foretell as present, and now absent, to them that sinned before, and to all the rest, that if I come again, I will not spare" (2 Cor. 13:2). "And if he will not hear them: tell the Church. And if he will not hear the Church, let him be to thee as the heathen and publican" (Matt. 18:17).

3. John 14:20—the same circumincession is to be found in a more particular way in (1) *Ubi Petrus, ibi ecclesia* and (2) the bishop in his diocese. What Peter is to the

universal Church that the bishop is to his diocese. St. Cyprian tells us "Christian, you ought to know that the bishop is in His Church and the Church is in its bishop" (Ep. LXIX). The Father is in His Son as His consubstantial splendour, as Christ is in His Church as His fullness and plentitude, and as the bishop is in his diocese as the fecundity of his priestly pontificate. Herein is the reason why the Church never abandons the titles to dioceses in which the faithful and clergy no longer reside—*in partibus infidelium*. The diocese may still be without priests or faithful, but it still lives in its bishops, like a father who has hopes of an heir. The torch of the diocese still burns because its episcopal chair is still occupied.

4. St. Paul reminds the Corinthians that they constitute one of the trials of the Church, by which she works out his salvation: "For there must be also heresies: that they also, who are approved, may be made manifest among you" (1 Cor. 11:19). In his epistle to the Galatians he contrasts the works of the spirit and the works of the flesh, and among the latter he numbers "heresies" (Gal. 5:20). St. Peter, who was divinely authorized to be the rock against heresies, was familiar with them during his own lifetime. "But there were also false prophets among the people even as there shall be among you, lying teachers who shall bring in sects of perdition and deny the Lord who bought them: bringing upon themselves swift destruction" (2 Pet. 2:1). St. Paul commanded his fellow worker Titus to avoid them. "A man that is a heretic, after the first and second admonition, avoid" (Titus 3:10).

5. The Church is made up of individuals but not of individualities. Being a divine human organism whose soul is the Holy Spirit, the life of any individual member depends on his obedience or subservience to the life of the whole. No cell of the human body can live in its perfection apart from the organism, but the organism can live without the cell. The cell lives its own individual life because of its incorporation into the organic life, and the baptized members of the Church live their spiritual lives because one with the Body of Christ. Individuality as expressed in the attempt to grow by cutting oneself off from the Mystical Body is just as fatal as in the biological order. For example, if a portion of a kidney is removed from its connective tissue and placed in a test tube with a nutrient member it will grow, but grotesquely. In the body its growth was orderly and limited, but when removed from social control its growth develops into unspecialized tissues which lose their quality as a kidney. It could be a kidney only on condition of its corporate fellowship with the rest of the body. So, too, the attempt to live in isolation from the Mystical Body by refusing to accept its corporate control or authority, results not only in unregulated development but in a degeneration of specialized function. The only way to avoid the peril of overestimating both ourselves and our ideas and our abilities as individuals is to keep them balanced by the authority which governs the regenerate society. That is why all heresies are nothing more or less than a gross exaggeration of a truth, and its over-emphasis, because isolated from other truths which counterbalance it.

## CHAPTER VIII

1. The Source of grace in Christ is the assumption of the human nature by the Word—the grace of union (3, q. 6, art. 6; 3, q. 7, art. 12). The grace of union produced in the human nature of Christ a created sanctity in a superior degree. The humanity of Christ, being an instrument of divinity with unity of the Divine Person, receives a grace corresponding to that personal union, and to such an extent that,

thanks to its plenitude, it flows over into us (*De Veritate*, q. 29, art. 5, c.). "Dicendum quod dare gratiam, aut Spiritum Sanctum, convenit Christo, secundum quod est Deus, auctoritative; sed instrumentaliter convenit etiam ei, secundum quod est homo; inquantum scilicet ejus humanitas instrumentum fuit divinitatis ejus" (3, q. 8, art. 2). The humanity of Christ without that union would have had no *sanctifying power*. Everything comes from Divinity, but *through* humanity.

2. The Passion of Christ is a kind of universal cause of salvation for the living and the dead. But a general cause is applied to particular effects by means of something special. Hence, as the power of the Passion is applied to the living through the Sacraments, which make us like unto Christ's Passion; so likewise it is applied to the dead through His descent into hell (3, q. 52, art. 1, ad. 2). Grace was bestowed upon Christ, not only as an individual, but inasmuch as He is the Head of the Church, so that it might overflow unto the members (3, q. 48, art. 1). The action of Christ's redemption in the Mystical Body is not that of the influence of His example alone. Since Christ's humanity is the instrument of the Godhead, therefore all Christ's actions and sufferings operate instrumentally in virtue of the Godhead for the salvation of men. Christ's Passion accomplished the salvation of men *efficiently* (3, q. 48, art. 6).

Because the Personality of Christ was Divine, it follows that the Divine Person could incorporate other human natures to Himself and thus form a Mystical Body. In assuming a human nature Christ potentially assumed all human natures. An act of our will by which we correspond to His grace changes our potential union with Him into actual union. The Church is therefore, as St. Thomas says above, "computatur una persona cum suo capite quod est Christus." Since He is the Head, then by the Passion which He endured from love and obedience, He delivered us as members from our sins, by the price of His Passion; in the same way as if a man by the industry of his hands were to redeem himself from a sin committed with his feet (3, q. 49, art. 1).

3. There are two erroneous extremes; one is to separate matter from God as false science sometimes does, by attributing it to chance; the other is to identify God and matter as false philosophy does when it becomes Pantheistic. In the virtuous mean is the philosophy of the sacramental universe which holds that matter is a ladder to the spirit, and the visible channel to the invisible.

4. "In the beginning was the Word, and the Word was with God, and the Word was God" (John 1:1).

5. "It is Christ, the person of Christ that is the sacrament par excellence, the first sacrament, the sole sacrament, since whatever we call a Sacrament is only a continuation of His symbolic and real action; symbolic, since He is a manifestation of God; real, because He is God given to us. Christ, by expressing the Divine and causing it to act; by employing to that end, as well as His soul, His suffering and glorified Flesh, after taming exterior nature; and then by founding, in order to carry on His Body and Soul, a visible society wherein the spiritual life depends on and uses sensible reality; Christ, by so doing, made Himself truly the Way, in the proper sense of the word. Every soul draws near to God through Him as by a rood of the flesh. Every soul touches God by means of those successive contacts whereof the sacrament of Baptism is the first, whereof the most holy humanity of Christ is the last" (A.D. Sertillanges, *The Church*, p. 139).

6. Our Lord was baptized as the inaugural act of His founding the Kingdom of God on earth. Baptism is for us too the inaugural act into the Church or the Kingdom of God on earth. Baptism has a double effect on the soul; it frees us from the original sin which infects all who were born of the flesh (except the Blessed Mother) and therefore made members of the race of Adam. By doing this it incorporates us into the life of the new Adam. Thus by the one and the same act, we die to sin and live to Christ. Baptism then is primarily a death, "We are buried with Him by Baptism into death" (Rom. 6:4). "All we who are baptized in Christ Jesus are baptized in His death" (Rom. 6:3). Cf. Chapter II.

7. Baptism makes the soul a member of the Mystical Body of Christ on earth (3, q. 63, arts. 1 and 2); Confirmation makes the soul more closely united with the Mystical Head in Heaven (3, q. 72, arts. 1 and 4). Penance restores him to the Mystical Body in case of sin (3, q. 84, art. 5 c.). Extreme Unction prepares the soul to pass from the Mystical Body on earth to the Mystical Body of the Church triumphant in heaven (Supp. 3, q. 30, art. 1, c.). The liturgy expresses a desire to have many priests present for the administration of this Sacrament. And if there be but one priest, the sacrament is still administered in the name of the Church of which this one priest is the minister and the representative. Thus does the Mystical Body witness to the passage from earth to eternal union with the Head (C.G., lib. 4, cap. 73). Matrimony sanctifies the soul in a mutual unbreakable union with his spouse, modelling it upon the eternal union of Christ for His Spouse the Mystical Body (Supp. 3, q. 45, arts. 1, 2; q. 47, art. 3; q. 59, art. 6). Holy Orders sanctifies the soul to carry the life of the Head to the members (Supp. 3, q. 36, art. 3, ad. 2). The Eucharist, to which all other Sacraments are founded, gives the soul intimate union with the Body, Blood, Soul and Divinity of His Lord and Saviour Jesus Christ (Supp. 3, q. 37, art. 2 and ad. 3. In 1 *Ep.* ad *Cor.* x. 16). Three sacraments imprint an indelible mark on the soul which it carries even unto the next world, seal us forever to one of the three offices of Christ, and hence may never be repeated. Baptism incorporates us to Christ the King; Confirmation to Christ the Teacher; and Holy Orders to Christ the Priest.

8. Homo potest operari ad interiorem effectum sacramenti in quantum operatur per modum ministerii (3, q. 64, art. 1).

9. *De Veritate*, q. 29, art. 5: Influence of the Head of the Mystical Body is not only internal by the infusion of grace which one has considered, but also *external* by ecclesiastical superiors who govern in the name of Christ. This *external* influence we considered in the two previous chapters.

## CHAPTER IX

1. "Dearly beloved, we are now the sons of God, and it hath not yet appeared what we shall be. But we know that, when He shall appear, we shall be like to Him" (1 John 3:2).

## CHAPTER XI

1. Matt. 10:40: "He that receiveth you receiveth Me, and he that receiveth Me receiveth Him that sent Me." Luke 10:16: "He that heareth you heareth Me; and

he that despiseth you despiseth Me; and he that despiseth Me, despiseth Him that sent Me." Matt. 27:40: "And saying, Vah, Thou that destroyest the temple of God, and in three days dost rebuild it, save Thy own self; if Thou be the Son of God come down from the Cross."

2. Luke 14:13–14: "But when thou makest a feast, call the poor, the maimed, the lame, and the blind: And thou shalt be blessed, because they have not wherewith to make thee recompense: for recompense shall be made thee at the resurrection of the just."

3. Matt. 5:44–45: "But I say to you, Love your enemies, do good to them that hate you, and pray for them that persecute and calumniate you; 'that you may be the children of your Father who is in heaven, who maketh His sun to rise upon the good, and bad, and raineth upon the just and the unjust.'"

4. Matt. 19:28: "And Jesus said to them, Amen, I say to you, that you, who have followed Me, in the regeneration, when the Son of man shall sit on the seat of His majesty, you also shall sit on the twelve seats judging the twelve tribes of Israel."

5. Luke 15:10: "So I say to you, there shall be joy before the angels of God upon one sinner doing penance."

6. 1 Cor. 12:13: "For in one Spirit were we all baptized into one Body, whether Jews or Gentiles, whether bond or free; and in one Spirit we have all been made to drink." Eph. 4:3, 4, 16: "Careful to keep the unity of the Spirit in the bond of peace." "One Body and one Spirit; as you are called in one hope of your calling." "From whom the whole body, being compacted and fitly joined together, by what every joint supplieth, according to the operation in the measure of every part, maketh increase of the body, unto the edifying of itself in charity." Eph. 2:18–22: "For by Him we have access both in one spirit to the Father. Now therefore you are no more strangers and foreigners; but you are fellow citizens with the saints and the domestics of God. Built upon the foundation of the apostles and prophets, Jesus Christ Himself being the chief corner stone. In whom all the building being framed together, groweth up into an holy temple of the Lord. In whom you also are built together into an habitation of God in the Spirit."

7. Rom. 12:4–6: "For as in one body we have many members, but all the members have not the same office. So we being many, are one body in Christ, and every one members one of another. And having different gifts, according to the grace that is given us . . . to be used according to the rule of faith." 1 Cor. 12:25: "That there might be no schism in the body; but the members might be mutually careful one for another." Rom. 1:9: "For God is my witness, whom I serve in my spirit in the gospel of His Son, that without ceasing I make a commemoration of you." Col. 1:9: "Therefore we also, from the day that we heard it, cease not to pray for you, and to beg that you may be filled with the knowledge of His will, in all wisdom, and spiritual understanding." Col. 4:12: "Epaphras saluteth you, who is one of you, a servant of Christ Jesus, who is always solicitous for you in prayers, that you may stand perfect, and full in all the will of God." 2 Thess. 1:11: "Wherefore also we pray always for you; that our God would make you worthy of His vocation, and fulfill all the good pleasure of His goodness and the work of faith in power." Eph. 6:17–19: "And take unto you the helmet of salvation, and the sword of the Spirit (which is the word of God). By all prayer and supplication praying at all times in the spirit and in the same watching with all instance and supplication for all the saints. And

for me, that speech may be given me, that I may open my mouth with confidence, to make known the mystery of the gospel." Heb. 13:18: "Pray for us. For we trust we have a good conscience, being willing to behave ourselves well in all things."

8. Sheen, *The Moral Universe*, chapter entitled "Purifying Flames."

9. Karl Adam, *The Spirit of Catholicism*, p. 104.

10. Rev. 21:14: "And the wall of the city had twelve foundations, and in them, the twelve names of the twelve apostles of the Lamb."

11. I John 1:3: "That which we have seen and have heard, we declare unto you, that you also may have fellowship with us, and our fellowship may be with the Father, and with His Son, Jesus Christ." John 17:20: "And not for them only do I pray, but for them also who through their word shall believe in Me."

12. Gal. 3:19: "Why then was the law? It was set because of transgressions, until the seed should come, to whom He made the promise, being ordained by angels in the hand of a mediator." Heb. 2:2: "For if the word, spoken by angels, became steadfast, and every transgression and disobedience received a just recompense of reward."

13. Rev. 7:10, 12: "And they cried with a loud voice, saying: Salvation to our God, who sitteth upon the throne, and to the Lamb." "Saying: Amen. Benediction, and glory, and wisdom, and thanksgiving and honour, and strength to our God for ever and ever. Amen."

14. Christ is the Head of the whole Mystical Body—From heaven He governs it in its entirety, and "though some are separated from the vision of Him, they are nevertheless united to Him by charity" (St. Augustine, *Evar. in Psalmos*, ps. 56, n. 1, P.L., vol. 36, col. 662).

15. The ministry of the elect in heaven to the faithful on earth is not limited to loving intercession. In addition to the communication through prayer and petition, there is also the communication through merit which may be effected in two ways: (1) In virtue of the unitive principle and cohesive force of the whole Mystical Body, namely, charity. John 17:21: "That they all may be one, as Thou, Father, in Me, and I in Thee; that they also may be one in Us; that the world may believe that Thou hast sent Me." John 13:35: "By this shall all men know that you are My disciples, if you have love one for another." Phil. 2:2: "Fulfil ye my joy, that you be of one mind, having the same charity, being of one accord, agreeing in sentiment." All who are united by charity which has been poured out upon us by the Holy Spirit gain something from the works of one another. Secondly, the communication of merit may be accomplished in virtue of the intention one makes in performing an act, in order that it might help another. Thus one in debt to God may have his debts paid through the generosity of another (Supp. 3, q. 71, art. 1). "The act of one becomes the merit of another through the medium of charity, by which we are all one in Christ" (Supp. 3, q. 13, art. 2, ad. 1). "Bear ye one another's burdens; and so you shall fulfill the law of Christ" (Gal. 6:2.)

Just as individuals have their treasury of merits which they may apply (a) in virtue of the common bond of charity (b) by intention, so too the Church has her own general treasury from which she distributes her riches by way of indulgences. Where did the Church get these merits? She got them through the superabundant merits of our Lord, the Blessed Mother and the Saints. This sacred patrimony or inheritance the Church can disburse to her needy members. Just as a rich man may set aside part of his fortune to help the poor, so too our Lord, who acquired infinite merits for us, and the Blessed Mother and the Saints who acquired more than they needed for their own individual salvation, put that superfluity into the "Spiritual Bank of the Church" which she dispenses to the spiritually poor, in virtue of Her Divine Commission to bind and loose. An indulgence then, is not a permission to commit sin, but rather a remission in whole or in part of the temporal punishment due to sin. They attest not only that every sin must be expiated "to the last farthing," but also to the unity of the Mystical Body of Christ. "That which gives value to indulgences is the unity of the Mystical Body in which many do penance beyond their debts" (Supp. 3, q. 26, art. 1).

16. 1 Cor. 13:8: "Charity never falleth away: whether prophecies shall be made void, or tongues shall cease, or knowledge shall be destroyed."

17. "The Eucharist is the sign of the unity of the Church. For that reason the efficacy of the Holy Eucharist of itself and in itself extends by way of sacrifice, to others than the ones who actually receive it" (Supp. 3, q. 25, art. 9, ad. 3).

18. The third communication of the members of the Church Militant one with another will be discussed in the following chapter.

## CHAPTER XII

1. Heb. 9:22. The relation between the reparation demanded of the individual and that made by Christ is discussed later in the chapter.

2. In theological language, Christ has merited for us de condigno, i.e., in strict equivalence. Creatures can merit de condigno for themselves an increase of sanctifying grace, but they merit for others only de congruo, i.e., by simple convenance.

3. "The charity of Christ presseth us: judging this, that if One died for all then all died; and that One died for all, that they also who live may not now live to themselves, but to Him who died for them and rose again" (2 Cor. 5:14, 15). This text awakens not the idea that Christ was substituted for us but rather that we are one with Him. For in order that Jesus may associate us with His death, it is essential that we should be wholly one with Him at the moment when He dies. We were one with Him not in *fact*, for we were not yet born, but we were one with Him by *right* for He "is the first born of every creature." His death becomes realized as mystically by faith and baptism. "We who are baptized in Christ Jesus are baptized in His death" (Rom. 6:3). Man's redemption has three steps: On Calvary redemption was accomplished by right, in principle, and in power; at baptism it is realized in fact and in deed, though imperfectly; in heaven it is finished and consummated.

## CHAPTER XIV

1. "Mary is after God and with God and under God the *efficient* cause of our regeneration because she begot our Redeemer, and because by her virtue, she merited by a merit of congruity this incomparable honour. She is the *material* cause, because the Holy Ghost through the intermediary of her consent took from her pure flesh and blood, the flesh and blood from which was made the Body immolated for the

Redemption of the world. She is the *final* cause, for the great work of Redemption which is ordained principally for the glory of God, is ordained secondarily for the honour of this same Virgin. She is the *formal* cause, for by the Light of a Light so very deiform she is the universal exemplar which shows us the way out of darkness to the vision of the Eternal Light" (St. Albert the Great, *Quaest.*, q. 146, t. XX, p. 100).

2. "Because of the association of suffering and of love between Mary and Jesus, Mary has rightly merited to be the co-Redemptrix of fallen humanity, the most powerful mediatrix in the whole world and, consequently, the dispenser of all the riches which Christ Jesus has won for us by His Blood and by His Death.... She merits for us *de congruo*, in the language of theologians, what Jesus Christ merits *de condigno*, and she is the supreme minister of the distribution of graces" (Pius X, *Ency. Ad diem illum*).

3. Encyclical: *Magnae Dei Matris.*

4. Benedict XV.

## CHAPTER XV

1. Matt. 26:26–28. "Christ in the Supper offered Himself up to death. *This is my Body*, He says, *which is delivered for you*, delivered unto death. *This is My Blood, which is shed for you in atonement for your sins.* My Blood which flows for you; is not that death? Death put indeed before us in a symbol, by means of that sacramental parting of the Blood from the Body; but death at the same time already pledged to God for all its worth, as well as all its awful reality, by the expressive language of that sacred symbol. The price of our sins shall be paid down on Calvary; but here the liability is incurred by our Redeemer, and subscribed in His very Blood. The flesh of the Lamb is here consigned into God's hands, for as much as it is assigned as our ransom" (*Catholic Faith in the Holy Eucharist*, edited by Fr. Lattey, S.J., 2nd ed., p. 115). "Christ after He had performed His work as a priest, said to His disciples: '*Do ye this in memory of Me.*' What He did, we do; we do as a memorial what He did as a prefiguration of His own passion. Our sacrifice presupposes then the death of the Lord as a thing of the passion. We offer the Death and Passion too; that is, the Victim of the Passion and Death, even as He did, but with this difference: He offered it to be immolated; we offer it as immolated of old. We offer the eternal Victim of the Cross once made and forever enduring. We offer it by the same rite that Christ used before us, by the rite of consecration, which in our hands as in His, constitutes a mystical-sacramental-symbolic-representative immolation, wherein lies the real and actual, the visible, audible and tangible oblation of what is represented, namely, the immolation of Calvary" (M. de la Taille, S.J., *The Mystery of Faith and Human Opinion*, p. 233).

2. What our Lord anticipated the night of the Last Supper, the Mass commemorates, even as He said, "Do ye this in memory of Me," or as St. Paul says, "As often as ye eat this bread and drink the cup, ye proclaim the death of the Lord until He come." In both cases, as Father de la Taille points out in his book already quoted, the sacrifice rests upon the same immolation, i.e., the Cross, but in two different ways; here *oblatio hostiae immolatae*; there *oblatio hostiae immolandae*. The Mass, then, as the Council of Trent points out, is a Sacrifice instituted by Christ. There is the same Priest and Victim in both the Cross and the Mass, namely, Christ. There

is, however, a different offering; on the Cross the offering was blood-stained; on the altars it is bloodless. Its worth and efficacy is derived from the Sacrifice of the Cross, the benefit of which is applied to us. The institution of the Sacrifice of the Mass goes back to the Supper, when Christ, who was about to deliver Himself up for us on the Cross, and who wished to endow the Church with a sacrifice commemorative of His own, first offered His Body and Blood under the appearance of bread and wine, and next appointed His apostles and their successors to renew that same offering after Him unto the consummation of the world.

3. There is only one sacrifice which is the sacrifice of Christ. In both Christ is Priest and Victim. But there is this difference: in the Mass He is no longer the sole Priest nor the sole Victim. In His Passion Christ offered Himself to the Father that He might beget His Mystical Body. In the Mass the Mystical Body now actually united with Christ, offers through Him and with Him the Victim of Calvary. In the Mass Christ the Priest has now associated with Him the instruments of His Priesthood. In the Mass Christ the Victim has associated with His Sacrifice on Calvary the state of victimhood of His Mystical Body. The principal Priest and Victim in the Mass is therefore Christ, without whom the Priesthood and sacrifice of the Mystical Body would be without value. The offering on Calvary constitutes, therefore, above all things else, the supreme offering. "But as every external sacrifice is a sign and symbol of an interior sacrifice, the Mystical Body offers the natural Body of Christ a seal, pledge and testimony of the offering of itself, of its own consecration" (Anger-Burke, *The Mystical Body of Christ*, p. 198).

4. *Sess.* 22, cap. 1.

5. The Church has the power to offer the Divine sacrifice, because it is one with Christ. In other words, the nature of the vital union of Christ and His Church is fundamental as an understanding of the Mass. A member of the Mystical Body can offer the sacrifice of Christ, because He is one with Christ: a living member of an organism whose Head is the risen Lord. By offering up the Victim of Calvary, the world concurs with the wish of Christ to save it, and adds the assent which was necessary as a condition to make the living act of reparation by Christ efficacious. "The Church under Christ is the offerer in every Mass. And the reason is that the Church is the Mystical Body of Christ. Apart from that Body no one can act representatively, nor by Divine agency. In every sacrifice of the Mass, no matter whether the priest be without a congregation or accompanied by the multitudes that fill St. Peter's, it is the Church as one Body which offers through His ministry" (M.C. D'Arcy, S.J., *The Mass and Redemption*, p. 115). After Christ had offered Himself on the Cross He continues to offer Himself in union with us through the ministry of His priests. As Pius XI stated in his Encyclical on Christ the King: "Christus sacerdos se pro peccatis hostiam obtulit, perpetuoque se offeret." Christ is therefore the Principal Priest and Victim in this Sacrifice, for if this great truth were ignored, our own sacrifices would be almost worthless. It is only because of our union with Him that they have value. And He is the Principal Priest, not because He instituted the Sacrifice, or commanded it to be repeated, but because He concurs actually in that sacrifice.

6. "Since the Church is the Body of this adorable Head, she learns from Him to sacrifice herself through Him" (St. Augustine, *City of God*, Book 10, Chapter 20). "The whole ransomed city, that is the Church and the Communion of saints, forms the universal sacrifice offered to God by the High Priest" (ibid., Book 10, Chapter 6).

7. The offertory collection to-day takes the place of these offerings of bread and wine.

8. The Priest is the visible official representative of the Head of the Mystical Body in this great act of sacrifice. It is the will of the Incarnate Word to be immolated, but the where and when and how are determined by the ministry of the priest. But in the Sacrifice of the Mass the priest does not act alone—he is the representative of the Mystical Body. Once the offertory of the bread has been made, the personality of the priest vanishes.

9. The offering of the chalice is a typical prayer of the Mass or the sacrifice of the priest and the people in union with Christ. "*We* offer to Thee, O Lord, the chalice of salvation. . . . And may the sacrifice *we* this day offer up be well-pleasing to Thee."

10. "So also Christ was offered once to exhaust the sins of many." "But this Man offering one sacrifice for sins, forever sitteth on the right hand of God. . . . For by *one oblation* He hath perfected forever them that are sanctified" (Heb. 10:12, 14).

11. St. Thomas says that Christ interceded for us in heaven in a two-fold manner: (1) by representation of His sacrificed humanity, (2) by actual and positive expression of the love He has for our salvation (*Comm. in Hebrews*, Sect. 4).

## CHAPTER XVI

1. 3, q. 73, art. 3.

2. 3, q. 73, art. 3, ad. 3.

3. 3, q. 73, art. 3.

4. Ibid.

5. Supp. 3, q. 37.

6. Supp. 3, q. 36, art. 2, ad. 1.

7. 3, q. 86, art. 4, ad. 3.

8. *Contra Gentiles*, lib. 4, cap. 73.

9. Ibid., cap. 78.

10. 3, q. 65, art. 3, ad. 1.

11. 4, d. 8, q. 1, art. 1, ad. 1.

12. 3, q. 65, art. 3.

13. *Sess.* XIII, Cap. 2.

## CHAPTER XVII

1. Rom. 8:19–23: "For the expectation of the creature waiteth for the revelation of the sons of God. For the creature was made subject to vanity: not willingly but by reason of Him that made it subject, in hope. Because the creature also itself

shall be delivered from the servitude and corruption, into the liberty of the glory of the children of God. For we know that every creature groaneth and travaileth in pain, even till now. And not only it, but ourselves also, who have the first fruits of the Spirit: even we ourselves, waiting for the adoption of the sons of God, the redemption of our body."

2. Rev. 10:5–6: "And the angel whom I saw standing upon the sea and upon the earth lifted up his hand to heaven. And he swore by Him that liveth for ever and ever, who created heaven and the things which are therein, and the earth and the things which are in it, and the sea and the things which are therein: That time shall be no longer."

3. Rom. 8:9, 11: "But you are not in the flesh, but in the spirit, if so be that the Spirit of God dwell in you. Now if any man have not the Spirit of Christ, he is none of His. And if the Spirit of Him that raised up Jesus from the dead dwell in you, He that raised up Jesus Christ from the dead shall quicken also mortal bodies, because of His Spirit that dwelleth in you." John 14:19: "Yet a little while and the world seeth Me no more. But you see Me: because I live, and you shall live."